Squaretail

Squaretail

THE DEFINITIVE GUIDE TO BROOK TROUT AND WHERE TO FIND THEM

Bob Mallard
Foreword by Ted Williams

STACKPOLE
BOOKS

Guilford, Connecticut

Published by Stackpole Books
An imprint of The Rowman & Littlefield Publishing Group, Inc.
4501 Forbes Blvd., Ste. 200
Lanham, MD 20706
www.rowman.com

Distributed by NATIONAL BOOK NETWORK

British Library Cataloguing in Publication Information available

Library of Congress Cataloging-in-Publication Data

Names: Mallard, Bob, 1958- author.
Title: Squaretail : the definitive guide to brook trout and where to find
    them / Bob Mallard ; foreword by Ted Williams.
Description: Guilford, Connecticut : Stackpole Books, [2019] | Includes
    index.
Identifiers: LCCN 2019005828 (print) | LCCN 2019006774 (ebook) | ISBN
    9780811766142 (e-book) | ISBN 9780811736572 (hardback : alk. paper) | ISBN
    9780811766142 (ebook)
Subjects: LCSH: Brook trout fishing—America. | Brook trout—America.
Classification: LCC SH689.3 (ebook) | LCC SH689.3 .M35 2019 (print) | DDC
    597.5/7—dc23
LC record available at https://lccn.loc.gov/2019005828

♾™ The paper used in this publication meets the minimum requirements of American
National Standard for Information Sciences—Permanence of Paper for Printed Library
Materials, ANSI/NISO Z39.48-1992.

Printed in the United States of America

This book is dedicated to the late Nick Karas. No one did more to bring brook trout mainstream and back into the limelight than Mr. Karas. Karas wrote a sporting column for *Newsday* from 1976 to 1997, which according to his son totaled more than 3,500 pieces, most of which were about fishing and hunting. Karas's angling prowess was so well known, it is said he had to change the name of his boat to keep local anglers from following him to his favorite spots. He was also a trained biologist. Karas authored six books, including his seminal *Brook Trout*, published in 1997. I bought a copy of the book soon after it came out and have had it in my library ever since. While I didn't fully appreciate the fact at the time, *Brook Trout* is one of just a few books dedicated solely to one species of fish—my favorite, *Salvelinus fontinalis*. When I first thought about writing this book, I went back through Karas's book to get a feel for what had changed in the 20 years since he wrote it. The answer was *much*, and this was part of what convinced me that this book needed to be written.

When all the routines and details and the human bores get on our nerves, we just yearn to go away from here to somewhere else. To go fishing is a sound, a valid, and an accepted reason for an escape. It requires no explanation.

—Herbert Hoover

CONTENTS

Conservation icon and mentor Ted Williams fishing for native "salters" on the Chandler River in Downeast Maine.
BOB MALLARD PHOTO

FOREWORD

What are we to make of the first comprehensive book that tells us where and even how to catch brook trout? Was it not the late dean of fly fishing himself, Robert Traver, who excoriated what he called "kiss-and-tell fishermen"?

From personal experience I know that Bob Mallard doesn't tattle on small, vulnerable brook trout water. But he has helped me understand something important about all wild fish, a truth that eludes many anglers: The number of people pursuing any given species is directly proportional to its long-term well-being. You can't seriously chase wild fish, brook trout especially, without becoming a passionate advocate. We need more, not fewer, brook trout anglers.

So carefully read this superb book. Follow the directions to the best brook trout haunts in our nation. And don't feel guilty about sharing what you learn.

You are in good hands. If there is a finer trout angler than Bob Mallard, I have not encountered one. (He is a wizard with a long wand.) Nor have I encountered anyone who knows more about wild brook trout and where to find them.

But it was not Mallard's knowledge or his casting prowess that forged our alliance and friendship. I tracked him down as a source for my articles because of his courageous defense of wild brook trout with a pen he wields every bit as deftly as a fly rod.

"God," a sage once proclaimed, "made brook trout last, after He had practiced on all the other fish." Markings on their green backs resemble grub trails on old bark. Chestnut flanks bear flecks of ruby, each ringed with a sapphire halo. Bellies are red as October swamp maples. Pectoral, ventral, and anal fins are trimmed with ivory. While lots of salmonids are bigger, none fights harder.

But Mallard teaches that the brook trout's true worth has little to do with its exquisite coloration or game qualities and much to do with the fact that it is part of a complicated and beautiful engine whose workings we don't understand but keep meddling with.

In his home state of Maine, Mallard has, with considerable personal sacrifice, confronted an angling population and management establishment slow to grasp that brook trout are native wildlife important in their own right, not just tasty table fare and providers of human sport. As Mallard has made clear in this book and elsewhere, wild brook trout are no less valuable to the nation than grizzlies or bald eagles.

This, alas, is news to most Americans. They measure the worth of trout in inches, seeking and demanding fish dispensed at roadside by hatchery truck—predominantly browns from Europe, rainbows from the Pacific Northwest, and "Frankenstein fish"—genetic cocktails mixed by hatchery technicians. These include tiger trout (forced hybrids of brown and brook trout), splake (forced hybrids of lake trout and brook trout), and palomino trout (mutant rainbows lacking pigmentation).

Diamonds are to paste what wild brook trout are to pallid, inbred domestic stock reared in concrete raceways that abrade tails and render pectoral fins fleshy stumps.

Could an awakening be near? Perhaps. Even in Maine there has been modest progress in management and public appreciation of brook trout. For a good deal of this we can thank Bob Mallard, the tireless rebutter of failed, anthropocentric notions that sadly linger from the days when "a trout was a trout" and managers flung species and subspecies around the continent like confetti. While we're more careful where we put trout these days, the old notion that they were placed on earth to bend our rods and tickle our palates is very much extant.

Because of state, federal, and private "bucket biology," which was de rigueur until about 1970, not all wild brook trout are native. In the West brook trout are aliens, frequently causing major ecological injury. Where they imperil native fish, no one is more ardently in favor of eliminating them than Bob Mallard. But in much of the West, brook trout exist where they either can't be eliminated or aren't doing significant harm.

For example, Mallard takes us to Yellowstone National Park's Blacktail Deer Lakes just off the road between Roosevelt and Mammoth Hot Springs. Sure, these brook trout aren't native. But they're wild and immaculate, and for now, they are here.

Enjoy brook trout wherever this book takes you. In their native range, support recovery wherever it is happening and help start recovery where it is not happening. Learn about and participate in the native fish movement.

Finally, remember these words of Robert Traver who quit the Michigan Supreme Court in order to fish for and write about wild brook trout, and who helped Bob Mallard spread the word about their true value: "Trout, unlike men, will not—indeed cannot—live except where beauty dwells."

—Ted Williams

ACKNOWLEDGMENTS

There are many people I wish to thank for directly or indirectly helping to make this book possible. It would be impossible to thank them all personally. I am, however, very grateful to all of them for their assistance. Thanks goes to:

Those who generously provided photographs and art in support of the book—especially the professionals who offered their wares. Every picture tells a story, every story needs a picture, and nothing tells a story like this better than a picture or painting of a beautiful wild native brook trout.

V. Paul Reynolds, publisher of *Northwoods Sporting Journal*, for publishing my first article. Thanks to Paul, I now work harder than anyone I know and for less money.

Thomas Ames Jr., author of *Hatch Guide for New England Streams*, *Fishbugs*, and *Caddisflies: A Guide to Eastern Species for Anglers and Other Naturalists*, for helping introduce me to a national audience.

All the publishers and editors I have worked with over the years who helped make me a better writer: Ken Allen, Crispin Battles, Kirk Deeter, Don Kirk, David Klausmeyer, Will Lund, Chris Major, Ben Mintz, Phil Monahan, Ross Purnell, V. Paul Reynolds, Naomi Schalit, John Shewey, and Harry Vanderweide, to name a few.

Brad Gage, New England Outdoors, for connecting me with Terry Gunn. Had I not met Terry, this book might not have happened.

Terry and Wendy Gunn for inviting me to contribute to their book *50 Best Tailwaters to Fly Fish*, and for the giving me the chance to write about Acadia National Park in their book *25 Best National Parks to Fly Fish*.

Terry Gunn, Lees Ferry Angler, for his encouragement and ongoing support, for suggesting that I do more writing, and for lobbying for me as a candidate to write *50 Best Places Fly Fishing the Northeast*—my first book.

Robert Clouse, publisher, Stonefly Press, for publishing my first two books and helping to expose my writing to the masses.

George Smith and Landon Mayer for inviting me to contribute to their books, *Maine Sporting Camps* and *The Hunt for Giant Trout*.

Thomas Ames Jr. and Tim Wade for taking time out of their busy schedules to write the forewords for my first two books.

Ted Williams for throwing his weight behind this book by contributing the foreword—he was my first and only choice. His ongoing advocacy to protect and preserve our wild native salmonids is unmatched. It's a great feeling when your heroes recognize your work.

David Peress for introducing me to the folks at Rowman & Littlefield Publishing, owners of Stackpole Books.

Jay Nichols at Stackpole Books for seeing the book, and brook trout, the way I did, and for helping me make this all work.

Artists Derek DeYoung, Nicholas Laferriere, A. D. Maddox, James Prosek, and Joseph Tomelleri for allowing me to use their art in support of articles, books, blog posts, presentations, and websites to help tell the native fish story.

Ted Williams and Clinton "Bill" Townsend, who through their tireless dedication to wild native fish, and their coaching, teaching, advising, and encouragement, instilled in me a true appreciation and respect for wild native fish and the places they live.

Edward Abby, Rick Bass, Rachel Carson, Dave Foreman, Aldo Leopold, Doug Peacock, David Petersen, Mike Roselle, Timothy Treadwell, Ted Williams, and all the other conservation writers out there for forcing me to look beyond what the mainstream and sporting media tells us, and delve deeper into the true status of, and threats to, our native species and wild places.

Emily Bastian, Murray Carpenter, Jonathan Carter, Gary Corson, Daryl DeJoy, Bradley Erdman, Charles Gauvin, Andy Goode, Cecil Grey, Dr. Michael Kinnison, Ted Koffman, John Lund, Bucky Owen, Roxanne Quimby, Naomi Schalit, Matt Scott, Dwayne Shaw, George Smith, Lucas St. Clair, Jym St. Pierre, Clinton "Bill" Townsend, Thomas Watson, Doug Watts, Ted Williams, and everyone else who has worked hard to protect and preserve Maine's wild native brook trout and the places they live.

Emily Bastian for being "Ms. Brook Trout" and working harder than anyone I know to help protect and preserve Maine's wild native brook trout.

Tom Dickens for convincing me to get back in the saddle and get organized, and for helping to get Native Fish Coalition off the ground. No one did more to make Native Fish Coalition a reality in its early days, and without Tom's vision and help it would not have happened.

Tom Dickens, Emily Bastian, Ben Brunt, Ted Williams, and the rest of the group for helping to keep Native Fish Coalition going and caring enough to donate their time.

My grandfather Franklin Brooks for planting the "fishing" seed in my head. Not sure where I'd be today if I had not found this island of sanity in what is often a crazy world.

The Beckwith family for sharing Camp U-No with me. I caught my first trout on a fly there—a 12-inch stocked rainbow from the Israel River that took a gray hackle fished dry, or however it landed, on a 7-foot, 5-weight fiberglass

Daiwa Gold Standard fly rod, Pflueger Medalist reel, and Cortland 444 line. I remember it like it was yesterday.

Bud Hawkins, the first person I ever met who had a true passion for fly fishing, for showing me how to tie my first fly using fur brushed from his old pet cat, Ma.

Craig Hallock for introducing me to Maine and pond-dwelling wild native brook trout. If not for him I might still be chasing stocked nonnative rainbows in Massachusetts with a spinning rod.

Tom Winslow for befriending me at Round Pond. Even though I was a young, hard-partying kid, he always took the time to talk to me, mentor me, and "try" to reel me in a bit. Round Pond was where I learned to truly appreciate wild native brook trout.

Erland Coombs for befriending me at Ripogenus Lake. Our forays into the woods and waters around Chesuncook were some of his last undertaken by vehicle and foot. Erland was a mentor of sorts and a truly good friend even though we were decades apart in age.

Kris Thompson and Pond in the River Guide Service; Kash Haley and Parkside & Main; John Blunt and Grant's Kennebago Camps; Bill Robinson and Dennys River Guide Service; Dwayne Shaw and Downeast Salmon Federation; Rob Burbank and Casey Mealey, and Appalachian Mountain Club; Jensen Bissell and Baxter State Park; Matt Libby, Matt Libby Jr., Jess Libby, and Toby Montgomery and Libby Camps; Igor and Karen Sikorsky and Bradford Camps; Lucas St. Clair and Elliotsville Plantation; Carolann Ouellette and Maine Office of Tourism; Nate Hill and Hill Country Guide Service; Andre Dionne and Bill Bernhardt and Cabins at Lopstick; Jon Howe and Tall Timber Lodge; Tom Freedman and Top Notch Fly Fishing; Geof Day and Sea-Run Brook Trout Coalition; Kevin Howell and Heath Cartee and Davidson River Outfitters; Mike Butler and family; Brian "Koz" Kozminski and True North Trout; Judy Fuller and Chris Lessway and North Branch Outing Club; Rich Paini, Jonathon Stiehl, and Ryan Loftice and TroutHunter; and everyone else who helped me while fishing for brook trout in their respective areas.

Emily and Larry Bastian, Tim and Lou Beckwith, Ben Brunt, Nate Hill, Jeff Levesque, Chris Major, Jeff Moore, Travis Parlin, David Peress, Kris Thompson, John Vacca, Dave Wysoki, and the rest of the "Brook Trout Gang"— here's hoping there are many more brook trout ahead for all of us.

And my wife, Diana, for hanging in there with me while I played fly fisherman, chased rainbows—and brookies, and otherwise refused to grow up.

The Nesowadnehunk Stream chapter is dedicated to Ray "Bucky" Owen and George Smith, two of the most influential outdoor figures in the history of Maine. Bucky is responsible for Maine's Quality Fishing Initiative, and George the State Heritage Fish law, arguably the two most important brook trout programs in the history of Maine. Both own camps on Nesowadnehunk Lake at what was once known as Camp Phoenix.

INTRODUCTION

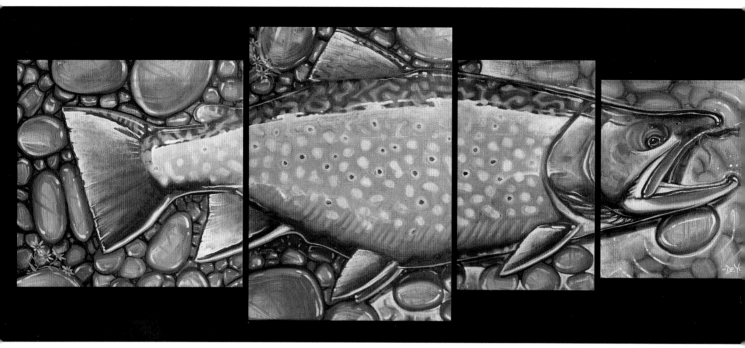

Four-panel brookie DEREK DEYOUNG ILLUSTRATION

The covers of most fly-fishing magazines are adorned with brown or rainbow trout, or some other exotic species. Bonefish, tarpon, permit, and peacock bass get more love from the fly-fishing media than brook trout, as do pike, muskies, and carp. Salmon, steelhead, and Arctic charr are better represented as well. Like a backup quarterback, brook trout don't get a lot of attention.

Yet prior to the introduction of brown trout in 1883 and rainbow trout in 1875, brook trout were the most sought after gamefish in the United States. They were written about in early books such as *American Anglers Book* (1864), *Fishing in American Waters* (1869), *Game Fish of North America* (1864), and *The Fishing Tourist* (1873). Brook trout donned the covers of early books and magazines and were arguably America's first gamefish.

Three states have named the brook trout their state fish: Michigan, Pennsylvania, and West Virginia. Five states have named the brook trout their State Freshwater Fish: New Hampshire, New Jersey, New York, North Carolina, and Virginia. Vermont designated the brook trout their State Cold Water Fish. In Maine, while not the official state fish—that honor belongs to the landlocked salmon, *Salmo salar sebago*—brook trout are classified as a State Heritage Fish along with the rare Arctic charr.

On average brook trout run smaller than other species of trout, and everyone knows that bigger is better these days. They are easy to catch—at least that's the perception. They don't jump or run or fight as well as some other species of trout.

Brook trout are not usually associated with the tailwaters, spring creeks, and reservoirs so popular with today's fly fishers. They are not found in famous places—at least by today's definition of "famous." You won't find brook trout in the Beaverhead, Bighorn, Green, Henrys Fork, Lees Ferry, Madison, Missouri, San Juan, or Yellowstone Rivers. You won't find them in Hebgen or Yellowstone Lakes. They are not present in Armstrong's, Nelson's, Silver, or Slough Creeks.

Brook trout are admittedly often found in obscure places. But you will also find them in the Allagash, Ausable, Au Sable, Batten Kill, Beaverkill, Kennebec, Kennebago, Magalloway, Neversink, Rapid, and Rapidan Rivers; Moosehead and Rangeley Lakes; and Big Spring and Willowemoc Creeks, all famous trout fisheries in their own right.

While best known as a small freestone stream fish, brook trout can also be found in large rivers, big lakes, and small ponds. They can even be found in tailwaters and spring creeks, as well as in tidal rivers and streams, estuaries, and open ocean. The Magalloway River in Maine is a trophy brook trout tailwater fishery. Big Spring in Pennsylvania is a limestone creek with a robust wild brook trout population. Lake Superior is home to giant brook trout known as "coasters." And sea-run brook trout, known as "salters," can be found in coastal streams from Maine to New York.

While most brook trout caught by anglers are small, and most likely have the smallest average size of any fish

Nine states have specialty brook trout license plates: Georgia, Massachusetts, North Carolina, Ohio, Tennessee, Vermont, Virginia, West Virginia, and Wisconsin. Pennsylvania Trout Unlimited has a non-registration plate, "Back the Brookie," as well. A movement is under way in Maine to create a brook trout plate. KENNY NELSON PHOTO

Jumping Trout, Winslow Homer (1889). Famed American painter Winslow Homer was also a brook trout fisherman. His 1892 painting, *A Brook Trout*, is one of the best-known depictions of the species, and his 1889 painting, *Jumping Trout*, also depicts a brook trout; a copy has hung in my home for over 20 years. His bamboo fly rod with his name on the case is housed at the American Museum of Fly Fishing in Manchester, Vermont.

that fly fishers target, it is not always the case. The Great Lakes, Maine, New Hampshire, and New York, as well as Labrador and Patagonia, and even a few western states, have waters that boast brook trout measured in pounds, not inches, and are trophy fisheries under any reasonable definition.

Admittedly, small brook trout in freestone streams might be the most gullible fish around. They have evolved to survive in a world where forage is scarce. But the heavily pressured and well-fed fish found in places like the Rapid and Magalloway Rivers in Maine will test the skills of even the most accomplished fly fisher.

Sure, some brook trout come to the net quite easily—but not all. Once while surrounded by rising fish on Henrys Lake that I assumed were cutthroat or cuttbow hybrids, it took us almost an hour and countless fly changes before we dialed it in. While the surface was littered with *Callibaetis*, it turned out that the fish were "dumb" brook trout gorging themselves on midge pupa. I have spent hours fishing for brook trout on a pond that seemed all but fishless, only to have it come alive with rises at the onset of a hatch. Other times I have been skunked on water I knew from personal experience held a solid population of brook trout. As those who have fished for brook trout in large rivers can attest, they know how to use the current and structure to their advantage as well as any other trout. And lake and pond brook trout are notorious for using weeds, submerged logs, and anchor ropes to avoid capture.

Brook trout are one of the most beautiful fish found anywhere. Large brook trout, especially males during the fall spawning season, are as impressive as any trout you will encounter. And small-stream resident brook trout are some of the most colorful fish you will ever see.

The first brook trout I ever caught was a stocked one, taken on a worm from Applebee Brook in New Hampshire's White Mountains. I was still in high school, or at least I was supposed to be.

My first 30-fish day involved stocked brook trout from a small impoundment in Whitefield, New Hampshire, known as Airport Marsh. I soon replicated my success on a small impoundment called Terrell Pond in Pittsburg, New Hampshire. In both cases the fish were caught on a Hornberg fished wet.

Closer to home, I caught 30 or so 8-inch freshly stocked brook trout on dries from a small meadow stream in northern Massachusetts. Known locally as Ash Swamp, it was my first "home water." I caught a 14-inch brook trout on a small bucktail a year or so later, and while beautiful, it was most likely a holdover.

My first large brook trout, a 16-incher, came from the upper Johns River in Carroll, New Hampshire. The fish took a light Cahill dry fly, and while it looked wild, it may have been a holdover, too. I took it back to camp to eat, something that has haunted me ever since.

The first unquestionably wild brook trout I caught was a 14-incher from Round Pond in central Maine. I was in my early 20s, and the fish took a large yellow Wulff that I had just tied on a folding picnic table at a remote campsite.

Like many anglers I soon got caught up in the "big fish" craze. I bought a drift boat and stopped fishing small streams and brook trout ponds altogether for roughly a decade. I became obsessed with trying to fish all the nation's best-known "trout" waters and made one hell of a dent in that project. And while brook trout had pretty much fallen off my radar screen, I made a trip to the Minipi region of Labrador to fish for "trophy brookies."

Driven by the collapse of my home river, the Kennebec in Maine, I bought a few short fly rods, a chestpack, and a fanny pack, and returned to the small streams of my youth, most of which were in the White Mountains of New Hampshire, the most beautiful place in the Northeast. I moved some old canoes around, revamped my pond gear, bought a couple of float tubes, and hit the remote brook trout ponds of central and northern Maine and northern New Hampshire with a vengeance.

Having now come full circle, I am once again an unapologetic brook trout fisherman. Wild native trout in natural environs are something truly special. And while I once had it and lost it, I will never make that mistake again. It's not size, numbers, or degree of difficulty, it's much bigger than that, and something you can't understand until you have found it.

I spent hours reading books, articles, papers, and blog posts in preparation for this book. I sorted through what I found, identified consistencies and inconsistencies, and took positions based on the reputation of the source, and to some degree the age of the material because things change, and in some cases our understanding of things changes. I also spent countless hours afield doing research, talking to people, collecting pictures, and, of course, fishing.

My travels took me to a limestone creek in Pennsylvania that is home to brook trout, some of which get quite large. I spent a day on a sprawling lake in Idaho that, while best known for its cutthroats and hybrids, has a robust population of brook trout. I fished for brook trout in a small pond in Yellowstone National Park, as well as a small stream in Cody, Wyoming.

There was the isolated hike-in headwater stream deep in the mountains of Pisgah National Forest in North Carolina, where pure-strain Southern Appalachian brook trout eke out a living in barely a half mile of water that plunges hundreds of feet over a series of drops, disappearing into a wooded hollow far below.

In Great Smoky Mountains National Park in Tennessee, we battled dense mountain laurel to catch an exceptionally beautiful fish that I accidentally dropped just before we could get a picture. I netted the fish from a small pocket of water using my hat, a trucker, which made a great improvised net.

Although I had lived in Massachusetts and Maine for nearly 50 years, I had never fished for sea-run brook trout. Armed with a short rod, a box full of small freshly tied

It would not be a stretch to call brook trout "America's Trout." In the history of American fly fishing, more anglers grew up catching brook trout than any other species of trout, char, or salmon. While this is most likely no longer the case (rainbows are probably the most frequently caught trout today), brook trout are where it all started.
DIANA MALLARD PHOTO

streamers, and a confusing mix of information and suggestions, I managed to catch a dozen or so brook trout from a small coastal stream in Cape Cod that emptied into a large bay within sight of the road.

In Acadia National Park, I watched close to 50 wild native brook trout that while only a few car lengths from the open ocean, were blocked by low tide and a stream that went intermittent just before reaching the crashing surf. On another stream in the park, I caught fish that were in tidal water with easy access to and from the sea.

I made a trip to Downeast Maine with mentor and fellow Native Fish Coalition founder Ted Williams, founding member and Maine chair Emily Bastian, and others as part of a volunteer survey project to identify populations of sea-run brook trout. Hosted by Dwayne Shaw, executive director of Downeast Salmon Federation, we canoed a river, catching small silvery brook trout all day long. I was so impressed with my trip to Downeast Maine and the robust and underfished sea-run brook trout resources we encountered that I returned twice more to fish several other rivers and streams.

The project also sent me to Maine's newest federal land, Katahdin Woods and Waters National Monument. Having not been there in a couple of decades, I was impressed with what I found, including a beautiful hike-in mountain stream teeming with wild brook trout.

I made several backpacking trips into White Mountain National Forest in New Hampshire, home to some of the most remote wild brook trout fishing left in New England. Nearly 4 miles up a trail off the end of a long dirt road, we caught close to 100 brook trout in just a day and a half. Backpacking for wild native brook trout represents, at least to me, fly fishing in its purest form.

While technically a where-to book, this is as much about fish as fishing, why-to as where-to, and what-to as how-to. It is about brook trout, a wildly varied, often overlooked and greatly underappreciated native gamefish in a world full of exotic, homogenized, and commercialized species, and a rare example of a natural fish living in natural places. While this book is not exclusively about wild native fish and natural waters, that is my primary focus. Stocked and nonnative fish and man-made or heavily altered environments, while covered, are the exception here, not the rule.

To write a book about brook trout and not point out how they, and their world, differ from other species of salmonids would be misleading, incomplete, and disingenuous. Brook trout are a unique fish living in a complex and rapidly changing world. They are remnants of a time when what swam in our rivers, streams, lakes, and ponds belonged there.

Brook trout are also the canary in the coal mine. They are an indicator species whose presence is indicative of a healthy aquatic ecosystem. While very much an eastern thing, "brookies," as brook trout are commonly referred to, have become somewhat of a poster child for the emerging native fish movement.

Brook trout will need friends if they are to survive, and the best way to accomplish this is through public awareness. For years I have used the where-to platform to promote conservation. I call it "conservation by destination." Unlike pure conservation writing, which is often preaching to the choir, where-to appeals to everyone, including those we need to reach most.

While hopefully enjoyable to read, this is not fiction. While hopefully informative, this is not a scientific paper. I have attempted to blend fish and fishing and write about them as I would speak to someone I met on the water. I hope you enjoy it. I hope you find it useful. And if you learn something along the way, that's great.

This book is not intended to supplant Karas's seminal book *Brook Trout*, as nothing can ever do so. It is not a textbook or literary work; it's a book about brook trout written by someone who has seen a whole lot of them. It is also not a kiss-and-tell where-to book, just a general guide to this amazing fish and the places they live.

It is important to note that I am not a trained biologist. I am an angler, writer, and observer of natural things. Much of what I know, or think I know, was learned in the field. As author Tom Ames once said, I am an "empirical" angler, and know what I know through hands-on experience, experimentation, and trial and error. I suppose the same can be said for my not-so-scientific "science."

In some ways my lack of formal education regarding fish is an asset, not a liability. I am not burdened by absolutes, textbook theory, and other things that can hamper one's ability to think outside the box. I do not have an academic reputation to protect that requires I be 100 percent sure of my position before stating it. But I am well-read, so most of what I believe has at least some basis in science.

I am analytical by nature. And while biased (like everyone else) to at least some degree, I think I am objective and willing to consider all sides of an issue. But as you know, research is only as good as the data available, and today that is somewhat of a problem as the internet has given voice to everyone, including people with bias, agendas, lack of experience, or, worse, absolute incompetency.

In a way I have been preparing for this book my entire adult life—without even realizing it. As a lifelong New Englander, fishing for brook trout is nothing new to me. In fact, I suspect I have spent more hours chasing brook trout than I have all other species of fish combined. I have fished for brook trout in rivers, streams, lakes, ponds, flowages, beaver ponds, and estuaries.

Brook trout have been a sort of salvation for me. They are what got me into the woods and off the beaten path. Brook trout introduced me to many of the things in nature I hold near and dear. They became a calling of sorts, and the primary focus of my advocacy efforts. Fishing for wild and native fish in natural places is what brings it all together for me.

This project has brought things full circle for me. It helped me collect my thoughts, get out of my comfort zone, and pay closer attention to what I was doing. It gave

Brook trout–themed consumer products, including T-shirts, underwear, belts, hats, eyeglass retainers, sun guards, phone cases, glasses and cups, beverage holders, fly-fishing tools, and fly boxes, have become quite popular. Brook trout art is equally popular, with artists like Derek DeYoung, A. D. Maddox, Andrea Larko, Karen Talbot, Alex Poland, and Samantha Aronson leading the charge. DIANA MALLARD PHOTO

The view from my new office. It sure beats the view of downtown Boston I used to have. BOB MALLARD PHOTO

me a more complete understanding of brook trout, and an even deeper respect and appreciation for them. It helped me understand why I do what I do, and how and why the preservation of wild native fish, especially brook trout, became more important to me than fishing.

Terminology

I use the terms *wild* and *self-sustaining* interchangeably to mean born in nature, not in a hatchery. When I use the term *native*, I mean fish that were historically present in the respective water, not just in the state or region. I don't subscribe to the "naturalized native" theory, which maintains that fish born in nature belong there regardless of their historic presence, or lack thereof.

I don't believe that native implies, or should imply, genetically pure. A nonnative fish can be genetically pure if they have not been compromised by hatchery fish or hybridization. A Sebago strain landlocked salmon living in Patagonia that has never been compromised by other strains of landlocked salmon is genetically pure. Ditto for Sunapee strain Arctic charr found in Idaho.

The term *heritage* has become somewhat synonymous with genetic purity. In Maine it is applied to both never-stocked-over fish and those that have not been stocked over in 25 years or more. To eliminate confusion, I do not use the term *heritage* to describe genetically pure

fish, only those protected under Maine's State Heritage Fish law.

I use the term *trout* loosely. In many cases I mean it figuratively, not literally. As has become the accepted practice in most fishing circles and the media, the term *trout* refers to both char and true trout. In Maine, when used alone, the word means brook trout. Pay attention to the context in which the word is used, and it should be clear as to what I mean.

I use the term *charr* to refer to Maine's Arctic charr; it is a regionally accepted spelling that seems to have originated in Canada, as many things in Maine do. When I refer to the genus of fish, I use the spelling *char*.

Lastly, I use the terms *population* and *fishery* interchangeably, usually for readability purposes so as not to use the same term too often. While I prefer *population*, as it implies fish, the term *fishery* implies fishing, and if it were not for fishing this book would never have been written.

While this book is a celebration of a unique, fascinating, and beautiful gamefish as well as a roadmap for where, and even how, to catch them, it is also a call to arms. If we are to preserve this beautiful fish for future generations, we need to stop the bleeding and fight to win back some of the ground we have lost. And while we're at it, we should take advantage of this wonderful resource and go fishing, as this is the best way to truly understand and appreciate it. And like golf, you don't have to eat the ball to enjoy the sport.

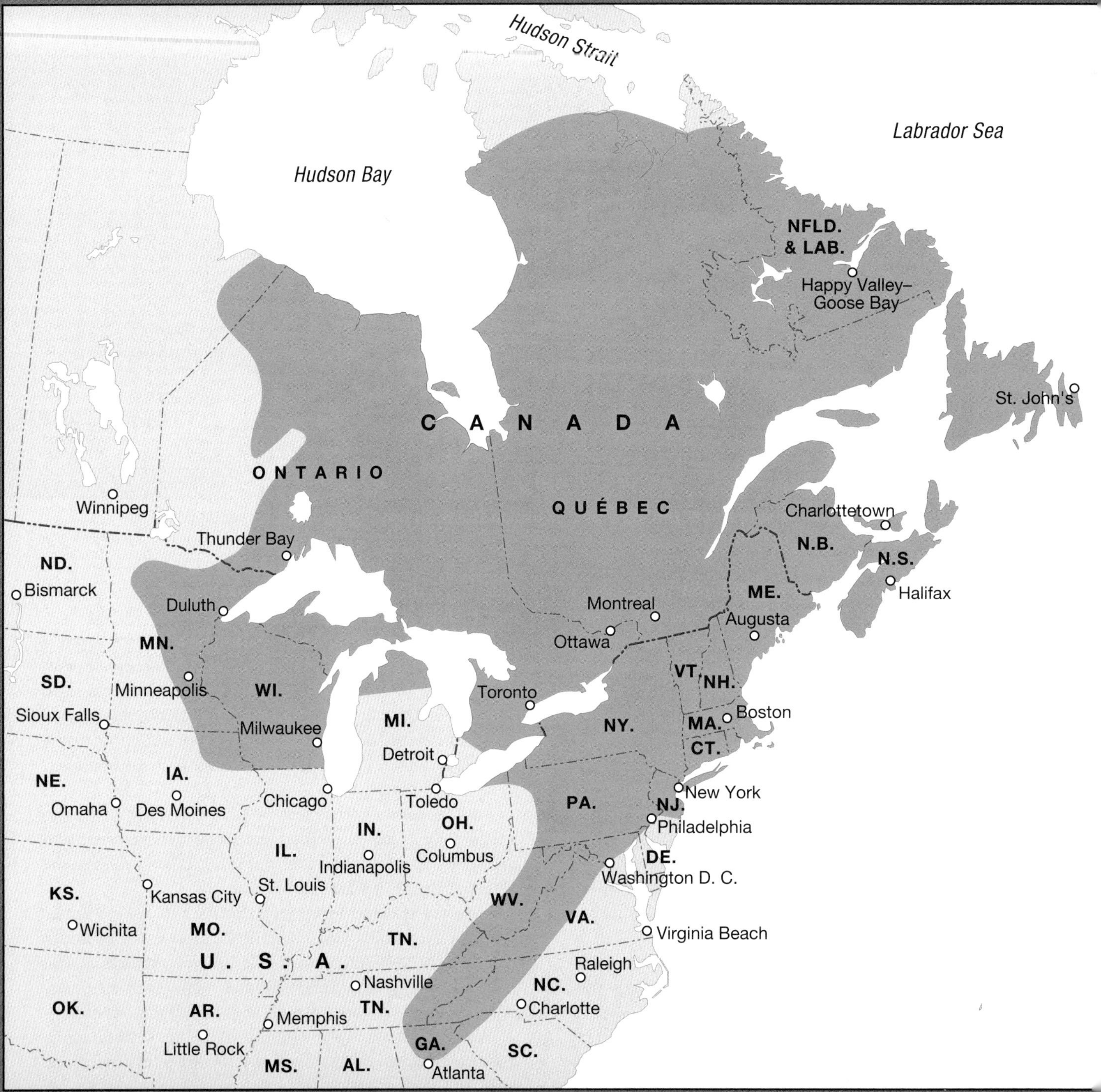

Brook trout native range map.

Brook Trout

Natural History

Brook trout have inhabited eastern waters since the glaciers retreated. They have been present in the Appalachian Mountain region for several million years. Brook trout are an indicator species, a sign of a healthy watershed and clean, cold water. They are often the first species to show signs of stress when environmental changes occur.

Originally referred to as *Salmo fontinalis* by naturalist Samuel Latham Mitchill in 1814, brook trout are now referred to as *Salvelinus fontinalis*. *Salvelinus* is a genus of salmonid. While occasionally applied to trout, it usually refers to char, or charr. *Salvelinus* are a member of the Salmoninae subfamily of the Salmonidae family. The term *fontinalis* is Latin for "of or from a spring or fountain," which refers to the cold, clean water brook trout are found in.

The name brook trout is misleading, for multiple reasons. Brook trout are not a true trout; they are a char. They are more closely related to Arctic charr, bull trout, Dolly Varden, and lake trout than they are brown trout, rainbow trout, and cutthroat trout. Brook trout are, however, the most trout-like of all char, demonstrating a similar life history and ecology and occupying similar habitat as that used by true trout, while often shunning habitat used by other char. Brook trout have several nicknames, including eastern brook trout, speckled trout or specs, brook charr, mud trout, common trout, squaretail, and, the most commonly used, brookie. Those found in the Great Lakes are called coasters and those that utilize saltwater habitat salters.

Native Range

Brook trout are one of the most widely distributed native trout in North America. They are native to the United States and Canada. Only lake trout and Arctic charr have a larger historic range. Brook trout can be found in the Canadian Provinces of Labrador, New Brunswick, Newfoundland, Nova Scotia, Ontario, Prince Edward Island, Quebec, and eastern Manitoba. They can be found in most Atlantic Ocean drainages as well as the James, Ungava, and Hudson Bay drainages. Brook trout are also one of the most widely distributed native trout in the contiguous United States. This includes the Appalachian corridor, a 100-mile-wide swath of land that extends from the top of Maine to northern Georgia. Parts of the Midwest and most of the Great Lakes were home to native brook trout as well.

Brook trout are native to most of Connecticut, Maine, Massachusetts, New Hampshire, New York, Pennsylvania, Vermont, and Wisconsin; much of Maryland and Rhode Island; parts of Michigan, Minnesota, New Jersey, North Carolina, Tennessee, Virginia, and West Virginia; and small sections of Georgia, Iowa, Kentucky, Ohio, and South Carolina. In many of these states they are the only native salmonid.

You can find native brook trout in the Great Lakes Basin, headwater tributaries of the Mississippi River, and most Atlantic Ocean drainages from Maine to Virginia. They can be found on both sides of the southern Appalachian Mountains as well, with those rivers and streams to the west draining into the Gulf of Mexico versus the Atlantic Ocean.

While brook trout were native to the Upper Peninsula of Michigan, the only place they were found on the Lower Peninsula was the Muskegon River system. They were not native to the Au Sable and Manistee Rivers, and their presence in the Boardman River is a source of debate. The only salmonid native to these fabled "trout" rivers were the now extinct Arctic grayling. Interestingly, according to a June 22, 2017, article by Gary Garth in *USA Today*, "Trout Fishing on Michigan's Pristine Au Sable River," brown trout of European origin were introduced to these waters a year before brook trout.

While native to most of the drainage, brook trout did not occur in most of the Lake Erie tributaries in Ohio. Many of these tributaries have since been stocked with brook trout and other species of trout, where they are reported to be doing quite well.

The southernmost populations of native brook trout in the world are found in northern Georgia in the headwaters of the Chattahoochee River in Chattahoochee National Forest. According to the Georgia Council of Trout Unlimited, wild brook trout inhabit roughly 140 miles of stream in the state. Twenty-four populations spread out across 36 miles are said to be Southern Appalachian strain.

Biology

When comparing similar types of fish, or any fauna for that matter, the application of scientific terms is not always consistent. For example, each type of cutthroat—Lahontan, Rio Grande, Bonneville, Greenback, Yellowstone, and so forth—is referred to as a separate subspecies; there is no simple cutthroat. Conversely, while there are two recognized subspecies of brook trout, the common form is referred to as a species.

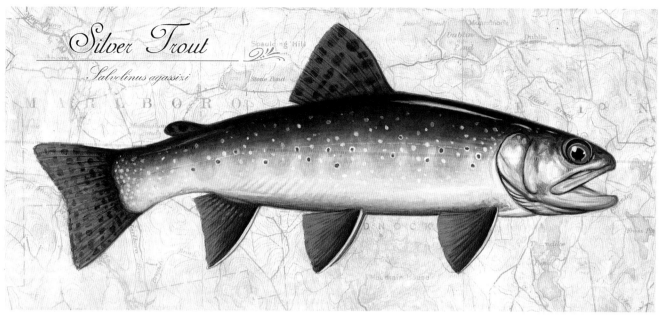

Extinct silver trout, which was believed to have been a subspecies of brook trout. MATT PATTERSON ILLUSTRATION

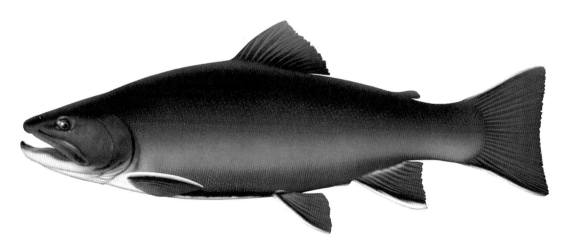

Aurora trout, a subspecies of brook trout. Notice the lack of spotting and vermiculation. CORY TREPANIER ILLUSTRATION

What constitutes a strain is even more complicated, and while slight genetic differences do exist, it is more a geographic than genetic categorization. While the scientific community generally recognizes a Southern Appalachian strain of brook trout that inhabits a multistate swath of land, Maine recognizes watershed-specific strains such as Kennebago and Nesowadnehunk.

In addition to species, subspecies, and strains, the term *form* is sometimes applied to brook trout to describe groups of fish that have a common life history. While genetically the same as other brook trout, and not confined to a geographic boundary like strains, these fish have adapted to a specific set of unique conditions.

Making things even more complicated is the fact that there are no definitive guidelines as to what is and is not a subspecies or strain, and what was thought to be a subspecies yesterday could be reclassified to a species or even a strain today, or vice versa, and what was considered a strain in the past could now be classified as a form.

Unlike many other trout, brook trout have few subspecies. The silver trout, *Salvelinus agassizii*, and aurora trout, *Salvelinus timagamiensis*, are the only two recognized subspecies. While sea-run brook trout and those found in the Great Lakes were once thought to be subspecies, they are now considered the same species as other brook trout.

The silver trout, once thought to be a form of lake trout or Arctic charr, is now believed to have been a deep-water form of brook trout. Last seen in Dublin Pond in New Hampshire in 1930, it is now extinct. This small brook trout, rarely growing above 12 inches, once inhabited Dublin/Monadnock Pond and Christine Lake in New Hampshire.

The aurora trout is native to two lakes, Whitepine and Whirligig, and their tributaries in the Temagami District of Ontario, Canada. While they were originally believed to be a separate species, they are now considered a subspecies of brook trout. Although their general coloration resembles a brook trout, they lack the spots and vermiculation found on brook trout. Having lost their native waters to acidification, they were introduced to other waters to save them and have since been restored to their native waters.

While not a true subspecies, the most genetically different group of brook trout is the Southern Appalachian strain. Native to parts of Virginia, Tennessee, North and South Carolina, and Georgia, their genetic markers are slightly different from other brook trout. Aesthetically, however, they look and behave similar to other brook trout. Even within their native range, pure-strain Southern Appalachian brook trout are somewhat rare due to decades of stocking.

Esteemed fisheries biologist Dr. Robert Behnke describes three forms of brook trout in his book *Trout and Salmon of North America*: A large lake form referred to as coasters found in the northern extremes of the range, a sea-run form that enters saltwater to feed and seek thermal refuge, and the common form found in lakes, ponds, rivers, and streams. All of these are part of the common species.

When it comes to water temperature, brook trout have the highest tolerance of warm water of any char. While they prefer water that is a bit cooler than true trout, they can survive in water that is too warm for most species of char. The optimal temperature for char is 50 to 57 degrees F; brook trout, however, can tolerate temperatures into the mid-60s. Conversely, true trout have an ideal temperature range of 57 to 65 degrees and can tolerate temperatures even higher. While they can survive temporary variations, brook trout's preferred temperature range is from the low 30s to the low 70s, with large fish being most affected by warm water.

Brook trout also have more general habitat requirements than most charr, inhabiting lakes, ponds, rivers, streams, estuaries, and saltwater. Brook trout prefer clear water. They are sensitive to pH and have very narrow requirements, typically in the 5.0 to 7.5 range. Many high-elevation brook trout populations were lost during the peak of the acid rain crisis. Brook trout also require highly oxygenated water and have a low tolerance for pollution.

Physical Description

The first drawing of a brook trout I could find was done by Dr. Jerome V. C. Smith and included in his 1833 book, *Natural History of Fishes*. Referred to as a "common trout," it has the general shape, spotting, and square tail found in brook trout, but it is an incomplete and somewhat inaccurate representation.

Brook trout, especially large spawning males, are one of the most beautiful salmonids. Even small brook trout can be extremely colorful. And while they are often at their most vibrant in the fall, some brook trout hold their colors year-round, especially those in mud-bottom beaver ponds and flowages. The dark colors found on some brook trout are most likely due to their chameleon-like tendency to try to blend in with their surroundings.

Brook trout have a dark green back with yellow-green marbled patterns called vermiculation. The flanks lighten in color as you move downward, transitioning into an orange or red. The bottom of the belly is an ivory-white

How the Brook Trout Got Its Spots

A Native American story says that brook trout did not originally have the colorful markings now found on their flanks. When Manitou, the Great Spirit of the Algonquins, went to visit the Iroquois, he became hungry. Stopping beside a pool in a stream surrounded by giant white pines and hemlocks, he saw that the water was full of trout. These trout were black and sans markings.

Manitou reached into the water and came out with the largest fish in the group. Upon inspecting it, he noted its beauty and strength, and decided to return it to the water rather than eat it. As the fish swam away its flanks began to turn silvery, and colored spots and halos appeared where the Great Spirit had touched it. Stripes where Manitou's fingers contacted the fish are still evident today in the form of parr markings.

Because of this encounter with the Great Spirit, brook trout were considered sacred to the Indians of the Six Nations, and they would not catch or eat them.

Note: This story is usually credited to the Shikellemus Indians. While there was a Native American named Shikellemus, to the best of my knowledge there were no Shikellemus Indians. Based on what I have been able to come up with, Shikellemus was a chief of the Cayuga band of the Iroquois, or Mingo, Nation. He was the father of Chief Logan, who is well known to history. ■

trimmed in black. Flanks are peppered with yellow-green spots, interspersed with blue-haloed red spots.

The tail, or caudal fin, of a brook trout is square with rounded corners. It is orange or yellow-green with wavy patterns or spots like those found on the back and flanks. The lower edge of the tail is white. The back and top edges are typically darker than the rest of the tail, and there is a small black line separating the white from the orange or green.

A brook trout's dorsal fin is large and sail-like. It is lighter green than the back and flecked with yellow-green spots or vermiculation lines. While I cannot prove it, based on anecdotal information I believe the dorsal fin may be somewhat proportionally smaller on lake and pond fish than it is on river and stream fish. If so, this is most likely due to its use as a rudder in moving water. The adipose fin on a brook trout is short and thick and colored like the dorsal fin. The pectoral, pelvic, and anal fins are orange and trimmed with white on the leading edge. A small black line separates the orange from the white in all cases.

The head of a brook trout is usually darker than the rest of the body. The top is covered in yellow-green spots and

While called "brook" trout, *Salvelinus fontinalis* is found in lakes and ponds throughout the northern extent of its native range as well as in stillwaters outside its range. DIANA MALLARD PHOTO

vermiculation lines. The lower jaw is white with a black trim separating it from the rest of the head. The cheeks are lighter than the top with less visible spots or vermiculation. A brook trout's eye is nearly black, and they have a pronounced lateral line midway up the flank that runs from the front of the tail to the gill plate.

Brook trout found in brackish water or saltwater are silvery with faint spots and pale bellies. When they move back into freshwater, they regain their more typical coloration and often very quickly. Those found in cold, clear lakes are often paler than those found in tannic rivers, streams, ponds, flowages, and lakes. Whether this is due to water chemistry, forage, or both is unclear.

It is also important to note that brook trout in general seem to demonstrate chameleon-like traits, getting lighter and darker depending on their surroundings. Spend a day electrofishing and you can watch the fish lighten in color after being placed in 5-gallon pails for processing. While I cannot prove it, it would be reasonable to assume that the same occurs in the wild.

Brook trout in small streams typically run from 3 to 6 inches, with 8-inch fish considered large. In small ponds their length range and average size vary considerably due to population densities, forage, competition, and angling pressure. In large lakes and certain rivers, brook trout can attain lengths of over 20 inches. The world-record brook

trout was in the 30-inch range. The average size is usually highest, but not always, where the population densities are the lowest.

Most brook trout caught from streams weigh well under a pound. Fish from lakes, ponds, and large rivers are often over a pound. Brook trout pushing 10 pounds are still caught in Canada, and fish up to 5 pounds are still caught in the United States. The world-record brook trout weighed close to 15 pounds. Brook trout size can be influenced by habitat, forage, competition, genetics, and angling pressure. Fish in streams tend to be smaller and grow more slowly than those found in lakes and ponds. Unusually cold water or short growing seasons (as in long winters) can also affect growth rates. Fish in the northern extremes of their range grow slower than those in the southern extremes due to a shorter growing season. Brook trout are often smaller where they are abundant and larger where they are not.

Habitat

Not all brook trout live in brooks, or even rivers. Some spend their entire life in lakes and ponds, some in rivers and streams, and some move between lakes and ponds and rivers and streams. Some even move between freshwater and brackish water or saltwater.

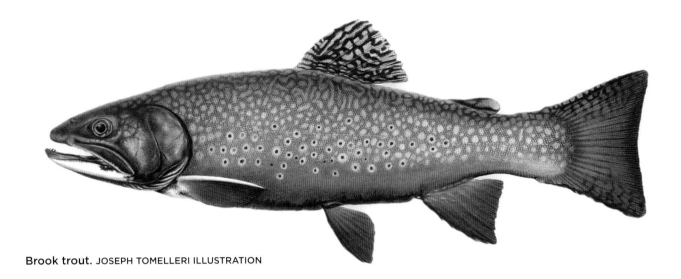

Brook trout. JOSEPH TOMELLERI ILLUSTRATION

While regularly applied to other species of fish, including salmonids, the terms *fluvial* (fish that live and spawn in streams and rivers), *adfluvial* (fish that are spawned and reared in tributaries but migrate to lakes and ponds), *lacustrine* (fish that live and spawn in lakes and ponds), *potamodromous* (fish that migrate between rivers and streams and lakes and ponds), and *diadromous* (fish that migrate between freshwater and saltwater) are rarely applied to brook trout, even though they demonstrate these behaviors.

Brook trout are also incredibly adaptable. Few species of salmonid utilize as many habitat types as brook trout and change habitat as often. A brook trout found in a lake today could show up miles up a stream tomorrow.

As streams warm or become low, brook trout often seek refuge in lakes and ponds. Habitat is altered, and sometimes significantly, by beaver activity, converting what was once a free-flowing stream to a slow and often shallow pond. When this happens, brook trout adapt to their new surroundings quite well, and quickly.

Brook trout with access to brackish water or saltwater often take advantage of such. Coastal streams teeming with brook trout in the spring can be all but devoid of fish in midsummer, the resident fish having moved to saltwater to escape warm or low water.

Life Cycle

Brook trout in small freestone streams rarely live more than a few years. In large lakes and rivers, especially in Canada, they can reach up to 10 years old. In ponds and lakes in the United States, they fall somewhere in between. Lifespan is influenced by biological and social factors such as water temperature, forage availability, angling pressure, harvest, and possibly genetics. Interestingly, the oldest brook trout on record were of hatchery origin and found well outside their native range in the High Sierras of California. As a result of the extreme conditions found in their high-elevation habitat and marginal forage, their metabolism was greatly slowed, and one specimen was reported to have lived for 24 years.

Freshly hatched brook trout are referred to as alevin, or sac fry. They have yolk sacs attached to their bellies and remain in the redd until they exhaust this built-in food supply. Once the yoke sac is gone, they leave the redd in search of food. When they lose their yoke sac, they are referred to as fry. Fry move into the shallows to forage on microscopic food sources and keep out of the way of predators, including adults of their own species. They develop vertical stripes along their flanks, known as parr marks, and are referred to as parr. Parr venture into deeper water where they feed on small insect larvae. The final stages of brook trout life are known as juvenile and adult.

While some brook trout spend their entire life in lakes and ponds or rivers and streams, some juvenile brook trout are born and reared in streams and move into lakes, ponds, or rivers as they mature. Others remain in streams and rivers their entire life.

Reproduction

Depending on conditions, brook trout can reach sexual maturity as early as two years old, and some biologists say earlier. They continue to spawn throughout their lives; unlike Pacific salmon, brook trout do not die after spawning.

Brook trout are fall spawners. Depending on the location, spawning occurs in September, October, or November. Fish begin to stage for spawning as early as mid- to late August. While many brook trout spawn in moving water, some demonstrate lacustrine behavior and spawn in lakes and ponds, usually near the shore.

Brook trout, especially males, become noticeably more colorful during spawning. Their bellies turn a brilliant orange or red, and while not as pronounced as salmon or brown trout, male brook trout develop a kype, or hooked jaw, during spawning.

In all cases, brook trout build redds in the gravel. Females construct a depression in the streambed using their tails to move sand and debris out of the way. In many cases redds are constructed where groundwater seeps up through the gravel. This is especially true in lakes and

Evidence of decades of beaver activity has turned this once free-flowing stream into a shallow meadow pond. Amazingly, the resident brook trout find a way to adapt to this type of habitat. RICHARD YVON PHOTO

ponds. The number of eggs produced by female brook trout is somewhat dependent on their size, with larger specimens laying more eggs than smaller ones. A typical female will produce roughly 500 eggs, a low number when compared to fish such as bass, pike, and smelt, which lay thousands.

Brook trout eggs are slightly denser than water. When laid they drop into the redd where the female buries them in loose gravel, leaving a slight mound. Male brook trout converge on redds to fertilize the eggs. They rub flanks with females, which stimulates the production of semen, or milt. Dominant males drive other males off the redds, which helps to reduce egg predation. The gestation period for brook trout eggs is roughly 100 days but can be as short as 50 or as long as 150. Brook trout eggs hatch in the early spring, typically in March or April.

Population Densities

Brook trout population densities can be abundant or sparse. They are usually most abundant where good stream spawning habitat is available. In cases where pond-dwelling fish utilize in-lake spawning habitat, populations are usually sparser. The term for this is *recruitment*, and it basically means spawning rates. High recruitment means high densities and low recruitment low densities.

Brook trout population densities are typically moderate to low where they are native. They can, however, be high in beaver ponds, lakes, and ponds with unusually high recruitment rates and some small freestone streams with light fishing pressure. As in most cases, Mother Nature has a way of working things out when we let her.

Brook trout population densities can be unusually high where they have been introduced. I have seen small streams in the Rocky Mountains with population densities of wild nonnative brook trout that far exceed anything I have seen where they are native. In many western streams brook trout populations have exploded to a point where they have pushed out native cutthroat. While I cannot prove it, I believe the high population densities of nonnative brook trout found in western streams is because brook trout have evolved to survive in conditions that would be considered marginal for most trout. Many freestone streams in the East are relatively infertile, with marginal forage, and are prone to warming and low water levels. Conversely, many western streams are fertile, cool, and apparently quite conducive to brook trout.

Brook trout are often small where they are abundant and larger where they are sparse. Unusually high population densities can result in what is referred to as stunting. True stunting is the presence of small older fish and the absence of large fish. In some cases the absence of large fish is the result of angler exploitation or minimum-length management, leading some to believe they are seeing stunting when what they are really seeing is simply a lack of older larger fish.

Feeding Habits

Brook trout are often referred to as opportunistic feeders. This is due to the fact that many live in what are relatively infertile environments such as natural freestone streams and oligotrophic lakes. In many cases insect hatches are unreliable, short-lived, and sparse. This forces brook trout to eat, or try to eat, pretty much anything that drifts or swims by.

Unlike most char, and like most trout, brook trout eat a lot of aquatic insects, especially larvae and pupa. They will, however, take advantage of all stages of mayflies, caddis, stoneflies, and midges. They eat dragonflies, damselflies, and boatmen as well. While brook trout eat all stages of damselflies including adults, they seem to focus mostly on dragonfly nymphs as opposed to adults. The same holds true for dobsonflies, with the hellgrammite larvae being much preferred over the adult.

Brook trout also eat terrestrial insects such as ants, beetles, bees, flies, moths, grasshoppers, and crickets. Like most trout, brook trout will gorge themselves on terrestrials when they are available. In Maine, ants and beetles trigger some of the best surface action of the season.

Dr. Behnke reports that when sharing the water with nonnative brown or rainbow trout, brook trout tend to feed on the bottom while the others feed subsurface or on top. While I generally agree with Behnke, I am not sure I agree with this assertion. I say this because I have caught brook trout on the surface where they overlap brown and/or rainbow trout, and in numbers that indicated no real species preference. It may, however, be true where the nonnatives are noticeably larger and more aggressive.

Large brook trout can be as piscivorous (minnow-eating) as any trout. They are known to eat chub, dace, sculpin, smelt, and other minnows. I know for a fact that they eat juvenile brook trout as well, as I have released small brook trout only to have them devoured by a larger brook trout. Brook trout will also eat mice, even fish of moderate size. Large rodent-eating brook trout are common in places like Labrador. Brook trout eat worms, caterpillars, leeches, crayfish, snails, salamanders, tadpoles and pollywogs, frogs, scuds and sow bugs, and fish eggs as well.

Because brook trout use their eyes to identify possible food sources and are not known for having great eyesight, they feed mostly, but certainly not exclusively, during the day. Like most trout they are especially active in the early morning and early evening, and sometimes feed at night when the moon is bright.

Place in the Food Web

Like many things in nature, brook trout are both predator and prey. They are preyed on by other fish including cannibalistically by members of their own species. In fact, in some cases large brook trout are the primary predator of small brook trout. They also serve as a food source for certain species of birds, mammals, and reptiles.

Herons, kingfishers, eagles, ospreys, cormorants, and loons all prey on brook trout. While herons and kingfishers are primarily a threat to smaller fish, eagles, ospreys, cormorants, and loons can feed on adult brook trout. The most effective and efficient avian brook trout predator, however, in my humble opinion, is the loon.

One fall during an unusually low water period, I saw where several large brook trout had been eaten by a great blue heron on the fabled Kennebago River in Maine, the scat, feathers, and scales on the rocks telling the gruesome tale. I once caught a large brook trout on Big Spring Run in Pennsylvania that had a hole clean though its flank, most likely the work of a heron.

Loons probably eat a higher percentage of brook trout than any other bird due to where they live and how they feed. I once had an overly aggressive loon steal a stringer of brook trout dragging behind my canoe. On numerous occasions I have had loons home in on the splashing of a hooked fish and try to take it right off the line on backcountry ponds in Maine. I watched friend Emily Bastian lose a 16-inch fish to a loon that surfaced and choked it down like a pelican. Things got so bad on one pond that we put 5-gallon pails in our canoes to hold fish until the loons lost interest.

While top-water opportunists are probably more of a threat to rough fish than trout, eagles and ospreys clearly eat some brook trout. I have seen both dive-bomb a large river, lake, or pond and come up with what I knew was a trout by its shape. In some cases the only trout present were brook trout.

Brook trout are preyed on by mink and otters as well. More than once I have found a pile of small brook trout heads at the base of a culvert, the scat piles showing it was the handiwork of a mink. I have seen groups of otters push through the water blowing up brook trout ahead of them. On several occasions I have witnessed otters dining on brook trout shoreside, oblivious or unconcerned with my presence.

I have seen the aftermath of what looked like raccoon/ brook trout interactions that went poorly for the latter. Coyotes have been documented feeding on cutthroat in Yellowstone National Park; could they do the same with brook trout elsewhere? And it is probable that like grizzlies and cutthroat trout, black bears consume at least some level of brook trout during spawning season when the bears are in hyperphagia and the trout are in small, shallow streams where they are vulnerable to predation.

I have seen snapping turtles feeding on brook trout, including a rather large brute choking down a 10-inch brook trout on the bottom of a clear coldwater swamp.

A rare Maine native Arctic charr. Found in just 11 native waters, they are the last Arctic charr in the contiguous United States and the southernmost Arctic charr in the world, and are said to be the oldest strains of Arctic charr in North America. BOB MALLARD PHOTO

And I suspect other species of turtle prey on juvenile brook trout when the opportunity presents itself as well.

Coevolution

Brook trout coevolved with Arctic charr, lake trout, landlocked salmon, and Atlantic salmon in certain waters in the northern part of their range. They also coevolved with lake whitefish, chub, dace, and sculpin. From roughly New York south, they did not overlap with any other salmonid and were the only native trout.

In Maine all native Arctic charr waters were also native brook trout waters. The same is true for most, if not all, native lake trout and landlocked salmon waters. Native Atlantic salmon shared the water with native brook trout in the Penobscot and Kennebec watersheds as well as many of the rivers and streams in the Downeast region.

In some waters in Labrador, brook trout coevolved with pike. When introduced where they are not native, pike typically cause the extirpation of, or seriously compromise, native brook trout populations. The same is true for smelt, which when they occur naturally can coexist with brook trout, but when introduced, especially in small ponds, can result in the demise of the latter.

Hybridization

Brook trout can, but rarely do, hybridize with other native char in nature. In fact, hybridization between naturally occurring species is relatively rare within the animal kingdom in general. Hybridization is usually the result of humans playing god and introducing one or more

species into an ecosystem. Even species that occur naturally together can respond differently when one or both is introduced.

While extremely uncommon there have been reports of naturally occurring brook trout/lake trout hybrids, referred to as splake, in Canada. A 13-pound specimen was taken in 1993 (noted in Karas's book). It was the result of a cross between a female brook trout and a male lake trout, the opposite of most hatchery-raised fish, and looked more like the former than the latter. The fish was also said to be fertile. Unfortunately, the way we have thrown fish around, and continue to do so, I don't believe we can ever be completely sure of what we are looking at or how it got there.

There are also reports of naturally occurring brook trout/Arctic charr crosses. Analysis of fish from the Fraser River watershed of northern Labrador in the mid-1980s found evidence of hybridization between brook trout and Arctic charr in six fish. It was even suggested that some hybrids backcrossed to one of the parent species. While rare elsewhere, it is possible that this is a somewhat regular occurrence in this watershed.

Splake are commonly raised in hatcheries and stocked around the country, including in what was historic brook trout water. In fact, Maine, the stronghold for native brook trout in the United States, is one of the biggest promoters of splake. While said to be sterile by many fisheries managers, Dr. Behnke refers to them as a "fertile" hybrid that "may reproduce in nature."

There are several waters in Canada that are reported to have self-sustaining populations of splake: Lake Agnes in Banff National Park and Lake 17 in Ontario are two.

Brook trout or splake? Note the unusual patterning on the head, limited red spots, and lack of blue halos around the red spots on this splake. Splake are not as easy to tell from brook trout as many anglers believe. CHARLIE PERRY PHOTO

A hatchery-raised brook trout/brown trout hybrid known as a tiger trout. We are seeing more each year of what appear to be wild tiger trout where brown trout have been introduced over brook trout. CHARLIE PERRY PHOTO

Per Fuller and Williams (1999), natural reproduction has occurred in Lake Huron as well. A report out of Michigan stated that "approximately 56 percent of Splake are fertile."

Backcrossed brook trout/splake hybrids have been reported as well. One example involved an over-the-limit "brook trout" court case in Leadville, Colorado, that Dr. Behnke told me about. Berst and McCombie (1975) reported brook trout/splake backcrosses in Glasgow Glen Pond, and Buss and Wright (1958) also reported

backcrosses. Hanson (1972) identified them in Redrock Lake, a native brook trout water.

Brook trout/Arctic charr hybrids, referred to as sparctic char, have been raised in hatcheries. Researchers at the State University of New York successfully crossed the species to create a fish that "captures the key desirable characteristics of its disparate parents." This was accomplished by combining the eggs of brook trout with the milt of Arctic charr.

Brook Trout Angling Records

The world-record brook trout, and by default the Canadian and North American record, was caught in Ontario, Canada, on July 21, 1915, by Dr. John William Cook. The fish came from Rabbit Rapids on the Nipigon River and was what is referred to as a coaster. It was over 30 inches long, had an estimated girth of 20 inches, and was weighed at 14.5 pounds 21 days after being caught, so it probably weighed close to 20 pounds when first landed.

Cook's brook trout is one of the longest-standing world-record fish, as well as one of the most controversial. In addition to who caught it and on what, there was some debate at the time as to whether the fish was a brook trout or a lake trout, which raises the question if it could have been a splake, as naturally occurring splake have been documented in the region.

Unfortunately, while modern science could have solved the mystery as to what the fish was, the mount was lost in a museum fire in 1990 and there is nothing left to test.

Canadian fishing records have proved somewhat elusive. There are no formal brook trout records for British Columbia, Newfoundland, Labrador, or Quebec. I found a report of a 10-pound, 11-ounce brook trout caught in Quebec in the late 2000s, and 10-pound brook trout are not uncommon in Labrador. A Manitoba, and possibly Canadian- and world-record brook trout was caught by Tim Matheson in 2006. A catch-and-release angler, he let the 29-inch fish that likely weighed over 15 pounds go and wasn't credited with the record. Provinces with formal brook trout records are as follows:

Tim Matheson of Manitoba, Canada, with a potential world-record brook trout caught from Barbe Lake and estimated to weigh between 15 and 17 pounds. To his credit, Mr. Matheson released the fish rather than killing it to secure a formal record. DOUG MCKENZIE PHOTO

- Alberta: 14 lbs., 14 oz., Unknown, 2009
- Manitoba: 10 lbs., East Blue Lake, 1988
- New Brunswick: 8 lbs., 14 oz., Tracadie River, 2016
- Nova Scotia: 6 lbs., 12 oz., Blackett's Lake, 1945
- Ontario: 14.5 lbs., Nipigon River, 1915
- Saskatchewan: 7.5 lbs., Loch Leven, 2004

The official brook trout record in the United States, a nonnative and most likely stocked fish of 11 pounds, 3 ounces, was caught in Deerfield Lake in South Dakota in 2007. The largest native brook trout, a 10-pound, 1-ounce fish, was caught in Lake Michigan in Wisconsin in 1999.

There are no state record brook trout for Alabama, Florida, Hawaii, Kansas, Louisiana, Mississippi, Missouri, North Dakota, Ohio, and Oklahoma—probably because there are no brook trout. Delaware only lists a record for "Trout," lumping all species into one and leaving the identity of the 11-pound, 10-ounce entry unclear. States with official brook trout records are as follows:

- Alaska: 3 lbs., 4 oz., Green Lake, 2012
- Arizona: 4 lbs., 15.2 oz., Sunrise Lake, 1995
- Arkansas: 5 lbs., North Fork River, 2002
- California: 9 lbs., 12 oz., Silver Lake, 1932
- Colorado: 7 lbs., 10 oz., Upper Cataract Lake, 1947
- Connecticut: 9 lbs., 3 oz., Blackwell Brook, 1998
- Georgia: 5 lbs., 10 oz., Waters Creek, 1986
- Idaho: 7 lbs., 1 oz., Henrys Lake, 1978
- Illinois: 7 lbs., 5 oz., Lake Michigan, 1998
- Indiana: 3 lbs., 15.5 oz., Lake Gage, 1973
- Iowa: 7 lbs., Fountain Springs Creek, 1996
- Kentucky: 3 lbs., 10 oz., Cumberland River, 2015
- Maine: 9 lbs., 2 oz., Mousam Lake, 2010
- Maryland: 6 lbs., 1.75 oz., Potomac River, 1999
- Massachusetts: 10 lbs., Ashfield Lake, 2008
- Michigan: 9 lbs., 8 oz., Clear Lake, 1996
- Minnesota: 6 lbs., 5.6 oz., Pigeon River, 2000
- Montana: 9 lbs., Lower Two Medicine Lake, 1940
- Nebraska: 5 lbs., 1 oz., Pawnee Springs, 1965
- Nevada: 5 lbs., 10 oz., Bull Run Reservoir, 1980
- New Hampshire: 9 lbs., Pleasant Lake, 1911

- New Jersey: 7 lbs., 3 oz., Rockaway River, 1995
- New Mexico: 5 lbs., Hidden Lake, 1996
- New York: 6 lbs., Silver Lake Wilderness Area, 2013
- North Carolina: 7 lbs., 7 oz., Raven Fork River, 1980
- Oregon: 9 lbs., 6 oz., Deschutes River, 1980
- Pennsylvania: 7 lbs., Fishing Creek, 1996
- Rhode Island: 3 lbs., 12 oz., Wyoming Pond, 1984
- South Carolina: 4 lbs., 10 oz., Chattooga River, 2010
- South Dakota: 11 lbs., 3 oz., Deerfield Lake, 2007
- Tennessee: 4 lbs., 12 oz., Caney Fork River, 2016
- Texas: 0.67 lb., Guadalupe River, 1984
- Utah: 7 lbs., 8 oz., Boulder Mountain, 1971
- Vermont: 5 lbs., 12 oz., Paran Creek, 1977
- Virginia: 5 lbs., 10 oz., Big Stony Creek, 1987
- Washington: 9 lbs., Wobbly Lake, 1998
- West Virginia: 7 lbs., 10 oz., Shavers Fork, 2004
- Wisconsin: 10 lbs., 1 oz., Lake Michigan, 1999
- Wyoming: 9 lbs., 11 oz., Green River Lake, 1976

There are references—as well as mounts, drawings, and paintings—of brook trout from Maine and the Adirondacks from before formal records were kept that were larger than the current official state record. Several fish housed at the Rangeley Outdoor Sporting Heritage Museum in Oquossoc, Maine, look as though they could have been records.

Sadly, the current Maine brook trout record had a clipped fin and may have been an accidentally stocked brood fish. While the fin-clip looked recent, there was no record of brook trout being stocked in the lake. Per Maine's Department of Inland Fisheries and Wildlife: "It is not known when this particular fish was stocked."

Sometime in the 1820s, Daniel Webster caught a well-publicized 14.5-pound brook trout, which would be more than twice the size of the current official record. A sea-run fish, it was caught from a mill pond on the Carmans River on Long Island, New York. Large brook trout, mostly sea-run, were reported from Massachusetts as well.

Brook Trout Landmarks

Upper Dam near Rangeley, Maine, separates Mooselookmeguntic and Upper Richardson Lakes. It is one of the most famous fly-fishing landmarks in the country and the birthplace of the Gray Ghost streamer. It was nationally known for its trophy wild native brook trout fishery, and some consider it the most famous brook trout fishery in the nation. Unfortunately, the historic structure was recently torn down and replaced with a modern one.

Lower Dam on the Rapid River was long synonymous with Maine fly fishing. It adorned the pages of magazines, books, catalogs, and calendars, but was recently dismantled under the guise of "public safety." All that's left are some rock pilings, old boards, and a plaque.

There is 2,500-pound brook trout sculpture at Promontory Point Park in Greeley, Colorado. Far from native brook trout range, the 11-foot-long, 7-foot-tall sculpture made from ceramic is nonetheless impressive. The statue was made by Peter Hazel and replaced a smaller one he did that was deemed unable to survive the harsh Colorado weather.

An equally impressive statue, actually a fountain, is in Kalkaska, Michigan. Formally known as the National Trout Memorial, it is referred to locally as the Fisherman's Shrine. The fish, said to be roughly 18 feet long, caused me to spin my rental car around for a better look while driving between historic Grayling and Traverse City. ▧

National Trout Memorial in Kalkaska, Michigan. Interestingly, it is located near the headwaters of the Boardman River, a disputed native brook trout water.
BOB MALLARD PHOTO

Historic Lower Dam on the Rapid River near Rangeley, Maine, the most recognized brook trout landmark in the state and one of the most recognized in the country. Sadly, it was torn down, ostensibly for "public safety."
DIANA MALLARD PHOTO

Brook trout are also crossed with brown trout to create what is referred to as tiger trout. Commonly raised in hatcheries by state fish and game agencies, most tiger trout you encounter will be stocked. However, reports of what are believed to be wild tiger trout are increasing. I recently saw a picture of what looked to be a wild tiger trout from New Hampshire. Introduced brook trout are also known to hybridize with native bull trout in the Columbia River basin in the northwestern United States.

Apparently, hatcheries have also experimented with brook trout/rainbow trout hybrids, according to Buss and Wright (1958): "and in nine yearling males originating from crosses of rainbow trout females x brook trout males. These fertile individuals have been backcrossed to the parental species with limited results to date."

One thing we know about hybridization is that we don't know nearly enough about it. When you start moving species around, all bets are off. As for the hatcheries, there are better ways to use our limited resources than creating new fish.

Nonnative Range

Like other trout, brook trout have been moved around, and more so than some realize. Even some of what many believe are native brook trout waters are not. Many high-elevation ponds in New York, New Hampshire, Vermont, and Maine were fishless prior to the introduction of brook trout. And, as noted earlier, the fabled Au Sable, Boardman, and Manistee Rivers in Michigan were not native brook trout fisheries.

Countless small, unheralded headwater streams in the West harbor populations of nonnative brook trout. In these cases brook trout have done to native cutthroat what browns and rainbows have done to brook trout in their native range. I have encountered nonnative brook trout in Arizona, Arkansas, California, Colorado, Idaho, Montana, New Mexico, Utah, and Wyoming. Even some famous blue-ribbon trout fisheries out west have at least some level of nonnative brook trout. The Fryingpan River in Colorado, Big Hole River in Montana, Lamar River and Soda Butte Creek in Yellowstone National Park, and Henrys Lake in Idaho come to mind. I caught nonnative brook trout in Tensleep Creek in Bighorn National Forest in Wyoming as well.

Brook trout have also been introduced to Europe, South America, and New Zealand. While not all attempts to establish self-sustaining populations succeeded, many did.

Fishing for nonnative brook trout in Tensleep Creek in Wyoming. DIANA MALLARD PHOTO

Tackle and Techniques

Former president and renowned sportsman Theodore Roosevelt hunted and fished in Maine. He spent time on the West Branch of the Mattawamkeag River, a native brook trout stream. While no one knows exactly what he did while in Maine, it would be reasonable to assume that at least some of that time was spent in pursuit of brook trout.

There are numerous photographs of former president Herbert Hoover holding brook trout. He once said, "There are only two occasions when Americans respect privacy, especially in Presidents. Those are prayer and fishing," as well as "All men are equal before fish." Hoover is reported to have spent time fishing for brook trout in Rangeley, Maine. Pioneer fly fisher Lee Wulff and his friend, legendary sportscaster friend Curt Gowdy, were avid brook trout anglers. They flew into the Labrador backcountry in

Wulff's famed Super Cub in search of giant wild native brook trout. Using a canoe that was lashed to the pontoons of the plane, they fished for brook trout that had probably never seen an angler. Their forays included the now famous Minipi watershed.

While much has changed since Presidents Roosevelt and Hoover and sporting legends Wulff and Gowdy first pursued brook trout, much has remained the same. Tackle has evolved considerably, but in some cases it has just come full circle. And we are employing tactics and techniques that early brook trout fishermen would never have dreamed of, but like tackle some of the techniques we purport to be new are actually just new iterations of old tactics.

In some ways, and probably more so than those who fish for other species, brook trout anglers have remained somewhat traditional in their approach to tackle and technique.

John Blunt, owner of historic Grant's Kennebago Camps near Rangeley, Maine, fishing the fabled Kennebago River. Drab colors, traditional vest, Maine Guide hat, and a Pflueger Medalist reel—it doesn't get anymore "brook trout" than that. DIANA MALLARD PHOTO

They are often tackle-minimalists, having honed their craft to a point where they know what they need and don't need. And they employ tactics because they work, not because they are new or trendy.

Brook trout anglers can be as different from other trout fishers as brook trout are from other trout. And there is a big difference between a brook trout angler and someone who fishes for brook trout. The former is singularly focused while the latter is an opportunist. The brook trout angler lives where wild native brook trout live; the opportunist does not.

Many hard-core brook trout anglers have little interest in nonnative trout and prefer wild to stocked fish. They often refer to brook trout as simply "trout" and nonnative trout as "brown trout" or "rainbow trout," as if the latter are somehow subordinate to the former. They get their information from friends, neighbors, and those they meet afield, not the internet or media. Brook trout anglers often describe hatches by their type, size, and color, not by Latin name or fly-fishing vernacular. They use terms like *keeper*, *limit*, *pan-size*, or other words that imply harvest even when it doesn't mean harvest. They are more likely to use the word *trophy* to refer to a large fish than the terms *hog* or *pig*, as there is no logical connection between brook trout and swine.

Brook trout anglers often shun flashy boats and brightly colored clothing, preferring a subtler and more stealthy approach. Their hats are as likely to have the logo of a pro sports team (often Boston, New York, or Atlanta) as they are a tackle manufacturer. And when it is a tackle manufacturer, it's as likely to be a sporting goods company as a fly-fishing company. Traditional vests, hip boots, and neoprene waders are by no means unheard of on brook trout water. And many brook trout stillwater anglers I know don't even own a pair of waders. Canoes are still the preferred watercraft on many brook trout waters, and traditional wicker pack baskets can still be seen on backcountry ponds in Maine.

But make no mistake about it, the brook trout angler is as dedicated and skilled as any other fly fisher. They know how to catch brook trout, and if you doubt for even a second the proficiency of so-called traditional brook trout anglers, spend some time on a remote brook trout pond fishing wet lines near one and you will understand what I mean.

Few anglers work harder for their fish than brook trout anglers. They deal with low densities when compared to western anglers. Because of where brook trout are found, they tend to spend more time in the backcountry than many other trout fishers and face worse conditions, including biting insects, than many other anglers.

No species of trout can be found in more varied habitats than brook trout. They inhabit streams, rivers, ponds, lakes, estuaries, and bays. They live in streams narrow enough to step across, rivers wide enough to require several double-hauls to cast across, and lakes so big they can only be fished from a large motorboat.

Brook trout vary in size more than most trout as well, running from less than 4 inches to over 20 inches, and from well under a pound to close to 10 pounds. As opportunistic feeders, brook trout feed on everything from tiny midge larvae to giant hellgrammite nymphs, minute Blue-Winged Olives (BWOs) to bulky stoneflies, inch-long dace to inches-long sculpin, and leeches, crayfish, and even mice.

Because of all these factors, the tackle and techniques best suited to pursuing brook trout vary radically depending on where you live, the type of water you fish, and to some degree the size of the fish you expect to encounter.

Tackle

At the component level, brook trout anglers use pretty much the same tackle all other fly fishers use. Like other anglers they are likely to have more than one rod and reel, several lines, something to wade in, a net or two, a couple of vests or packs, maybe a watercraft or two, an assortment of tools and chemicals, and myriad flies.

What makes brook trout anglers somewhat unique, however, is the fact that the range of tackle at the component level is greater for brook trout than for many other species. This is due to the broad range of fish sizes that brook trout anglers encounter, as well as the various types of water they fish. What works on a tiny mountain stream does not work on a lake or pond—at least not well.

RODS

There is no real length and line-weight range for brook trout fishing. A range of 6- to 10-foot and 2- to 7-weight, which is accurate, would be of no value, as it represents a huge percentage of the rods sold today. Add slow-action to fast-action, and glass to graphite, and it is even more vague. And if you are a backcountry angler, multi-piece rods of more than four pieces can be a good idea. While rivers can be fished with conventional "trout" rods, small brook trout streams require specialty products to effectively fish them. And lakes and ponds present unique challenges as well, and this varies depending on the type of watercraft you are using.

Small freestone streams present a challenge to fly fishers. Tight quarters, low canopy, and short casts are the rule, making rods in the 5- to 7.5-foot range a good choice. Due to the short casts and small fish, slow-action rods, including glass and bamboo, work best. For the same reasons, rods in the 2- to 3-weight range are your best bet.

Tenkara rods have made inroads with small-stream anglers over the last decade. While relatively new to the United States, Tenkara fishing has been around for a couple of centuries in Japan. These simple telescopic rods are used without a reel, and the fly is more dropped than cast. At lengths up to 12 feet, you can reach fish that would be tough to reach with a traditional fly rod. While Lefty Kreh once referred to Tenkara as a "fad" and said it wouldn't last, the jury is still out.

For large streams and small rivers, I prefer an 8-foot, 4-weight medium-action rod, as it gives me a bit more length and distance without overwhelming what are often small fish. If you fish large rivers, a standard 9-foot,

Short light-line fly rods—including glass and bamboo—small-arbor click-and-pawl reels, compact chestpacks and fanny packs, and small nets are all you need for fishing the typical small brook trout stream. DIANA MALLARD PHOTO

5-weight, all-purpose, medium-action "trout rod" will suffice. If you like throwing streamers, you may want to consider a 6-weight. If you nymph a lot, you may want a longer rod in the 10- to 11-foot range.

If you fish lakes and ponds, a standard 9-foot, 5-weight fast-action rod is the best all-around option. If you fish from a personal watercraft, consider a 10-foot, 5-weight rod, as the longer length helps lift line off the water and keep your backcast out of the water. And if you do a lot of wet-lining in lakes and ponds, a 6-weight can be a great option. Anglers fishing mice and big streamers for large brook trout in Canada, Patagonia, and parts of the United States often use 7-weights.

REELS

For small streams a click-and-pawl reel is all you need. In fact, these are often the only reels that balance well with short, light rods. Capacity is not an issue as you will rarely, if ever, see your backing or, for that matter, even the midpoint in your fly line. I often size down to reduce weight and to balance my outfit, allowing for no more than 50 yards of backing, and often less.

For most other applications a standard trout reel will work just fine. In rivers, ponds, and lakes you should allow for 75 yards or more backing. In places like Labrador and

Patagonia, a larger reel with a minimum of 100 yards of backing is recommended.

LINES

So-called all-purpose floating fly lines work best for stream and river brook trout fishing. The short front tapers work well in pocketwater and for short casts, while allowing you to switch between match-the-hatch dries, attractor dries, dry/droppers, wets, and small buggers and streamers. While subtle colors may or may not spook fish less, they are never a bad idea. On rivers, lakes, and ponds, consider a textured line, as they cast a bit farther.

While sink-tip lines are not necessary on streams, it's a good idea to carry one when fishing rivers. Lines with tips in the 5- to 7-foot range with medium sink rates work best for large streams and small rivers, and tips in the 10- to 15-foot range with fast sink rates work best for large rivers.

You should have two or more lines when fishing lakes and ponds: a floating and one or more sinking. So-called distance lines in subtle colors are your best bet for dry-fly fishing, as they help you reach out and present the fly delicately. If you use only one sinking line, it should have a medium sink rate. If you can justify two, add a fast-sinking line for when the fish are deep. And always use so-called density-compensated or uniform-sink lines, as they help you detect hits. Intermediate lines can be helpful when fish are in the shallows or feeding just below the surface.

LEADERS

Like rods, the best leader to use depends on the kind of water you are fishing, as well as whether you are fishing a floating or sinking line. Leader length is also somewhat influenced by the length of the rod you are using, as it helps to keep them somewhat the same. While a 9-foot rod can cast a 12-foot leader well, a 9-foot leader can be tough to manage with a 6-foot rod. Also, if your leader is too long, it will be tough to manage in tight quarters and make short casts difficult.

Short leaders are your best bet for streams. Consider standard leaders in 5X in the 6- to 7.5-foot range for dries, and 6-foot 4X to 5X fluorocarbon leaders for streamers and wets. Fluorocarbon helps get your fly down when using a floating line, which is usually the case. One company makes a 6-foot pocketwater leader that is great for short rods on small streams.

The rule on rivers is "as long as you can handle." Leaders from 9 to 12 feet work best for dry-fly fishing. Go long for small flies and shorten up for large flies. While 5X leaders are your best bet most of the time, move up to 4X for large flies and down to 6X for small flies. For streamers and buggers consider fluorocarbon leaders in the 6- to 9-foot and 3X to 4X range.

Leader length is critical on lakes and ponds because the surface is often flat. The rule of thumb is "the longer the better." Standard leaders in the 9- to 15-foot range are your best bet for dries, going shorter for large flies such as *Hexagenia* patterns and longer for small flies such as midges. Use 5X for small flies and 4X for large flies. For subsurface fishing consider a 9-foot 4X fluorocarbon leader.

TIPPET

As a rule you should use fluorocarbon tippet regardless of whether you are tying on a dry dropper or a sinking dropper. With a low light refraction and a weight that is slightly heavier than water, it is less visible to fish and gets your tippet just below the surface. When dry-fly fishing for finicky fish, consider using fluorocarbon to your first fly as well.

When fishing small streams, you only need a few spools of tippet: 5X standard and 4X and 5X fluorocarbon. On rivers, lakes, and ponds, consider 4X to 6X standard and 3X to 6X fluorocarbon. If you do a lot of fishing, consider so-called guide spools, as they save money and reduce waste.

And be sure to check your tippet at the beginning of each season to make sure it has not degraded.

Not all tippet is created equal. Pay close attention to the diameter-to-strength ratios, as they vary considerably from one manufacturer to another, as well as from one product to another within a manufacturer. For example, non-fluorocarbon 5X can run from 3 to 6 pounds in breaking strength. While this may not matter when fishing for small fish, it can make a huge difference with big fish. Another thing to consider is that standard and fluorocarbon tippet have very different diameter-to-strength ratios. In some cases 5X fluorocarbon can actually be stronger than 4X non-fluorocarbon, moving the break-point to your lead fly, not your dropper.

FLIES

As opportunistic feeders, brook trout eat a broad range of foods. This includes classic match-the-hatch insects, terrestrials, small minnows, leeches, crayfish, and just about anything else they can get their mouths on. In fact, brook trout sample pretty much everything that comes their way.

While there are hatches on the typical small freestone streams that brook trout inhabit, they are often short-lived and somewhat sparse. As a result, attractor dry flies are often your best bet. This includes patterns such as humpies, Wulffs, Coachmen, small Stimulators, beetles, ants, crickets, and small hoppers. Brightly colored patterns often work best, as they are easy to see in fast-moving water. Small streamers such as Mickey Finns, Black-Nose Dace, and Muddlers, as well as classic wet flies such as the Parmachenee Belle, are your best bet for subsurface.

For brook trout in rivers and large streams, your fly selection should be pretty much the same as what you use for other species of trout. The issue of forage is more about

No mayfly brings big brook trout to the surface like the giant *Hexagenia*. My Hexagenius pattern has a realistic low profile, floats high, and won't spin your leader. BOB MALLARD PHOTO

water type than fish species, and all trout in a river eat basically the same thing. A broad selection of mayflies, caddis, and stoneflies in a variety of sizes, colors, and stages is a good bet. The same thing applies to streamers and bugers—variety is key as it allows you to experiment a bit.

Brook trout in lakes and ponds feed on things they don't necessarily encounter on rivers and streams. Dragonfly and damselfly patterns are important to the stillwater brook trout angler. So are leeches, and patterns without coneheads work better than those with them because they swim more naturally. The same goes for nymphs; consider using patterns without beads. The hatches found on lakes and ponds are different from those found on most streams and rivers and include burrowers such as *Hexagenia*.

Many pond brook trout anglers in Maine use brightly colored streamers such as Mickey Finns, orange and yellow Muddlers, and the ever-popular Hornberg in gray, yellow, green, and red. Local variations include the Hornberg/Muddler hybrid (aka Horny Muddler), as well as numerous versions of Marabou Muddlers.

I think it's fair to say that brook trout anglers are more likely to use local patterns than are other anglers. The opportunistic feeding habits of brook trout have caused serious brook trout anglers to get creative and develop patterns that work on their local waters and, by default, most likely many other brook trout waters.

In Maine, brook trout anglers fish local patterns such as the Devil Bug, Maple Syrup, Wood Special, Wardens Worry, Montreal Whore, BTO—Big Trout Only, and my own Brook Trout Killer. I have seen similar patterns with equally entertaining names in neighboring New Hampshire and Vermont, as well as New York and Virginia.

WADERS

Like just about everything else involving brook trout tackle, what you use for waders—and I use the term figuratively—is dependent on the type of water you are fishing as well as the time of year.

Most of the time you can wet-wade small streams. In fact, wet-wading is often the most comfortable option, as small-stream fishing is usually more active than wading rivers. Neoprene socks or sock/gravel guard combinations help make up for the loss of a neoprene wader booty, as well as help keep debris out of your boots and your laces tied. In the spring and fall you may want to consider hip boots, and stockingfoot breathable versions are preferred as they allow you to use whatever type of wading boots work best. While somewhat hard to find, stockingfoot hip boots are still made but are often only available through big box companies.

For large streams and rivers, as well as personal watercraft, your basic waders will work just fine. And if the conditions allow, just wet-wade, as it is easier and more comfortable.

BOOTS

Small-stream fishing is different from wading large streams and rivers. You often must walk to get there, and once there you usually cover more water, and faster, than you do when fishing a river. The uneven terrain and slippery rocks can be challenging as well. And the fact that you are in and out of the water and often walking in mud and vegetation makes things even more complicated.

Hybrid rubber/felt sole wading boots are great for fishing backcountry streams because they offer good traction on the trail as well as safe footing in the water. DIANA MALLARD PHOTO

Gear lanyards are a great way to carry your tools while fishing small streams. They are light, compact, and easy to access and come in many sizes, configurations, and colors. BOB MALLARD PHOTO

While felt soles work great on slippery rocks, they are not good for walking through the woods or climbing in and out of the water to avoid obstacles. If you use felt soles, consider buying studded felt or a set of add-on studs or cleats to improve traction on the trail and while climbing in and out of the stream on what are often muddy banks.

Rubber soles are great for hiking but can be less than ideal on the slippery rocks often encountered on freestone streams. If you use rubber soles, you should consider studded or barred rubber or a set of add-on studs or cleats to help you navigate the slippery rocks while not hampering your ability to walk on trails.

One company offers a boot with a hybrid sole that combines a rubber lug sole with a flush felt insert. This design provides solid traction on the trail and great performance in the water, and works well while climbing up and down banks. Add a few studs and they are even better. Another company makes a series of boots with interchangeable soles. This allows you to walk in using one sole and fish in another if you choose. Or simply use the sole that is best for the conditions you are fishing in at the time.

When fishing from a personal watercraft, you may want to consider rubber soles, as you are often entering the water on sand or mud and standing in mud when in the water. Avoid studs as they can damage your fins, and look for boots with stiff sides so your fins don't pinch your feet.

PACKS

Fanny packs, sometimes referred to as lumbar packs, are a great option for small streams where you rarely encounter water more than waist-deep, and when you do it is easy to get around it to avoid swamping your pack. They are comfortable, cool, and out of the way, and allow room for water and a snack. When fishing with a fanny pack, consider a gear lanyard to keep your tools handy.

In larger streams and small rivers, you may want to consider a small chestpack that you don't have to take off every time you encounter waist-deep water. Pare it back to just what you need to lessen the weight. Sling packs are another option.

Tech packs are a great option for wading large rivers, as they allow you to carry a wide range of flies and tippet as well as a spare spool and extra layer of clothing. Today's so-called tech packs are much more comfortable than old-style vests because they get the weight off your neck and onto your shoulders.

Gear bags are best for boat anglers, as they get your tackle off your person and onto the floor of your boat, into a storage box, or under the seat. They are roomy and easy to access and allow you to carry pretty much whatever you need, including boating safety items. If you fish from a personal watercraft, consider a small chestpack.

NETS

Carrying a net can help reduce fish-handling and lessen the likelihood of breaking flies off in fish's mouths while trying to remove them. Nets also allow you to cradle fish in the water while they recover. Size your net to the fish you expect to encounter and always use shallow net bags, ideally in rubber, as the fish are easier to remove and the less abrasive rubber is better for the fish.

Long-handled nets are best for fishing from a boat; you can reach out without risking falling out or tipping over, a real possibility, and something I have witnessed on more than one occasion. Nets with large hoops work best, as they are easier to get fish into. As for length, there is plenty of room in the boat, so use it.

So-called float tube nets are best for fishing from personal watercraft. They have medium-length handles and midsize hoops. This allows you to reach out a bit, yet still be able to store the net in what is often limited space. Consider nets that float, and, if not, invest in a net leash in case you drop your net, which you most likely will eventually do.

WATERCRAFT

Watercraft for brook trout fishing run the gamut and include everything from motorboats to drift boats to rafts to rowboats to canoes to kayaks to personal watercraft such as float tubes and pontoon boats.

Small, open motorboats can be good for fishing lakes and large ponds. Many brook trout anglers prefer large square-stern canoes, so-called freighter canoes, and classic designs such as Grand Lakers and Rangeley Boats. Boston Whalers, duck boats, and other skiffs are also used.

If you mostly fish small ponds, a canoe is one of your best options as it allows you to move around easily and quickly. If you prefer to stay put and want a bit more stability, consider a small rowboat or rowing skiff. Many anglers like to fish from a kayak because they are comfortable and easy to carry. While not common in brook trout country, I suspect some are fishing from stand-up paddleboards.

While not usually the case, drift boats can be used on some brook trout rivers. Rafts can be used on others that are too small, shallow, or rocky for drift boats. Some northeastern fly fishers pole flat-bottom canoes, and some traditional anglers from the Midwest still paddle and pole classic Au Sable River Boats.

For those who want to get off the beaten path and explore a bit, nothing works like a float tube. This compact and light watercraft can be pumped up and carried on your back or deflated, carried in a backpack, and pumped up at the shore. While slow to take hold in brook trout country, I am seeing more and more each year.

Tim Beckwith fishing a remote hike-in brook trout pond in New Hampshire. Float tubes allow anglers to fish waters that cannot effectively be waded or fished from shore. Consider a lightweight compact model for backcountry use.
BOB MALLARD PHOTO

Brook trout in small streams take advantage of woody debris to avoid predators and ambush food. Anglers must employ nonconventional techniques and make short, precise casts to reach these fish. DIANA MALLARD PHOTO

Techniques

Like tackle, brook trout technique varies wildly depending on the type of water you are fishing, and even the time of year. Like most trout, brook trout eat both subsurface and on the surface. They take all stages of aquatic insects, minnows, and, as stated earlier, pretty much anything that comes by or passes their nose. As such you need to adjust your technique to the situation you are faced with at any given time.

Working downstream on small streams allows you to hit every pocket, especially when using streamers and wets or skittering dries—a deadly tactic. But there are times when an upstream approach is necessary so you don't spook the fish. Since fishing streamers upstream can be difficult, you may want to fish dries or dry/droppers when working upstream.

So-called dapping, or reaching out with the rod and dropping the fly where you want it, is useful when fishing small pocketwater. While it can be done downstream or upstream, it is most effective when working downstream, especially if you keep a low profile and avoid casting too much of a shadow. Some prefer a longer rod for this.

When working downstream on small streams, you should roll-cast as much as possible to avoid tangling in streamside vegetation and canopy and snapping flies off on rocks behind you. When fishing upstream make short, quick, precise casts and avoid false-casting wherever possible to lessen the likelihood of getting caught in the trees and bushes.

It is easy to break your rod on small streams by banging it on the branches above you. A quick look behind before you cast can help prevent an early end to your fishing day, an expensive rod repair, and the inconvenient temporary loss of your favorite stream rod. Sidearm casts, roll-casts, and bow-and-arrow casts can help prevent these mishaps.

River fishing for brook trout is like river fishing for any other trout. What you do for rainbows and browns usually works for brook trout because the fish are eating pretty much the same things. One exception—but by no means a rule—is streamer size, with brook trout less likely to take a very large pattern than the more piscivorous brown trout.

Lake and pond fishing present a unique challenge. Distance, accuracy, and presentation all come into play. When fishing lakes and ponds, it's best to limit your false casts, as this can put fish down. Slapping the water behind you with your line spooks fish as well. When fishing dries, consider casting only to fish you can see, and if you must blind cast do so quietly.

Learning to read riseforms to determine direction of travel can be a huge help to the stillwater fly fisher. Unlike trout in streams and rivers, lake and pond fish are always moving, and dropping a fly where they *were* is not nearly as productive as where they are *going*. Look for the "pillow" of water at the edge of the rise, as it is generally on the direction-of-travel side of the rise.

The author casting to a brook trout that is actively feeding on emergers. Distance helps, and accuracy is critical when fishing stillwaters. Learn to read riseforms and cast to where the fish is going, not to where it has been. CECIL GRAY PHOTO

Native Fish Coalition Maine state chair Emily Bastian executing a bow-and-arrow cast in a small, tree-choked salter stream in Acadia National Park in Maine. Sometimes this is your only option. BOB MALLARD PHOTO

Public Access

Laws regarding trespass, especially access to water, vary considerably from state to state. Some laws are clear, others not so. It is important that anglers understand these laws and know where they are at all times to help avoid unpleasant, and potentially costly, conflicts with landowners and law enforcement.

In some states the landowner owns the water, in others they own the streambed, and in still others they own neither. In those states where landowners own the streambed, the rules for gaining access to the water are different from those dictating what you can do once you are in it. Where the landowner owns the streambed, while you may or may not float through, you usually cannot wade.

Some states require landowners to post their land if they do not want you on it; some do not. In cases where posting is required, most states have laws regarding how landowners must post, including how far apart signs must be and even the size of the signs. Where posting is not required, it is up to the angler to determine who owns the land and to gain permission, sometimes in writing, before accessing the property.

Many states have a so-called navigable waterway law. While these do not entitle you to trespass on private property, they do allow you to float, and sometimes wade, within the high-water mark, assuming you entered the water on public property (or private property where you have permission to do so) and the water meets the definition of navigable, which varies from state to state.

In some states, landowners whose property abuts a waterway own the riverbed to the middle of the waterway only. If they own the land on both sides, they by default own the entire riverbed. This means that wading, dropping an anchor, or even rubbing the bottom with your boat might be considered trespassing. In other cases only those who own both sides own the riverbed.

Massachusetts law guarantees access to navigable waters. The public also has the right to "passage up and down the stream in boats or other craft, for purposes of business, convenience, or pleasure" in navigable waters. But navigable is determined based on "waters where the tide ebbs and flows," and nonnavigable waters are those "above the ebbing and flowing of the tide."

In Virginia, waters and their beds are owned by the state and deemed to be public unless they are subject

A gate on private property in central Maine prevents drive-in access. Walk-in access, however, is guaranteed under Maine's Great Ponds Act. Not all states have such a law, and laws applicable to moving water often don't apply to stillwater. BOB MALLARD PHOTO

to a grant that predates the current law. Anglers fishing the popular Jackson River who refused to leave when asked to were sued by a landowner for trespass, and a judge found that the landowner's case was valid due to the apparent existence of such a grant.

North Carolina has a navigable water law that defines such waters as a "public trust." The definition of navigable is clear and favors anglers: "[I]f a body of water in its natural condition can be navigated by watercraft, it is navigable in fact and, therefore, navigable in law, even if it has not been used for such purposes." This does not, however, allow you to get out on the banks, or necessarily give you the right to wade.

In Tennessee, navigable streams are in the public domain. Landowners have title to the low watermark, which can be underwater at times, making things a bit complicated. If a stream is "shallow as to be unfit for transportation and commerce," the streambed is "wholly and absolutely in the owners of the adjoining land."

A "great pond" is a lake or pond held in trust by the state for public use. It is generally defined as natural waters over 10 acres. Some states have a clause that allows for the inclusion of larger man-made waters. In Maine, New Hampshire, and Massachusetts, the term is used in both common law, or judicial precedent, and formal statute dating back to colonial times.

Maine has a law that guarantees "access or egress," including overland, to natural lakes and ponds larger than 10 acres and man-made waters over 30 acres. It does not apply to public water supplies. While the landowner can block vehicular access, they cannot stop you from walking or flying in. However, walking around once you are in there is subject to general trespass laws.

A similar law in New Hampshire applies to "great ponds and artificial impoundments of 10 acres or more." It does not apply to natural lakes and ponds that were less than 10 acres before being "raised by damming."

Most states have some form of sportsman harassment law. These laws protect sportsmen in the legal pursuit of fish and game from overzealous landowners. If you feel you have been unfoundedly harassed while fishing, walk away and contact a game warden to resolve the issue rather than get into a conflict with the landowner. And take a picture of the offending party if you can do so without escalating things. ∎

While small fish may circle around a bit, and sometimes a lot, large fish often feed in a straight line. So if you want big fish, chase them, and by that I mean get out ahead of straight-line feeders and get a fly in front of them. As a rule, but there are exceptions, large fish also make less of a disturbance when feeding than small fish.

When fish are not looking up on a lake or pond, don't try to make them come to you; go to them. Referred to as wet-lining, fishing with a sinking line is an effective and efficient way to catch brook trout in stillwater. While it may look easy, wet-lining requires a lot of skill and patience. One of the hardest things to determine, but of utmost importance, is what depth the fish are at. Retrieval speed is likewise critical and is best done by trial-and-error.

Maintaining constant contact with your fly is key to effective wet-lining, as the takes are far subtler than you might expect. Keep your line taut and learn to set to any resistance no matter how minor, as bumps, hits, stops, and tugs are only a fraction of what is going on down there. Most of your takes will be nothing more than a hesitation in your retrieve, and you must set the hook to seal the deal. One way to help detect strikes is to keep the top 2 feet of your rod in the water and pointing toward your fly.

How to set the hook is an issue with wet-lining as well. With your rod tip pointed at the fish, it is usually best to strip set as you would in saltwater. As soon as you have hooked the fish, however, put the rod to the side and use it to absorb the shock and put pressure on the fish. And be careful to not let the fish get into the weeds or around your anchor line.

When fishing for brook trout—or any trout for that matter—you should cover as much water as possible and never stay in one place too long. This holds true for small streams, rivers, lakes, and ponds. If the trout did not respond to your last 40 casts, they most likely won't respond to the next 40. This is especially true in what are often sparsely populated brook trout waters.

WHERE TO GO

Brook trout can be found in Canada as far north as northern Quebec and as far west as central Ontario and eastern Manitoba. Like Canadian angling records, their presence farther west is unclear and poorly documented.

In the United States brook trout can be found from Maine's border with Canada to just north of Atlanta, Georgia, and throughout the Great Lakes region as well. Nonnative brook trout can be found throughout much of the Rocky Mountains and Southwest. They are present on the West Coast as well as the Dakotas, Nebraska, Arkansas, and even Texas.

Regardless of where you live in the United States, if there are trout to be found you are rarely more than a day's drive from brook trout. These beautiful gamefish swim in beaver ponds, flowages, ponds, lakes, reservoirs, streams, rivers, tidal waters, and estuaries and bays.

NATIVE WATERS

W hether in a river, stream, lake, pond, flowage, or estuary, there is nothing like fishing for wild native brook trout in a natural, remote, and unspoiled setting. Whether you can drive there for the day, do so as part of a weekend getaway, or must fly to make it happen, everyone should experience wild native brook trout in a natural setting at least once in his or her life. Big or small, all wild native brook trout are a treasure. Add a remote and undeveloped setting, and it just doesn't get any better—and represents what is to me fly fishing in its purest form.

A beautiful wild native brook trout from heavily developed and densely populated Massachusetts. This fish, a trophy brook trout to most anglers, was caught barely two hours from bustling downtown Boston.
BOB MALLARD PHOTO

Big Spring Creek
(PENNSYLVANIA)

Big Spring Creek is located in central Pennsylvania, just over two hours from Washington, DC. It is one of the few major limestone creeks in the state that still supports a viable wild brook trout fishery. While some limestone creeks still have populations of wild brook trout, they are usually remnant, and most of Pennsylvania's wild brook trout are now found in small freestone streams. Located near the town of Newville, the world-famous Big Spring Creek emanates from a large bubbling spring. It is roughly 6 miles long, terminating at Conodoguinet Creek, and is said to be the fifth-largest spring in Pennsylvania with a flow of 27 cfs.

The water in Big Spring Creek is gin clear with year-round temperatures in the high 40s and low 50s. It has the sand bottom and dense aquatic vegetation found in classic limestone creeks, as well as the rich insect life and robust sow bug biomass, a form of crustacean. It is basically the same type of environment as an English chalkstream.

Big Spring has a rich angling history going back more than 75 years. It was a favorite of Vince Marinara, Charlie Fox, and the Fly Fishers' Club of Harrisburg faithful. It also has a history as a working stream, once powering several mills. Old pictures show dams and stone and brick buildings. While most are gone, you can still see the remnants of a few of these structures along its course.

The first blow to the brook trout in Big Spring Creek was the introduction of nonnative and highly invasive brown trout. These fish competed with the native brook trout for food and space, and as they grew large on the veritable buffet of food, they became predators of juvenile and

A large wild brook trout from the placid, gin-clear waters of Big Spring Creek in central Pennsylvania, the last well-known limestone creek in the state with a significant wild brook trout population. MATTHEW SUPINSKI PHOTO

Big Spring Creek looks, smells, and fishes more like an English chalkstream than a Northeast brook trout stream. Note the angler lying flat in the grass to keep a low profile to avoid spooking fish. MATTHEW SUPINSKI PHOTO

even small adult brook trout. A 30-inch, 15-pound brown trout specimen caught by Don Martin in the 1940s could have eaten even the biggest brook trout in the creek.

In the early 1970s, the Pennsylvania Fish & Boat Commission built a hatchery at the headwaters of Big Spring Creek. Soon after, the native brook trout population began to decline. A study in the late 1990s determined that the hatchery effluent was the cause. In 2000, citizens lobbied to close the hatchery, and a year later a decision was made to close it. By the late 2000s the brook trout population had rebounded, with electroshocking surveys turning up wild brook trout up to 18 inches, making Big Spring once again the finest native brook trout limestone creek fishery in the state.

My history with Big Spring goes back over 30 years. I first discovered it during what was considered a down time, but even then I felt it was worth going out of my way to fish there. While the section of fishable water was short, the size of the fish was impressive. And although there were giant browns and rainbows, it was the large, beautiful brook trout that kept me coming back.

As a lifelong New Englander, I'm not easily impressed by brook trout because I see a whole lot of them, and some very large ones. But the brook trout in Big Spring Creek impressed even me. Several I caught were as big as any I had seen outside of Maine and Canada. They were as beautiful as any brook trout I had ever encountered, too,

their coloration resembling that of a Southern Appalachian brook trout more than those found in New England.

The stretch of Big Spring Creek of most interest to fly fishers starts just below the old hatchery and extends downstream roughly a mile, but the amount of fishable water is increasing due to improvements in water quality. The creek is closed to fishing from its headwaters down approximately 100 feet. Below this is what is referred to as the "ditch," part of a designated Heritage Trout Angling section. This long, slow run holds some of the largest fish in the stream, but is difficult to fish due to pressure and the flat, clear water. The Heritage Trout Angling section is open to fishing year-round and is restricted to fly fishing only, barbless hooks, and catch-and-release.

As you move downstream on Big Spring Creek, the regulations get less protective. This does not mean, however, that the fishing is not worthy of your attention—it most definitely is. As the water quality improves and the insect life increases, the trout are spreading out more.

When fishing Big Spring Creek, it is best to stay out of the water. Stirring up the bottom can spook fish holding downstream, and any unnatural noise or vibration will stop fish from feeding temporarily. You must move slowly along the bank, paying attention so you don't step in a hole. Keeping a low profile is a good idea, and in fact necessary. Casting to specific fish, ideally those actively feeding, is always your best bet. Blind casting should be

Large brook trout finning in the gin-clear water of Big Spring Creek. BOB MALLARD PHOTO

reserved for low light; when the water is choppy, high, or off-color; or when no fish are showing.

Brook trout in Big Spring Creek feed on insects, sow bugs—referred to locally as cress bugs—and minnows. Both midges and mayflies are present. While hatches are rarely what you would call epic, they are usually reliable and are improving. Sulphurs and BWOs are the most important hatches. Terrestrials are available in the spring and summer, especially ants, beetles, and crickets. Sow bugs are available year-round. Sculpin are the predominant minnow.

Unlike many small-stream brook trout that often come to a fly quite recklessly, the fish in Big Spring Creek are not easy to fool. In fact, they are as selective as any trout I have fished for, which is part of the allure of the creek—wild native brook trout in a technical spring creek environment.

The story of Big Spring Creek is still being written. It has had more ups and downs than almost any trout fishery in the state. Every time you think it is up, something happens to take it back down again. Every time you think it is down, something happens to bring it back up. The latest challenge facing the brook trout of Big Spring Creek is

rainbow trout. Since the hatchery was removed, the wild rainbow trout population has increased significantly. But for reasons that are not completely clear, it appears that the brown trout population has dropped off. Some fear that the nonnative rainbow trout could displace the native brook trout as they have elsewhere, a legitimate concern.

Rainbow trout grow bigger than brook trout, and since bigger is better today, rainbows are popular with anglers. It would also be difficult at best to eradicate the rainbows without negatively affecting the brook trout. So once again we find ourselves faced with a decision that pits what is "best" against what is "right." In this case, while rainbows may be viewed as "best" from a pure angling standpoint, as a native species brook trout are "right."

Many consider Big Spring Creek the finest brook trout fishery in Pennsylvania. It is a technical fishery for wild native brook trout in a limestone creek environment. There are fish here that would be considered a trophy in most other brook trout waters. The habitat is improving due to the decommissioning of the hatchery, as well as ongoing habitat work being done by the state and volunteers. Maintaining a healthy wild native brook trout population would be the perfect end to the story.

Cupsuptic River (MAINE)

The Cupsuptic River near historic Rangeley is the Rodney Dangerfield of Maine brook trout rivers—it gets no respect. While just the fourth-"best" brook trout river in Rangeley, fifth if you count Upper Dam, move the Cupsuptic River anywhere else in the country and it would most likely be the finest self-sustaining native brook trout river in the area.

The name Cupsuptic comes from the Abenaki Native American tribe and means "a closed-up stream." If you go there you will understand what they meant, as the canopy and shoreline vegetation literally closes up the stream in some places.

The Cupsuptic River flows through a rugged, remote, and undeveloped valley. To the east of the river lies a string of mountains that represent some of the tallest in the area, including Kennebago Divide, Snow Mountain, and Twin Mountains. It flows north to south and is part of the Androscoggin River watershed. The area in and around the Cupsuptic River is heavily wooded and home to beaver, black bear, coyote, lynx, mink, moose, otter, snowshoe hare, and white-tailed deer. Eagles soar overhead, ruffed grouse drum in the woods, and loons call on the lakes and ponds. There is very little development, no power, and limited cell coverage.

Beginning at tiny Cupsuptic Pond near the Canadian border at the bottom of a small tongue of land that extends 8 or so miles into Maine, the Cupsuptic River runs roughly 24 miles before terminating at Cupsuptic Lake just northwest of Oquossoc, home of the Rangeley Outdoor Sporting Heritage Museum. The river is a series of riffles, runs, pools, and waterfalls. The water remains cool as a result of coldwater tributaries and springs.

The Cupsuptic River above Big Falls is great small-stream wild brook trout habitat in a remote and unspoiled setting accessible only by dirt road. DIANA MALLARD PHOTO

The Cupsuptic River downstream of Big Falls. The river changes from waterfalls and fast, shallow, rocky runs to deep, slow water, all of which is home to wild brook trout. DIANA MALLARD PHOTO

Sandwiched between the fabled Kennebago River to the east and the popular Magalloway River to the west, the Cupsuptic is often overlooked by visiting anglers. One reason is that the road into the fabled Rapid River, the finest brook trout river in the country, is just 5 miles away. Even Upper Dam, a historic but very short stretch of water, gets more attention than the Cupsuptic. This is good news for those looking for some solitude in an area that sees a lot of anglers.

As trout rivers go, the Cupsuptic has a solid pedigree. It terminates at Cupsuptic Lake, an above-average wild brook trout fishery. Fabled Rangeley Lake drains into Cupsuptic Lake via the Rangeley River, a seasonal trophy brook trout fishery. Cupsuptic Lake is part of Mooselookmeguntic Lake, a famous brook trout water in its own right, which enters Upper Richardson Lake at the renowned Upper Dam. Upper Richardson enters Lower Richardson Lake at what is known as the Narrows. Middle Dam, at the outflow of Lower Richardson, is the beginning of the nationally known Rapid River.

Like many of Maine's trout streams, the Cupsuptic River suffered from damage resulting from decades of logging and driving logs downstream to the mills. The Maine Department of Inland Fisheries and Wildlife, with help from the Rangeley Region Guides and Sportsmen's Association, has done studies to ascertain the feasibility of habitat restoration. In the late 1990s they identified

degraded areas. Grade control structures were constructed to address sediment transport that was affecting large pools that provide critical refuge. Efforts to improve the stream are ongoing.

Today the Cupsuptic River provides ideal habitat for wild brook trout. The lower end of the river is critical spawning and nursery habitat for trout and salmon from Cupsuptic and Mooselookmeguntic Lakes. Large fish from the lakes enter the lower river to spawn in the fall. They also move into the river in the spring to feed on spawning smelt. Right behind the smelt are suckers whose eggs they gorge on. Upstream, the river is home to a year-round resident population of brook trout.

While large lake-run brook trout up to 20 inches can be encountered in the lower river at certain times of year, most of the fish caught in the middle and upper reaches of the Cupsuptic are relatively small, averaging 6 to 8 inches. Fish up to 12 inches are caught, and specimens larger than that are possible. And the brook trout are as beautiful as any found in the area.

Access to the Cupsuptic River is better than that found on some other rivers in the area. Dirt roads parallel the river for much of its length, allowing you to move around. But getting in and out of the river can be a challenge. While wading is easy in many places, parts of the stream are best fished from a canoe. The areas around the Lincoln Road Bridge, Little Falls, and Big Falls are popular with fly

Classic freestone water on the middle Cupsuptic River. An upstream approach allows for good drifts while helping to not spook fish. DIANA MALLARD PHOTO

fishers. There are formal "wilderness" campsites available for a fee, some of which are found near scenic Big Falls.

Brook trout in the Cupsuptic River feed on small minnows, insects, and fish eggs. Smelt are present in the lower river in the early spring, as are sucker eggs. Dace and sculpin are available throughout the river year-round. Insects include mayflies, caddis, and stoneflies. Terrestrials are available in the summer. Hatches start in early to mid-May and continue into the early summer. There is a brief resurgence in the early fall, with insects hatching intermittently until the season closes.

The Cupsuptic River is open to fishing from April through September. The entire river, including its tributaries, are restricted to fly fishing only. There is a 5-fish limit and 6-inch minimum length limit in the upper river. From Little Falls to Cupsuptic Lake there is a 2-fish limit with a 10-inch minimum length limit, and only one fish may exceed 12 inches. After August 15 there is a 1-fish limit throughout the entire system. The river fishes well throughout the season, especially in its upper reaches.

The Cupsuptic River offers some of the best small-stream fishing for brook trout in the greater Rangeley area. While the fish are not large like those caught in the lower Kennebago, Magalloway tailwater, or Rapid River, they are healthy and beautiful. It is also less crowded than the better-known rivers, making the fish a bit easier to catch, which is not necessarily a bad thing. And as I said in the beginning of the chapter, if the Cupsuptic River was located anywhere but in Rangeley, Maine, it would be one of the finest wild brook trout rivers in the area.

Dead Diamond River (NEW HAMPSHIRE)

The Dead Diamond River in New Hampshire is not only the finest wild native brook trout watershed in the state, but also the finest in New England outside of Maine, one of the finest in the Northeast, and, it would be fair to say, one of the finest in the country. It's the best native brook trout river most brook trout aficionados have never fished.

Located in extreme northeastern New Hampshire near the Maine border, the Dead Diamond River is part of a large, remote wilderness watershed. Along with the Swift Diamond River, numerous secondary streams, and several ponds, it is a wild native brook trout watershed of national significance. Almost all the rivers, streams, and ponds in the watershed are home to native brook trout, most of which are wild.

The Dead Diamond River is just short of 20 miles long. It begins in Atkinson and Gilmanton Academy Grant. Much of the river is located in Second College Grant, known locally as Dartmouth Grant. Its headwater tributaries extend into the towns of Pittsburg, a well-known fishing destination, Clarksville, and Dix's Grant. In addition to

resident brook trout that average 8 to 10 inches, fish up to 18 inches enter the lower river in the spring and fall and during high water periods.

Second College Grant is an unincorporated township in Coos County. It is owned and managed by Dartmouth College, granted to the college in the early 1800s. There are trails and cabins available for Dartmouth students, employees, and alumni that are maintained by the Dartmouth Outing Club and Dartmouth Outdoor Programs Office. It covers an area of approximately 27,000 acres, and is bordered by Dix's Grant to the west, Atkinson and Gilmanton Academy Grant to the north, Wentworth's Location to the south, and Maine to the east. The highest point is Mount Tucker at 2,840 feet above sea level.

While Second College Grant was historically managed for forestry to help offset operating costs, timber harvesting was suspended in the 1970s for evaluation. Prior policies were reviewed and replaced with sustainable programs that limited cutting—both how much and where. Today the land is managed for wildlife and recreation, as well

A large wild brook trout caught from the Dead Diamond River in the early spring. When angling pressure goes up, the best thing to do is go down—which means small nymphs fished on the bottom. DIANA MALLARD PHOTO

The author and guide Tom Freedman fishing the lower Dead Diamond River in New Hampshire. The land along the river is owned by Dartmouth College and is closed to vehicular traffic. Walk-in access is allowed. DIANA MALLARD PHOTO

as so-called sustainable forestry. This has benefited native flora and fauna, including brook trout.

The Dead Diamond River is a tributary of the Magalloway River, considered by many to be the second-finest self-sustaining native brook trout river in the country. The Magalloway empties into Umbagog Lake just north of where the Rapid River, considered by most to be the finest self-sustaining native brook trout river in the country, enters the lake. Large brook trout migrate throughout the entire system, including the Dead Diamond River.

The Dead Diamond River begins at the confluence of the East Branch Dead Diamond River and Middle Branch Dead Diamond River. The West Branch Dead Diamond River joins just downstream; its tributaries include Hellgate Brook, Pisgah Brook, Roby Brook, and Rowell Brook. The Little Dead Diamond River enters the river roughly 2 miles below that; the South Branch Little Dead Diamond River is its only tributary. The Swift Diamond River enters roughly a mile above its termination.

Other tributaries to the Dead Diamond are Lamb Valley Brook, Loomis Valley Brook, and Tracy Brook. There are two small ponds in its headwaters: Beaver Pond and Lamb Valley Pond. Two streams within the watershed are formally designated as Wild Trout Management waters by the state: Lamb Valley Brook and Loomis Valley Brook.

The Swift Diamond River is approximately 18 miles long and is the second-largest river in the watershed. It begins at Diamond Pond in Stewartstown, a stocked rainbow trout lake, and ends at the Dead Diamond River, flowing through Dixville, Dix's Grant, and Second College Grant. The headwaters of the Swift Diamond extends into Clarksville. Brook trout average between 6 and 8 inches long, but fish up to 12 inches are caught.

In addition to Diamond Pond, there are two other trout ponds in the headwaters of the Swift Diamond River— Little Diamond Pond and Nathan Pond—both of which hold brook trout. Its tributaries are Alder Brook, Bennett's Brook, Four Mile Brook, Gulf Brook, Keyser Brook, Larry's Brook, Nathan Pond Brook, Roaring Brook, South Valley Brook, Squeeze Hole Brook, and Tracy Brook. One, Alder Brook, is a formally designated Wild Trout Management water.

The Dead Diamond River is open to fishing from January through September. From its confluence with the Swift Diamond River to its termination at the Magalloway River, it is managed for catch-and-release, and tackle is restricted to single-hook barbless artificial lures and flies only. Above the Swift Diamond River, the limit is 5 fish or 5 pounds, whichever comes first, with no minimum length limit and no tackle restrictions.

A large brook trout from the Dead Diamond River in northeastern New Hampshire, the finest wild native brook trout river in the United States outside of Maine. Notice the scars behind the gill plate and forward of the tail; it looks as though the fish may have been caught in a state fish and game net at one point.
DIANA MALLARD PHOTO

The three Wild Trout Management waters—Alder Brook, Lamb Valley Brook, and Loomis Valley Brook—are open to fishing from January through Labor Day, but are closed in the fall to protect spawning fish. They are managed for catch-and-release, and tackle is restricted to single-hook barbless artificial lures and flies only. These waters are not stocked and are maintained solely through natural reproduction. There are only 13 so-designated streams in the state.

All other rivers and streams in the Dead Diamond River watershed are open to fishing from January through October 15, with a 5-fish, 5-pound limit, no minimum length limit, and no tackle restrictions.

Little Diamond Pond and Nathan Pond are formally designated Trout Ponds. Both are stocked and open to fishing from the fourth Saturday in April through October 15. The limit on brook trout is 5 fish or 5 pounds. There is no minimum length limit, and the use of live fish as bait is prohibited to help prevent the spread of nonnative and often highly invasive baitfish.

Hatches in the Dead Diamond River watershed start in May and continue into the end of the season. Mayflies, caddis, stoneflies, and midges are all present. The ponds get damselfly and dragonfly hatches in the summer as well. Summer also brings terrestrials such as ants and beetles. Fish also feed on leeches and small minnows—primarily sculpin, dace, and juvenile trout.

There are both stocked and wild brook trout in the Dead Diamond River watershed. Fish run from 6 to 18 inches, with the occasional larger fish caught. The watershed offers a mix of large streams, small rivers, lakes, and ponds. In addition to the three designated Wild Trout Management streams, wild fish can be found in the headwaters of many of the tributaries as well as the lower Dead Diamond River.

New Hampshire Fish & Game have been studying the Dead Diamond River for roughly seven years to determine if it warrants further protection. It is New Hampshire's best wild native brook trout fishery, a tributary of the Magalloway River, and part of the same watershed as the fabled Rapid River, the two finest wild native brook trout rivers in the nation. Nowhere in the state can you find larger wild native brook trout in a riverine environment. If there is a river in New Hampshire worthier of absolute protection, I have not seen it.

Dennys River (MAINE)

The Dennys River is located in northeast, or Downeast, Maine. It begins at Meddybemps Lake and flows 23 miles before terminating at Dennys Bay at a place called Hells Vestibule. It is one of the fabled Downeast Salmon Rivers, and prior to being dammed was said to have accounted for up to 20 percent of the wild native Atlantic salmon found in the United States.

One of the wildest, most remote, ecologically diverse, and intact streams on the Atlantic coast of the United States, the Dennys River is home to Maine's highest concentration of nesting bald eagles and rare species of freshwater mussel and mayfly. It still has all of its native fish species, including federally endangered Atlantic salmon and sea-run brook trout, the latter of which is covered in detail later in this book.

The Dennys River is one of the most robust, and everchanging, sea-run fish ecosystems found in the East. While the Atlantic salmon are admittedly not doing well and are propped up almost exclusively through stocking, their close cousin the brook trout has remained stable and may

be regaining lost ground. Smelts, alewives, and eels are also doing well.

Known by the Passamaquoddy as Kethonosk, the Dennys River was named after an Indian who hunted the area. Using nets made of cedar bark, they came to the river to trap "frostfish," either tomcod or smelt, during their annual migration from the ocean to the river to spawn. These fish served as an important source of protein at a time when food was scarce. They also fished for Atlantic salmon and, it would be fair to assume, brook trout.

In the early days of European settlement, the Dennys River was a source of dispute. Prior to establishing a formal border between the Loyalists and Revolutionaries, who had rights to the land was constantly challenged. To some the border was the Dennys River, to others the St. Croix River, known at the time as the Schoodic or Skutik River.

Later the Dennys was the scene of the so-called salmon wars between the citizens who wanted to angle for these prized fish, the federal government that wanted to save the fish, and a state that wanted to maintain control over

A large sea-run brook trout caught by Emily Bastian from the fabled Dennys River in Downeast Maine. Like many salters the fish fell for a small streamer. BOB MALLARD PHOTO

While often too deep to wade, the Dennys River can be waded in certain areas. Don't overlook the slow sections, as fish congregate around the numerous and easy-to-overlook springs. EMILY BASTIAN PHOTO

this socially and economically important iconic species. While things have quieted down, the fishery is closed, Atlantic salmon are nearing extinction, and the fabled Dennys River Sportsman's Club is abandoned and in disrepair after roughly a century of operation. Formed after a major dam removal initiated by the founding members, the club included famed boxer Jack Dempsey.

Sea-run brook trout, known as salters and growing to lengths of 18 inches or more, were once so numerous that salmon anglers complained they were interfering with their "fly drifts." While diminished from their historic highs, the wild native sea-run brook trout of the Dennys River appear to be doing pretty well.

Sea-run brook trout are a diadromous form of fish, migrating between freshwater and saltwater. They live and spawn in freshwater but move into saltwater to feed and seek thermal refuge. This is different from truly anadromous fish such as salmon, which live in saltwater and enter freshwater to spawn.

Part of the reason the brook trout of the Dennys River are sustaining is an aging and declining human population, which has reduced pressure on the resource. The Downeast region has the oldest population in the state, and after a brief bump-up in the early 1990s, the population has steadily declined to early 1970s levels. Young people aren't fishing to the degree their parents and grandparents did,

which takes pressure off the resource. And many folks who fish have shifted to nonnative bass, which, while taking pressure off brook trout, creates other and more dangerous problems such as the spread of bass into trout habitat, which has already happened.

The Dennys River is one of the northernmost sea-run brook trout rivers in the United States. And while it is not the easternmost salter stream in the United States, it is the easternmost salter river. A 20-mile section of the Dennys River is believed to be the longest unbridged stretch of coastal river in New England. Some think it may be the longest on the Eastern Seaboard. Regardless, the Dennys is one of the most remote rivers you will find on the Atlantic coast, and this is part of what makes it so special.

While I had fished the Dennys River before while attempting to find Atlantic salmon at a time when I didn't have a clue as to what they were, where to find them, or how to catch them, I didn't know how good the river was until I fished it with Bill Robinson, owner of Dennys River Guide Service. Accompanied by Bill, Dwayne Shaw, executive director of Downeast Salmon Federation, and Emily Bastian, chair of the Maine chapter of Native Fish Coalition, we drove deep into the woods, slid a pair of canoes down a hill, and headed off in a swarm of blackflies.

While my salters to date had been small, less than 8 inches, the first fish I caught on the Dennys River, at 10

Due to its remoteness and long stretches of deep, slow water, the Dennys River is best fished from a canoe. Home to the largest salters in New England, it's well worth the effort. EMILY BASTIAN PHOTO

inches, was the largest sea-run brook trout I had ever seen. During the course of the day, we landed many fish in the 8- to 10-inch range, several 12-inch fish, and one silvery fish that went 14 inches. While I spent as much time, or more, taking pictures, as I did fishing, it was the finest sea-run brook trout fishing I had ever experienced.

Brook trout in the Dennys River can be found where you would expect to find them, in riffles and deep holes, as well as the many subtle, easily missed spring holes that the average brook trout angler would slide right past without even making a cast. Fish can be pretty much anywhere, so it is best to leave no water unfished.

The Dennys River is the crown jewel of Maine sea-run brook trout rivers. That the river has flown under the radar, at least as a brook trout fishery, for as long as it has is more a testimony to where it is than what it is. And by that I mean its location in northern coastal Maine as opposed to the more popular western or central interior Maine.

Nearly the entire length of the Dennys River is permanently protected by the State of Maine, Downeast Coastal Conservancy, The Nature Conservancy, and Downeast Salmon Federation to help preserve its rare Atlantic salmon population. The Dennys River is best fished from a canoe, as access can be difficult and getting around once you are there even more so due to long sections of deep water.

Brook trout in the Dennys River can be caught on streamers, nymphs, and dries. Locals are purported to use mouse patterns to entice some of the larger specimens. Anglers should be prepared to encounter federally protected Atlantic salmon parr, which must be released immediately and unharmed.

The Dennys River is open to fishing from April through September. It is managed under general law regulations: unrestricted bait, 5 fish, 6 inches. An approximately 200-foot section is closed to fishing to protect Atlantic salmon.

The Dennys River is arguably the finest sea-run brook trout fishery in the country. If fly fishing for wild native sea-run brook trout—and some of the larger salters you will ever find—in a remote, unspoiled, uncrowded, and historic setting is what you are after, the Dennys River is the place to find it. And the possibility of seeing a rare, endangered Atlantic salmon in its native spawning grounds seals the deal, at least for me.

Kennebago Lake (MAINE)

Kennebago Lake is located near historic Rangeley, Maine. It is the largest fly-fishing-only water in Maine and said to be the largest east of the Mississippi. At 1,700 acres, it is 300 acres larger than the second biggest in Maine and nearly 1,200 acres larger than the third. It is believed to be the first lake in Maine with that designation, the regulation having been in place since at least the late 1920s.

Kennebago Lake is approximately 15 miles east of New Hampshire and 10 miles south of the Canadian border and lies at approximately 1,800 feet above sea level. It is nearly 5 miles long and three-quarters mile wide with a maximum depth of roughly 115 feet and an average depth of nearly 70 feet. It is part of the headwaters of the fabled Kennebago River, and one of only five waters in Maine designated as a Wilderness Gem Lake.

The Kennebago Indians, members of the Abenaki tribe of the Algonquin nation, once called the area around Kennebago Lake home. They hunted, fished, and camped at what is known as the Causeway. Loggers drove timber down the lake, into the Kennebago River, and down the Androscoggin River to the mills in Berlin, New Hampshire. Early in the Civil War, young men looking to avoid the fighting established a remote camp on the lake at what is now known as Skedaddler's Cove. They survived by trading furs for supplies.

Starting in the early 1900s, steamships transported tourists up Kennebago Lake. While they were eventually replaced by motorboats, the remains of the last, *Kennebago III*, can still be seen on the shoreline. During prohibition, alcohol was smuggled from Canada and rowed down the lake, usually under the cover of darkness, to furnish the sporting camps. President Herbert Hoover, an avid angler, and Maine governor Percival Baxter, father of Baxter State Park, stayed at the lake.

Kennebago Lake has a rich fly-fishing heritage. It has been home to one or more sporting camps since 1875. While the first was Kennebago Lake House, the most famous is Grant's Kennebago Camps, started by Ed Grant in 1875 and the only remaining commercial business on the lake. Cornelia "Fly Rod" Crosby, Maine's first registered guide, guided on the lake. Fly fishers came from all over the Northeast to fish for brook trout that reached 4 to 8 pounds. They came by foot, buckboard (riding or walking behind), train (referred to as a rail bus), and eventually automobile.

Shoreside guest cabins at historic Grant's Kennebago Camps on Kennebago Lake. Classic wooden Rangeley Boats are still the watercraft of choice for many visiting fly fishers. DIANA MALLARD PHOTO

Kennebago Lake is believed to be Maine's first fly-fishing-only lake and said to be the largest fly-fishing-only water east of the Mississippi. DIANA MALLARD PHOTO

Kennebago Lake is classified as a Principal Fishery for brook trout by Maine's Department of Inland Fisheries and Wildlife. It is the 50th-largest such lake in the state. The lake is also a formally designated State Heritage Fish water, a designation given to lakes and ponds that have not been stocked in at least 25 years. It is the fifth-largest such water, and while once heavily stocked, it has not been stocked since 1954.

Brook trout are native to Kennebago Lake. They are self-sustaining and average 10 to 14 inches. Fish in the 16-inch range are fairly common, and fish larger than that are caught. A 7-pound fish caught from the lake was sent to Harvard University professor of zoology Louis Agassiz in the late 1800s, who confirmed it was in fact a brook trout, not a lake trout as some assumed. Even today fish up to 4 or more pounds are caught.

Interestingly, Kennebago Lake is also home to a remnant and rare-to-Maine population of nonnative wild brown trout, some of which attain weights of over 5 pounds and represent the largest pond-dwelling wild brown trout caught in the state. Where they came from is unclear.

Hatches on Kennebago Lake start in late May and run through July. They pick up again in the fall and end in mid- to late October. The first hatches are mayflies such as Black Quills and March Browns. *Hexagenia*, Maine's largest mayfly, hatch in July. Caddis start hatching in June and are present through July. Ants and beetles are available in June and again in October. Summer brings dragonflies and damsels. The primary fall hatch is chironomids, or midges.

Kennebago Lake is open to fishing from April through October, one of the few wild brook trout ponds in Maine open in October. Tributaries close after August 15 to protect spawning brook trout. The lake is usually ice-free by mid-May, but ice-out can come as early as the beginning of May. The bag limit on brook trout is 5 fish, and the minimum length limit is 6 inches; only one fish may exceed 12 inches.

There are commercial and private camps on Kennebago Lake. The camp owner bylaws recommend motors no larger than 10 horsepower. Most people adhere to this, keeping noise, speed, and traffic to a dull roar. They discourage towing activities such as waterskiing. The bylaws also suggest that you allow "2 to 3 cast lengths between anchored boats."

Kennebago Lake is located behind locked gates and accessible by dirt road only, which helps control access and limit pressure. The closest paved road is roughly 5 miles away as the crow flies, but the dirt road in is closer to 10 miles long. Other than those who own or lease property behind the gates, access is best gained by staying at Grant's or one of the rental cabins in the area, or by hiring a guide who has a key to the gates, as walking in is not practical. Grant's is located on the water on the west end of the lake, or "foot," as it is called. They have a fleet of restored Rangeley Boats that make you feel like you have stepped back in time.

Kennebago Lake is a beautiful place. The fly-fishing-only regulation along with voluntary restrictions on motor size make it oddly peaceful for a lake its size. Moose and deer can be seen wading the shallows, and beavers and muskrats swim in the coves. Loons are always present, their haunting calls often the only thing breaking the night silence. Kennebago is one of the finest large brook trout lakes in Maine. In a state where the brook trout is king, that speaks volumes.

Kennebago River (MAINE)

The Kennebago River is located in western Maine near historic Rangeley. It is arguably the most famous brook trout river in the country from a historical standpoint. It is also one of the finest in the nation, second only to the Rapid and Magalloway Rivers.

The name Kennebago refers to a Native American tribe that inhabited the area. It means "people of the land of sweet flowing waters." There is a place they called Indian Rock, where the river flows into Cupsuptic Lake. The book *Squire Rangeley's Township* states: "Once near an old landing on the Kennebago we found an ancient but well-preserved 'jack' for night still hunting of moose. It bore the marks of careful Indian handiwork." It also states that "a shaded point between Lake Cupsuptic and the outlet stream from the Kennebago and Rangeley Lakes was an ancient Indian burial place."

The Kennebago River is roughly 25 miles long. It begins at Big Island Pond north of the Boundary Mountains near Maine's border with Canada. A few miles below the pond, the river enters Long Pond, barely discernible on some maps. Below the pond the river flows approximately 8 miles before entering Little Kennebago Lake, a quality wild brook trout pond. A couple of miles after exiting the lake, the outlet of Kennebago Lake, the largest fly-fishing-only lake in Maine, enters the river at what is known as The Logans. From here it runs roughly 8 miles before emptying into Cupsuptic Lake. Just before entering the lake, the river picks up its largest tributary, the Rangeley River. The only dam is at Kennebago Falls just below the confluence with the outlet of Kennebago Lake.

Beginning in the 1860s word began to spread about the large brook trout being caught from the river. By 1868 the

The lower Kennebago River gets a run of large brook trout from Cupsuptic and Mooselookmeguntic Lakes in the spring and fall. While these fish will hit a streamer early in the run, once they have been in the river a bit, they are best targeted with nymphs. DIANA MALLARD PHOTO

The Kennebago River in western Maine during the fall. Big wild brook trout and beautiful scenery make this the quintessential New England brook trout river. DIANA MALLARD PHOTO

Oquossoc Anglers Association had been established where the river enters Cupsuptic Lake, an arm of Mooselookmeguntic Lake. It is believed to be the first river in Maine designated as fly fishing only, a regulation that has been in place since at least the late 1920s.

Brook trout are native to the Kennebago River; the river is not stocked. The three lakes—Long, Little Kennebago, and Kennebago—along with the river's tributaries are not stocked either. Even sprawling Mooselookmeguntic and Cupsuptic Lakes have not been stocked with brook trout since 1984. The brook trout you encounter are wild. The Maine Department of Inland Fisheries and Wildlife uses the "Kennebago strain" of brook trout in its hatcheries for stocking elsewhere, a testimony to the performance, aesthetics, and genetics of these fish. There are introduced landlocked salmon in Kennebago River as well; they too are wild.

The Kennebago River consists of a series of long, slow sections interrupted by riffles, runs, mild rapids, and pocketwater. It is wadable for much of its length, although you will have to get out to navigate around some of the deeper pools. While very few anglers do it, the section from Steep Bank Pool down to Cupsuptic Lake is best fished from a canoe, using it as a taxi to get from place to place and a casting platform when it is too deep to wade.

For the purposes of fishing, the Kennebago is often broken into four sections. The first is from Big Island Pond to Little Kennebago Lake. This section receives the least

pressure and is home to a resident population of brook trout in the 6- to 10-inch range. Larger fish, up to 18 inches, enter the lower end of this section from the lake in the spring and fall.

The second section runs between Little Kennebago Lake and Kennebago Lake and includes The Logans. This short section of river is somewhat seasonal. While some fish remain in the river year-round, most of what you will encounter are fish that enter the river in the spring and fall from the two lakes. At this time fish up to 18 inches are possible.

The third section runs from Kennebago Lake to the Kennebago River Road Bridge. This nearly 6-mile section of river is home to resident brook trout in the 6- to 12-inch range. Much larger fish, up to 20 inches or more, are found in the lower end of this section in the fall. These are spawning fish from Cupsuptic and Mooselookmeguntic Lakes.

The last section runs from the bridge to Cupsuptic Lake. It includes the fabled Steep Bank Pool. Large brook trout move into this section from the lake below in the spring, usually mid- to late May. They follow the suckers on their annual spawning migration to gorge on their eggs. Trophy-sized fish of up to 4 pounds or more—and some of the most colorful you will ever see—enter the river from the lake in the fall to spawn.

While there is good public access from Steep Bank Pool down to Cupsuptic Lake, access to the rest of the Kennebago is very limited. A gate just above Steep Bank, along

Author hooked into a large brook trout on the middle Kennebago River. They don't come to the net easily.
DIANA MALLARD PHOTO

with another located just downstream of Little Kennebago Lake, restricts public access to roughly 8 miles of river. Public access is available from less than a half mile below the lake to just under 4 miles above it. From there to the headwaters, access is restricted by gates.

In Maine, if you own both sides of a river or stream, you own the streambed. If you own just one side, you do not. In the case of the former, you can float through, but cannot wade or anchor if it is posted. In the case of the latter, you can wade or anchor as long as you enter the water via public property. Regardless, the owners of the land along the Kennebago have not restricted foot or even bike access, just vehicles. Vehicle access is limited to camp owners, their guests, and guests of businesses operating inside the gates, and even this is restricted to some degree.

Brook trout in the Kennebago feed on insects, minnows, and eggs. Mayflies, caddis, and stoneflies are all present. Hatches start in mid-May and run into the early summer. Dragonflies, ants, and beetles are present in the summer. Minnows include smelt, dace, and sculpin. The former is available primarily in the early spring, the latter two year-round. Trout gorge themselves on sucker eggs soon after the smelt run subsides.

The Kennebago River is open to fishing from April through September. A short section on the lower river known as the "spawning beds" closes after September 15 to protect spawning fish. The entire river, including the ponds as well as the tributaries, is restricted to fly fishing only. Bag and length limits vary depending on where you are. The river is catch-and-release after August 15.

Along with the nearby Rapid and Magalloway Rivers, the Kennebago is one of the top three native brook trout rivers in the country. Many believe it has the most beautiful brookies in Maine, me included. The river runs through a beautiful and historic area, and traffic is somewhat limited due to the gated access. It may be the most beautiful brook trout river in Maine as well.

Kennebec River (MAINE)

The Kennebec River is located in central Maine. It is my "home river" and has been for roughly 20 years, and it was my "home-away-from-home river" for 25 years before that. While best known for its nonnative brown trout and Maine's finest wild rainbow trout fishery, it is also a brook trout fishery of note.

The Kennebec is the second-largest river in Maine. It is 170 miles long and drains an area of approximately 5,970 square miles. It begins at roughly 1,025 feet above sea level and ends at the ocean, dropping over 1,000 feet along its way. Its source is Moosehead Lake, the largest lake in the state and wholly within New England. The Kennebec exits the lake in two distinct branches, East and West Outlets, separated by roughly 5 miles, a geographic anomaly.

The Kennebec River has a rich fly-fishing history. Author Arthur Macdougall's fictional character Dud Dean, Maine Guide, plied his trade on the river in the 1920s and 1930s. Roscoe Vernon Gaddis, better known as Gadabout Gaddis, filmed his Emmy-nominated television show, *The Flying Fisherman*, on its banks in the 1960s and 1970s. The river was also the site of one of the first major dam removal projects in the nation, Edwards Dam in Augusta, done mostly to benefit fish.

Brook trout are native to the Kennebec River and many of its tributaries. Today they are found mostly from Moosehead Lake to just below Abenaki Dam in Madison. They are rare below this point and, if encountered, are either drop-downs from above or a tributary. While most of the fish found above Caratunk Falls in Solon are wild, those found below are primarily stocked. Brook trout are stocked in both Outlets, with the East Outlet providing by far the best fishing of the two. While primarily a spring and fall

The remote and rugged Kennebec Gorge is home to some of the largest river-resident brook trout in Maine outside of Rangeley. Getting to them is the real challenge. CHRIS RUSSELL PHOTO

landlocked salmon fishery, it puts up some large holdover brook trout up to 18 inches. The West Outlet has mostly small fish and is infested with nonnative smallmouth bass.

There are wild brook trout from the confluence of the Dead River, another wild brook trout river of note, down to Wyman Lake. They run from 6 to 16 inches, with larger fish caught. Most are found in narrow, fast runs and deep pools, and while there are plenty of brook trout there, they are not always easy to find. There is a decent wild brook trout population below Wyman Dam in Bingham. Fish up to 12 inches are caught, and reports of larger fish come in from time to time. They share the water with rainbows, landlocked salmon, and, recently, smallmouth bass, all of which outnumber them. While brook trout can be caught anywhere at any time, they tend to be found around the mouths of small streams.

Brook trout are a secondary species below Caratunk Falls and Abenaki Dam, both of which are managed for stocked brown trout, and the former for wild nonnative landlocked salmon as well. They are stocked in the spring and fall but rarely, if ever, hold over.

The best brook trout fishing on the Kennebec River, by far, is below Harris Dam in what is known as the Kennebec Gorge. This roughly 10-mile section of river begins at Harris Dam and ends just above the Kennebec's confluence with the Dead River. The maximum depth of the gorge is roughly 240 feet, and it has an elevation drop of roughly 225 feet. It is remote, and the most rugged stretch of river in New England.

The brook trout in the Kennebec Gorge are wild. They run from 6 to 18 inches inches, but the average is closer to 12 inches. According to studies they have some of the best length-to-weight ratios in the state. They are also very strong from living in a rugged freestone environment subject to daily flow rates that change more than tenfold, and high-water events more than twice that.

Access to the Kennebec Gorge is easiest at the two ends, just upstream of the Route 201 bridge and immediately below Harris Dam. And while there are very few formal trails to the water, there are a few other spots where you can gain access, but they require a long ride on dirt roads and a steep descent down to the water.

Flows in the Kennebec Gorge are feast or famine, with low water in the 325 cfs range and high water in the 5,000 cfs range. The gorge serves many masters, the most influential being power generation and whitewater rafting. There are scheduled raft releases as well as formal agreements referred to as "fish flows" that give anglers low-water periods in the evening and morning. They are, however, not binding, and power needs and Mother Nature trump all.

The Kennebec Gorge can be waded in low water, but even then it is not easy. There are large boulders and slippery rocks, and the water can come up at any time and without warning. It is impossible, and dangerous, to wade

The wild brook trout from the upper Kennebec River have some of the best length-to-weight ratios in Maine. They get that way on a diet of large stoneflies and minnows. BOB MALLARD PHOTO

Well-known Maine outdoor personality George Smith fishing the Kennebec Gorge. Access is best gained by raft and should only be attempted by skilled rowers with knowledge of the river and its flow regime. BOB MALLARD PHOTO

in high water. Recent changes have resulted in a phased release, which, while providing some level of warning that the water is coming up, shortens the duration of the low water periods. There is also a horn at the dam that announces releases. Unfortunately, it can't be heard more than a few hundred yards away from the dam, and waders must do so with utmost caution.

Fishing from a rowed raft is the best way to fish the Kennebec Gorge. This allows you to cover more water while addressing some of the safety and access issues noted above. It requires an intimate knowledge of the river, hard work, and solid rowing skills, and is best done by hiring a guide familiar with the river.

The primary spawning tributary for the upper Kennebec River's brook trout is Cold Stream, which enters the river from the west near the end of the gorge. The stream is part of an important public land, covered later in this book, and is the finest wild native brook trout stream in the area.

The upper Kennebec River is open to fishing from April through October. Prime time is mid-May through mid-July

and September through October, with late July through August best fished early or late. Tackle is restricted to artificial lures only, and there is a 2-fish, 14-inch limit on brook trout.

Brook trout in the Kennebec River feed on insects and minnows. Hatches start in mid-May and run right into the fall, and include mayflies, caddis, and stoneflies. There are golden stones throughout the river and giant stones in the Kennebec Gorge, and the fall BWO hatch is one of the best in the state. The predominant minnows are sculpin and fallfish, with smelt found immediately below Harris and Wyman Dams. Fish are caught on dries, nymphs, buggers, and streamers.

The Kennebec is one of the longest brook trout rivers in Maine, and the Kennebec Gorge the most remote float in New England. The river is rugged and beautiful, with limited development. There are no paved roads into the gorge, and a conservation easement prevents logging below the top of the gorge, or the crown. Most of the brook trout you encounter will be wild, making it a truly special place.

Magalloway River (MAINE)

The Magalloway River is located in western Maine near historic Rangeley. It is arguably the second-finest wild native brook trout river in the country after the nearby Rapid River, and one of the most famous. Brook trout in the lower river are measured in pounds, not inches. And all the fish in the river are wild; there is no stocking. President Eisenhower fished the river in 1955; a streamside plaque commemorates his visit.

Native Americans camped along the banks of the Magalloway 10,000 years ago, their ancient campsites now buried beneath Aziscohos Lake. They hunted migrating woodland caribou, now extirpated from the region. Metallak, "The Lone Indian of the Magalloway," hunted, trapped, fished, and guided the area. He was reputed to have lived to be 120 years old and ridden a bull moose. Nearby Parmachenee Lake was named after his daughter. There is a mountain, pond, and island named after him, as well as a number of clubs and businesses.

The Magalloway River can be divided into three sections for the purpose of fishing: upper, middle, and lower. In total there is nearly 30 miles of river, not including 15-mile, 6,700-acre Aziscohos and 900-acre Parmachenee Lakes, both solid wild native brook trout fisheries in their own right. Each section of river varies considerably in size, topography, flow regime, and the fishery itself.

The Magalloway River begins at the confluence of several small streams near the Canadian border. Known as the Upper Magalloway, it flows approximately two and a half

Emily Bastian with a large brook trout from the Magalloway River, considered by many to be the second-finest native brook trout river fishery in the United States after the nearby Rapid River. That is what we call a happy angler.
LARRY BASTIAN PHOTO

Large brook trout gorge themselves on sucker eggs in the early spring on the Magalloway River. Find the suckers and you will find brook trout just downstream of them. TRAVIS PARLIN PHOTO

miles before emptying into Parmachenee Lake. It is a small freestone stream flowing through a working forest managed for pulpwood. Access is via a network of unmarked roads, some of which are gated and restricted to camp owners and guests of a sporting camp located on the lake. Most of the trout are in the 6- to 12-inch range. Larger fish in the 16- to 20-inch range enter the lower end in the spring, fall, and after heavy rains. The spring fish are in search of an easy meal—spawning smelt and sucker eggs. The fall fish are there to spawn.

Below Parmachenee Lake at what was known as Black Cat Dam begins what is referred to as the "Middle" Magalloway. This short stretch of river flows approximately a mile and a half before terminating at Aziscohos Lake. At roughly 30 to 40 feet wide, it resembles a large stream or medium-sized river. Access is via dirt roads that parallel both shores or boat. Water levels vary seasonally and bump up as the result of rain. Likewise, water temperatures vary noticeably throughout the season. Brook trout average between 6 and 12 inches, with much larger fish caught. In the spring smelt enter the river on their annual spawning run, drawing large brook trout and landlocked salmon into the lower river. Soon after the smelt drop back to the lake, the suckers enter the river and the cycle is repeated. In the case of the former, the trout are in search of minnows, in the latter eggs.

The dam at the outlet of Aziscohos Lake creates Maine's finest tailwater fishery, the "Lower" Magalloway. Cold water released from the dam provides season-long fishing even during the warmest of years. The river drops roughly 250 feet in elevation in the first mile, with much of the flow diverted a quarter mile downstream by pipe to a power station. Between the dam and the power station is a series of drops, pools, and pocketwater that hold fish. However, it is below here that the best fishing is found. From the power station to Wilsons Mills the Magalloway is a rugged freestone river. Below Wilsons Mills it is a meandering stream. Brook trout in this section average between 12 and 16 inches, fish over 18 inches are common, and fish over 20 inches are always possible.

Flows in the upper and middle Magalloway typically run between 50 and 150 cfs. Flows on the lower river generally run in the 300 to 600 cfs range. The entire river is subject to spikes during spring runoff and after rain. There are also scheduled releases on the lower river in the summer in support of whitewater recreation that run from 900 to 1,200 cfs. The Magalloway is a wading river, with floating only possible from Wilsons Mills down. Some fly fishers use boats or canoes to gain access to where the river enters the lakes.

Brook trout in the Magalloway feed on insects, minnows, crayfish, and fish eggs. Insects include mayflies, caddis, stoneflies, and midges, the latter of which are found

Larry Bastian fishing the fabled Mailbox Pool on the lower Magalloway River in Maine. The Mailbox Pool probably gives up more large fish than any two other spots on the river. EMILY BASTIAN PHOTO

mostly in the lower river. Hatches start in mid-May and continue into the early summer. There is a brief resurgence in the early fall when Blue-Winged Olives and Slate Drakes hatch. Hatches start earlier on the lower river than they do on the middle and upper river due to the tailwater effect. Smelt are present mostly in the early spring, with dace and sculpin available year-round.

The upper and middle Magalloway are relatively easy to fish, and what works on most brook trout water will work there. Due to the pressure the lower Magalloway is best fished with nymphs. And while fish will take streamers, they rarely take them in the traditional way; streamers are usually best fished by casting them upstream and bringing them back low and slow versus fishing them down and across. Brook trout in the Magalloway will take mice and large terrestrials at certain times as well.

The Magalloway is open to fishing from April through September. The entire river is restricted to fly fishing only. There is a catch-and-release restriction on brook trout below Aziscohos Lake. Above the lake there is a 1-fish limit, and all trout less than 6 inches and greater than 12 inches must be released. After August 15 the middle and upper river are catch-and-release to protect spawning fish.

The lower Magalloway is usually fishable by the season opener, with most of the fish found in and around Wilsons Mills at that time. The middle and upper river are often inaccessible until early May due to poor road conditions. During spring runoff, much of the river can be temporarily unfishable due to high water. While the lower river remains cool enough to support trout year-round, the middle and upper river are best fished in the spring and fall.

Brook trout in the Magalloway are very migratory. They are found in specific places at certain times of year. Rain or unseasonably cold or warm temperatures can move them around as well. Look for fish in the lower ends of the three sections in the spring and after rain, and close to the dam on the lower river in the summer.

Due to the presence of nonnative and highly invasive smallmouth bass in the Rapid River, the Magalloway River may be Maine's, and by default the nation's, best hope for maintaining large wild native brook trout in a riverine environment. Strict regulations on the lower river have helped it meet its potential, in spite of what is a high level of traffic. Enjoy this special resource and treat it with care, as it may be our last best hope.

Moosehead Lake (MAINE)

Moosehead Lake is located in central Maine just over four hours north of Boston. It is the largest lake in Maine and the biggest wholly within New England. It is the second-largest native brook trout lake located entirely within the United States after Lake Michigan, and the biggest even partially in the United States after the Great Lakes and Lake Champlain. It is also considered the largest "mountain lake" in the eastern United States.

Moosehead Lake lies at roughly 1,025 feet above sea level. It drains an area of approximately 1,250 square miles. The surface area of the lake is approximately 75,000 acres, and its total volume is said to be over 4,000,000 acre-feet. The lake measures 40 miles at its longest point and 10 miles at its widest point. The average depth is 55 feet, and the maximum depth is nearly 250 feet. There are roughly 400 miles of shoreline, and it is home to more than 80 islands, the largest of which are Sugar, Deer, and Farms Islands.

The Native American name for Moosehead Lake was Sebamook or Sebemook. An impoundment on the upper West Branch Penobscot River just north of the lake bears the name Seboomook today. The current name, Moosehead, is believed to be a reflection of the lake's shape.

Mount Kineo, located on a small peninsula halfway up the lake, is one of the most recognizable landmarks in Maine. Its 700-foot cliffs rise straight up from the lake on the southeast side of the mountain. Native Americans came from throughout the region to collect flint from the mountain for use in spears and arrows. Known as siliceous slate or hornstone, it is the largest such deposit in the country.

European settlers first came to the area in the early 1800s. Kineo was home to a resort starting in the late 1840s. It succumbed to fire in the late 1860s and again in the early 1880s. In 1911 it was purchased by the railroad. At the time it was the largest waterfront hotel in the country. The rail to the resort was discontinued in the early 1930s, leading to its sale. The hotel was demolished soon after. Its golf course, built in the 1880s, is still in operation today and believed to be the second-oldest course in New England.

The northern end of Moosehead Lake serves as the boundary between the Kennebec and Penobscot watersheds, the two largest in the state. There is a historic canoe portage between the lake and the West Branch Penobscot River located at aptly named Northeast Carry. The portage is located at the site of a trail that was used by native inhabitants for thousands of years, and later to move logs to the West Branch to be floated to the mills downstream. It was also used by Henry David Thoreau in the mid-1840s,

and he makes numerous references to Moosehead Lake in his book *The Maine Woods*.

Moosehead Lake is part of one of the finest native brook trout watersheds in the country. Its two largest tributaries, the Moose and Roach Rivers, are solid wild brook trout fisheries and two of the best native brook trout rivers in the country. The lake is the headwaters of the fabled Kennebec River, which exits the lake via two distinctly different streams, West and East Outlets, a geographic anomaly. (Both the Kennebec River and Roach River are covered in separate chapters in this book.)

Moosehead Lake is a self-sustaining brook trout fishery. According to Maine's Department of Inland Fisheries and Wildlife, the lake has not been stocked with brook trout since 1998. Brook trout average a foot in length, with fish between 14 and 16 inches fairly common, and trout up to 20 inches caught.

Moosehead Lake is open to ice fishing from January through March, and open-water fishing April through

A Maine Department of Inland Fisheries and Wildlife biologist surveys fish from Moosehead Lake. This is a trophy by any standard and a sign of what the lake is capable of producing. A protective slot limit and some additional ice fishing restrictions could help the lake meet its potential. KYLE MURPHY PHOTO

A panoramic view of sprawling Moosehead Lake from atop Mount Kineo. Moosehead is the largest lake in Maine and wholly located in New England, and the biggest "mountain lake" in the eastern United States. EMILY BASTIAN PHOTO

September. Practically speaking, the fly-fishing season starts in mid- to late May when the lake becomes ice-free. There is a 1-fish, 14-inch limit on brook trout, including on the lower end of all tributaries as denoted by red posts or the first upstream bridge. There are no tackle restrictions.

Hatches on Moosehead Lake start soon after ice-out and continue into the fall. Mayflies, caddis, and midges are all present. The giant *Hexagenia* hatches in early July. Flying ants, beetles, dragonflies, and damsels are important summer forage. Throughout the season trout feed on minnows, mostly smelt, leeches, and crayfish.

You need a large boat to effectively, and safely, fish Moosehead Lake. Motorboats are your best bet, as they allow you to cover more water and get off the water quickly when the lake kicks up, and it can kick up at any time. As a result, while canoes, kayaks, and small boats can be used, you should stay close to the shore and pick your times wisely, which means early morning and late afternoon.

Moosehead Lake is served by the lakeside tourist community of Greenville. This four-season destination offers lodging, dining, retail, and services. Greenville Junction down the road has some services also, as does Rockwood, roughly halfway up the west shore of the lake. Lily Bay State Park, located approximately one-quarter of the way up the lake on the east shore, offers lakeside camping. Beyond this, development on the lake is sparse and limited to mostly private camps.

Greenville is home to the steamship *Katahdin*, built by Bath Iron Works in 1914. It was originally used to transport tourists up the lake to the sporting camps. Later it was used to tow rafts of logs down the lake to be run down the Kennebec, and was part of the nation's last log drive in 1975. This National Historic Landmark is still in operation today, taking visitors on tours of the lake.

Large lakes in Maine are fished primarily by ice anglers and trollers. When you consider that fly fishers utilize Yellowstone Lake in Yellowstone National Park, Hebgen Lake in Montana, Henrys Lake in Idaho, and other large lakes around the country, it makes one wonder what Maine fly fishers might be missing by not fishing Moosehead Lake.

Moosehead Lake is a beautiful and relatively lightly developed lake—especially for a lake its size. Wild brook trout, some of which are quite large, cruise its shoreline, coves, and tributary mouths, sipping flies off the surface unnoticed by the fly-fishing masses. That more anglers do not take advantage of this unique trophy wild native brook trout resource is amazing.

Nesowadnehunk (MAINE)

Nesowadnehunk is Abenaki for "swift water between mountains." It is the name of two lakes, two streams, a stretch of river, and a waterfall: Nesowadnehunk Lake, Little Nesowadnehunk Lake, Nesowadnehunk Stream, Little Nesowadnehunk Stream, Nesowadnehunk Deadwater, and Nesowadnehunk Falls. It is also the name of a campground in Baxter State Park, Nesowadnehunk Field Campground. It is often spelled Sourdnahunk, a phonetic representation. Locally it is sometimes pronounced "soudyhunk."

Little Nesowadnehunk Lake is the headwaters of the Nesowadnehunk watershed. It is connected to Nesowadnehunk Lake via a short flowage referred to on some maps as Nesowadnehunk Stream. Nesowadnehunk Lake is the source of well-known Nesowadnehunk Stream, and Little Nesowadnehunk Stream is a tributary of Nesowadnehunk Stream. Nesowadnehunk Stream is a tributary of the fabled West Branch Penobscot River, joining it just below Nesowadnehunk Falls. Nesowadnehunk Deadwater is just above the falls.

Nesowadnehunk has a rich brook trout heritage. Nesowadnehunk Lake, Little Nesowadnehunk Lake, Nesowadnehunk Stream, and Little Nesowadnehunk Stream are all home to wild native brook trout. The small lake and streams have never been stocked, and the large lake was last stocked in 1956. Both lakes are classified as State Heritage Fish waters. The Nesowadnehunk Lake strain of brook trout has been used in the Maine state hatchery system for decades.

Nesowadnehunk also has a great fly-fishing heritage. Both Nesowadnehunk Lake and Little Nesowadnehunk Lake are fly fishing only. At nearly 1,400 acres the former is the second-largest fly-fishing-only water in the state, behind fabled Kennebago Lake in historic Rangeley. Nesowadnehunk Stream is one of the few fly-fishing-only small streams in the state.

Anglers fly-fishing Nesowadnehunk Lake from boats at dusk. Arguably Maine's most-fished wild brook trout lake, there are times when it looks more like a bass tournament than a recreational trout fishery. DANIEL STRAINE PHOTO

Emily Bastian fishing Nesowadnehunk Stream. One of Maine's few fly-fishing-only streams, it traverses Baxter State Park before emptying into the fabled West Branch Penobscot River just below Nesowadnehunk Falls.
LARRY BASTIAN PHOTO

The centerpiece of the Nesowadnehunk watershed is Nesowadnehunk Lake, located just west of Baxter State Park, where roughly a mile of its northeast shoreline serves as part of the park's western boundary. It is approximately 10 miles northwest of Mount Katahdin, the highest point in Maine and the northern terminus of the famous Appalachian Trail, which can be seen from most of the lake.

Nesowadnehunk Lake lies at 1,380 feet above sea level. It has six small inlets, the largest of which is the outlet of Little Nesowadnehunk Lake. The southernmost end of the lake is sometimes referred to as the Nesowadnehunk Thoroughfare, the lower 1,000 feet down to a small dam at the outlet of the lake, which is closed to fishing to protect spawning brook trout.

Nesowadnehunk Lake is the 33rd-largest self-sustaining brook trout lake in the state, and the eighth-largest State Heritage Fish water. It has a maximum depth of 46 feet, with an average depth of roughly 17 feet. It is likely that no lake, pond, river, or stream in Maine gives up more brook trout to the frying pan than Nesowadnehunk Lake, a testimony to the health of this unique wild native fishery.

A sporting camp known as Camp Phoenix operated on Nesowadnehunk Lake from 1896 to 1988. Located on the southeast shore, the cabins and main lodge are now privately owned and part of a condo association. Access is gained via Baxter State Park. There is a public campground on the southwest end of the lake and a private one on the northwest shore. There are two boat launches: the public campground and a public site at the northeast corner of the lake.

Nesowadnehunk Lake is one of the most popular fly-fishing lakes in the state and has been for generations. To call it a "wild brook trout factory" would be fair. Fish numbers are unusually high and appear to be some of the highest in the state. The average fish is between 10 and 12 inches, and trout up to 14 inches are not uncommon. Oddly, fish larger than 14 inches, while caught, are rare. It would be interesting to see if a slot limit that protected large trout could improve the top end.

Little Nesowadnehunk Lake has long been known as a "big fish" pond. While the average is smaller than in the big lake, the top end is higher with fish up to 18 inches or more caught. At just 100 acres it is much smaller than the big lake. It is also a shallow lake, with a maximum depth of just 20 feet and an average depth of only 15 feet.

Nesowadnehunk Stream is nearly 15 miles long, most of which lies within Baxter State Park. It is paralleled by a dirt road starting about a third of the way up from the West Branch Penobscot all the way to the lake. The road is rarely more than a half mile from the stream, and usually much less, and it is often within sight of the water. A large freestone stream, it changes from rocky to sandy substrate throughout its course. Nesowadnehunk Stream is popular with brook trout anglers and has been for decades. It is one of the most heavily fished waters in Baxter State Park, and by far the most popular stream. The lower end of Nesowadnehunk Stream is remote and offers some of the best fishing on the stream, as well as some of the biggest fish.

Nesowadnehunk Deadwater and Nesowadnehunk Falls are located on the West Branch Penobscot. While there are wild native brook trout there, they are best known for their landlocked salmon, considered by many to be the finest river-dwelling landlocked salmon in the state, and arguably the country. Brook trout can be caught in the deadwater during hatches but are purely incidental below the falls.

Trout in the lakes feed on insects, minnows, leeches, and crayfish in the big lake. Mayflies, caddis, midges, dragonflies, damselflies, and terrestrials are all present. The big lake has a very strong, and popular, Green Drake—or, more accurately, *Hexagenia*—hatch. The minnows are mostly dace, and like most ponds in Maine, leeches are plentiful. The big lake's rocky bottom makes it ideal habitat for crayfish, and fishing crayfish patterns on the bottom with a sinking line can be productive.

Hatches start in late May and run through late July. Insects hatch sporadically throughout the summer and pick up again in the early fall, running until the end of the season. The first hatches are mayflies such as Black Quills and March Browns. *Hexagenia* hatch in early July and run through the month. Caddis start hatching in June and are present through July. Ants and beetles are available in June. Summer brings dragonflies and damsels. The primary fall hatch is midges.

Both lakes and the stream are open to fishing from April through September. Practically speaking, the season doesn't begin until the lake is free of ice, sometime in early to mid-May. The daily limit on the big lake and stream is 5 fish with a 6-inch minimum. The small lake has a 2-fish, 10- to 12-inch limit; only one fish can exceed 12 inches.

While the large lake is best fished from a small motorboat, canoes and kayaks can be used as long as you don't venture too far from where you put in, as the lake can kick up without warning, making it hard, and dangerous, to get back. The small lake is best fished from a canoe, kayak, or float tube.

The views from Nesowadnehunk and Little Nesowadnehunk Lakes are some of the best in the state, and include Doubletop Mountain and Mount Katahdin. Nesowadnehunk Stream is one of the most beautiful in the state. If lots of wild brook trout in the 6- to 12-inch range, with the chance of larger fish, in a beautiful setting are what you are looking for, Nesowadnehunk is the place.

A typical wild native brook trout from Nesowadnehunk Lake. While the average size is good, true trophies are rare.
DIANA MALLARD PHOTO

Nipigon River (ONTARIO)

The Nipigon River was the source of the current world-record brook trout, and has long been considered one of the finest, if not the finest, wild native brook trout rivers in the world. It is home to coaster brook trout, and is one of the finest trophy brook trout rivers outside of Labrador. Coasters are a potamodromous form of brook trout that spend part of their life in the large lakes of the upper Great Lakes regions. Once plentiful, coaster numbers have been significantly reduced as a result of dams, angler exploitation, logging, and the introduction of nonnative fish. Many populations have been extirpated.

The Nipigon River is located in the Thunder Bay District in northwestern Ontario, Canada. It begins at Lake Nipigon and ends at Nipigon Bay on Lake Superior. The river is roughly 30 miles long and drains an area of approximately 1,000 square miles. It is a large river at 150 feet to over 600 feet wide. It starts at 853 feet above sea level and ends at 600 feet above sea level, a drop of just over 250 feet, an average of only 8 feet per mile.

Native Americans lived in the area around the Nipigon River starting roughly 9,000 years ago. It is believed they first came to the area while following migrating caribou herds. Rock art found at the mouth of the Nipigon River predates the arrival of Europeans by a few thousand years. While European fur traders came to the area in the mid-1660s, they did not establish a permanent trading post until the late 1670s.

By the mid-1870s, recreational fishing had become a major industry on the Nipigon River. Known throughout Canada and the midwestern United States for its large brook trout, people came from all over to be guided on the river by native guides, who would mount fish skins on birch bark and frame them in wood, a type of taxidermy not found anywhere else. Visitors would bring these mounts home as a memento of their trip.

Three dams—Alexander Dam, Cameron Falls Dam, and Pine Portage Dam—were built along the Nipigon River and have compromised the fishery. Another, Virgin Falls Dam,

A large Nipigon River brook trout. Regardless of reports to the contrary, while not what it once was, the Nipigon is still one of the finest brook trout fisheries in the world. NICHOLAS LAFERRIERE PHOTO

A beautiful wild native brook trout from the Nipigon River—as nice as they get and a trophy by any rational standard.
JAMES SMEDLEY PHOTO

was decommissioned. These dams block coaster brook trout from reaching critical spawning habitat, as well as lessen their ability to migrate throughout the Nipigon system.

On July 21, 1915, Dr. John William Cook of Fort Williams (some say Port Arthur), Ontario, reportedly caught the largest brook trout ever recorded. This world-record fish is by default the Canadian and North American record as well. The fish was caught at Rabbit Rapids on the Nipigon River. It was a coaster, said to be over 30 inches long, with an estimated girth of more than 20 inches. The fish weighed 14.5 pounds 21 days after being caught, so it probably weighed close to 20 pounds when first landed.

The Nipigon River brook trout is one of the longest-standing world-record fish. It is also one of the more controversial ones. In addition to questions as to who really caught it, and on what, there was also some debate at the time as to whether the fish was a brook trout or a lake trout, or possibly even a splake, as naturally occurring brook trout/lake trout hybrids have been documented in the region.

Unfortunately, we will never really know who caught the fish or what they caught it on, or if in fact it was a brook trout. Although modern DNA could have solved the mystery as to what the fish was, the mount was destroyed in 1990 when the museum that was housing it was lost in a fire. What we do know is that this, and many confirmed, trophy brook trout have been caught from the Nipigon River over the last hundred or so years.

Prince Edward, Prince of Wales, was guided on the Nipigon River in 1919. The mount of a large brook trout he caught hangs on the wall of the Archives of Canada.

It has been reported that another 14-pound brook trout was caught on the same day and in the same rapids as Dr. Cook's record fish. And Dr. Cook is said to have caught two 6-pound brook trout at the same time on a tandem fly rig the day he caught his record fish.

The Nipigon River is one of hundreds of tributaries to Lake Superior. Brook trout can be found from its source at Lake Nipigon to Lake Superior. Resident brook trout run from 8 to 12 inches, with fish larger than that caught. The river is also home to coasters, large brook trout that move between the river and the big lakes. Some of the largest brook trout caught outside of Labrador come from the Nipigon River.

Lake Nipigon and many of its tributaries are home to brook trout as well. The lake is home to coasters, too, many of which enter the tributaries in the fall to spawn. Resident fish can grow to trophy size as well.

Brook trout in the Nipigon system feed on insects and minnows. While Dr. Cook's world-record fish was caught on a minnow imitation, it was said to be full of what were believed to be caddis. Due to its size the Nipigon River is best fished from a boat, and ideally a motorboat so you can get around and back to where you started when you are done.

While the Nipigon River will never be what it once was, it is much better than some want to admit, and still a wild native brook trout fishery of international significance. Brook trout over 20 inches and from 5 to 7 pounds are still caught, and fish up to 10 pounds are possible, and in a place that is easy to get to and affordable to the average angler.

Pierce Pond (MAINE)

Pierce Pond is located just east of Pierce Pond Mountain in Pierce Pond Township, Somerset County, Maine. It is as much a region as it is a specific body of water. In addition to Pierce and Upper Pierce Ponds, the area is home to 17 small ponds, all of which hold brook trout. Many of these ponds can be reached via trails from Pierce Pond, and others via a network of dirt roads, some of which are open to public access.

Pierce Pond has attracted sportsmen and outdoor enthusiasts for generations. They come to boat, camp, hike, hunt, view wildlife, and, of course, fish. Author Arthur Macdougall Jr. wrote about Pierce Pond in his popular Dud Dean series. His articles appeared in *Field & Stream* in the 1930s. His books, including *Dud Dean: Maine Guide*, *Dud Dean and His Country*, and *Where Flows the Kennebec*, are highly sought after.

The Pierce Pond watershed is one of the most beautiful areas in central Maine. Its relatively undeveloped rugged landscape, extensive forest lands, and numerous lakes and ponds provide habitat for a broad and diverse range of plants, birds, mammals, and fish. Black bear, beaver, bobcat, coyote, lynx, moose, otter, and white-tailed deer are all present. So are eagles, loons, ruffed grouse, and woodland ducks. It feels like you are much farther away from civilization than you actually are.

Pierce Pond is accessible by dirt road or floatplane only, and many of the roads into the area are gated. There are two sporting camps and several private cabins on Pierce Pond, and several campsites on Upper Pierce Pond, a couple of which are located on islands.

Pierce Pond is arguably the finest medium-sized wild brook trout lake in the state east of Kennebago Lake and south of Nesowadnehunk Lake, both of which are featured in this book. If judged solely by the size of its fish, the northern line would be pushed up into the fabled Allagash Region. Add fly-fishing-only and catch-and-release

An angler with a wild brook trout from Pierce Pond, home to the largest pond-dwelling brook trout in Maine east of Rangeley and south of Moosehead Lake, and one of the most beautiful places in Maine. COURTESY MAINE WILDERNESS WATERSHED TRUST/R. PELUSO

The author portaging a large freighter canoe between Pierce Pond and Upper Pierce Pond. The local guides know the water so well they motor through. DIANA MALLARD PHOTO

restrictions and it would most likely be the finest medium-sized wild brook trout lake south of the Allagash Region.

Pierce Pond is connected to Upper Pierce Pond by a short thoroughfare. Locals refer to the larger of the two, Pierce Pond, as Lower Pierce Pond and Middle Pierce Pond. When referred to in this way, the boundary between Lower Pierce and Middle Pierce Ponds is delineated by what is known as Caribou Narrows. Located roughly two-thirds of the way up the lake, this narrow shallow section is easily identified by its large island.

In total Pierce and Upper Pierce Ponds cover 1,650 acres. The average depth is 39 feet; the maximum depth is 185 feet and found in the larger lake. The ponds sit at roughly 1,150 feet above sea level. It is classified by the state as a body of water of "statewide significance." It is not, however, classified as a State Heritage Fish water due to an ongoing and ill-advised nonnative landlocked salmon stocking program.

Pierce Pond is classified as a Principal Fishery for brook trout. The brook trout are native and self-sustaining—it was last stocked with brook trout in 1995. Brook trout in Pierce Pond average over a foot long, fish in the 14- to 16-inch range are common, and fish over 20 inches and more than 4 pounds are caught. The fishing logs at one of the sporting camps show a surprising

number of fish caught each year that would be considered trophies anywhere else.

Six ponds—Dixon, Fish, Grass, Helen, High, and Pickerel—are self-sustaining and classified as State Heritage Fish waters. Two ponds, Fish and Helen, have never been stocked and contain genetically pure fish. Dixon, Grass, High, and Pickerel Ponds have never been directly stocked, but may or may not have received stocked fish from another source. All six ponds are restricted to fly fishing only. One, Pickerel Pond, is catch-and-release.

The outlet of Pierce Pond, Pierce Pond Stream, empties into the Kennebec River where the fabled Appalachian Trail crosses. Once the site of a steamship shuttle, its hull still visible in the woods just downstream of the confluence, hikers are now ferried across the Kennebec in canoes manned by volunteers. There are several scenic waterfalls on the stream. Brook trout can be found in the upper end and sporadically throughout the stream.

Trout in Pierce Pond feed on insects, minnows, and leeches. Mayflies, caddis, and midges are all present. Spring brings Black Quills and March Browns, and early summer brings *Hexagenia*, which lure large brook trout to the surface. Flying ants, beetles, dragonflies, and damsels are important summer forage. Early spring and fall bring midges. Fish are caught on smelt imitations as well,

Pierce Pond, the best brook trout lake in Maine east of Rangeley and south of Nesowadnehunk Lake. If measured solely on the size of the fish, the line would move noticeably farther north. COURTESY MAINE WILDERNESS WATERSHED TRUST

especially in the spring. Leech patterns can work at any time. Pierce Pond offers anglers one of the best chances in the state to catch a trophy brook trout on a dry fly.

Pierce Pond is open to fishing from April, or ice-out, through September. Tackle is restricted to artificial lures and flies only. There is a 2-fish limit on brook trout, the minimum length limit is 10 inches, and only one fish may exceed 12 inches. And while not explicitly prohibited, large boats are rarely seen on the lake due to the limited access. Most boats you see will be square-stern canoes and traditional Rangeley Boats and Grand Lakers. Personal watercraft such as Jet Skis are prohibited.

The following comes from the Maine Department of Inland Fisheries and Wildlife: "Water quality in Pierce Pond is excellent for coldwater gamefish. Brook trout reproduce in sufficient numbers to provide for a fine fishery. Spawning habitat for salmon, however, is limited and annual stockings are made to maintain a fishery." This begs the question, why are we stocking over wild brook trout, and how much better could the brook trout fishery be without the additional mouths to feed?

Pierce Pond is a special place, and those who frequent it are very loyal to and protective of it. Guests at the two

Loons are a common sight on Pierce Pond. Their haunting calls are often the only thing that breaks the night silence. EMILY BASTIAN PHOTO

sporting camps come year after year, and in many cases have done so for decades. It's not unusual to see three generations of family eating dinner together at one of the sporting camps. That this trophy wild native brook trout resource is within a couple hours' drive, half of which is on dirt roads, of Maine's capital in Augusta makes it all the more special. Thanks to the tireless efforts of the Maine Wilderness Watershed Trust, which has prevented shoreline development on Pierce Pond, the area in and around Pierce Pond has a strong public advocate. The Trust's goal is to protect this invaluable and irreplaceable resource in perpetuity.

Dud Dean

Dud Dean was a fictitious Maine Guide who plied his craft on the upper Kennebec River and surrounding streams and ponds in central Maine. The creation of author Arthur R. Macdougall from Bingham, Maine, stories about Dud Dean graced the pages of books and magazines during the golden age of American outdoor sports, including a stint in *Field & Stream* in the 1920s and 1930s.

Dud Dean put the Kennebec Valley on the sporting map. His legacy is still evident today with the 2001 rerelease of some of his stories in book form, *Remembering Dud Dean*, and the formation of a now defunct native fish advocacy group around the same time called the Dud Dean Angling Society. A small pond along the upper Kennebec River bears his creator's name, Macdougall Pond.

At a time when flannel, wool and cotton clothing, rubber boots, and felt hats were standard attire, Dud Dean took to the woods and waters of the Kennebec Valley with fly rod in hand in search of brook trout and landlocked salmon. His travels took him to the upper Kennebec River, the Moose River, Enchanted Pond, and Pierce Pond, all home to wild native brook trout.

Fictitious Maine Guide Dud Dean caught brook trout throughout the fabled Kennebec Valley during the golden age of outdoor sports. BOB MALLARD PHOTO

Rapid River (MAINE)

This is the seventh book project I have worked on in the last five years. The other books were about tailwaters, the Northeast, trout towns, Maine sporting camps, national parks, and trophy fish. All were where-to books. One body of water was covered in four of these books, the Rapid River in Maine. It was the only water in Maine, and one of only several in New England, to make the tailwater and trophy fish books, and the first water featured in the Rangeley, Maine, chapter in the trout towns book.

The Rapid River is the finest self-sustaining trophy native brook trout river in Maine and, in fact, the United States. If catching a trophy wild native fluvial brook trout is your goal, the Rapid River gives you the best chance to do so without going to Canada. In general, the Rapid River is the premier trophy wild native salmonid fishery in Maine, New England, and possibly the East. To call it one of the finest self-sustaining native trout fisheries in the nation would be fair.

The Rapid River is located in western Maine near historic Rangeley. It starts at Middle Dam, the outlet of Lower Richardson Lake, and ends at Umbagog Lake on the Maine–New Hampshire border. It is interrupted by aptly named Pond in the River roughly a mile below Middle Dam. The Rapid is a short river, with a total length of just 6 miles, including the pond. As its name implies, the river has a steep gradient, dropping roughly 200 feet from beginning to end.

The now defunct Lower Dam on the Rapid River was the most recognized fly-fishing landmark in Maine for generations. This historic stone and wood dam was used to

A large brook trout caught from Second Current on the Rapid River in the early spring. Interestingly, it took a bubble gum–pink San Juan worm after everything that was supposed to work failed to produce. KRIS THOMPSON PHOTO

The now defunct historic Lower Dam on the Rapid River. Nothing says, or said, "brook trout" like Lower Dam. Torn down in the name of public safety, the Rapid River will never feel quite the same. DIANA MALLARD PHOTO

help drive logs down the river to Umbagog Lake and on to the Androscoggin River. It graced the covers of magazines and the pages of books, calendars, brochures, and more recently websites, and was synonymous with Maine brook trout. The victim of safety concerns and potential liability, the structure was torn down less than a decade ago. All that remains of fabled Lower Dam are some log cribbing, rock pylons, and a shoreside plaque.

Louise Dickinson Rich wrote several books within casting distance of the Rapid River. Her most famous, *We Took to the Woods*, was written in 1942 while staying at Forest Lodge just downstream of historic Lower Dam. The small complex was owned and occupied by the Rich family from 1933 to 1944 and served as Louise's summer residence until 1955. The property was added to the National Register of Historic Places in 2008. Forest Lodge looks pretty much the same today as it did when Ms. Rich lived there. Her office and vintage typewriter are more or less how she left them.

The area surrounding the Rapid River is densely forested. The land abutting the river is protected by a conservation easement prohibiting development and logging within 165 feet of the water. Development is limited to a handful of rustic buildings. The only power is found at Middle Dam, and cell coverage is spotty at best. Access is via a network of unmarked dirt roads and is restricted by locked gates. Vehicle access is limited to those with property on the river and their guests. Otherwise you must walk 20 to 40 minutes or paddle across Pond in the River from its south end.

The Rapid River is one of the few places where we do almost everything right. Tackle is restricted to fly fishing only and single-hook, single-point barbless flies. It is catch-and-release on brook trout, and there is a 3-fish, 12-inch limit on landlocked salmon to encourage harvest to help lessen competition for food and space. Pond in the River is managed under the same tackle and harvest restrictions as the river. While the river is not stocked, some level of stocked fish enter the river from the lakes above and below. There is also wild nonnative landlocked (Atlantic) salmon in the Rapid River, introduced in the late nineteenth century by the state.

Brook trout in the Rapid River are measured in pounds, not inches. They average over a foot long, fish up to 16 inches are common and up to 20 inches are not uncommon, and fish larger than this are caught. They are also some of the most beautiful brook trout you will ever see, and that says a lot when you consider that brook trout are one of the most beautiful fish there is.

The Rapid River is a rugged freestone river. It is a mix of pocketwater, runs, riffles, and pools throughout its

Brook trout in the Rapid River can be found in pools, runs, and fast water. While the highest densities are found in named sections such as First and Second Current, fish can be found in small, subtle holding areas as well.
DIANA MALLARD PHOTO

length. It is primarily a wading river due to the numerous drops and obstacles, but is not easy to wade due to the uneven bottom, slippery rocks, and heavy current. Some anglers use canoes and small boats to gain access to spots not reachable by wading. Much of the river can be accessed via a network of informal trails and dirt roads.

Flows on the Rapid are controlled by Middle Dam, located at the outlet of Lower Richardson Lake. They average between 300 and 800 cfs and can run as high as 5,000 cfs during spring runoff or after a heavy rain. The river is best waded at 300 to 650 cfs. Above this wading can be difficult and even dangerous.

The Rapid River is open to fishing from April through September. A short section below Lower Dam is closed to fishing after September 15 to protect spawning brook trout. Pond in the River is closed to fishing July and August to protect brook trout that enter the pond in search of thermal refuge. Practically speaking, fishing begins when the snow has melted enough to gain access to the river, usually in mid-April. The section of the Rapid River above Pond in the River can fish well in the early spring, even while there is still ice on the pond. It takes a bit of time for fish to move into other sections of the river. Peak

fishing is in May and June and again in September. Fishing slows down in the summer when the water warms up and the fish move into the pond. The fishing starts to pick up again in mid- to late August when the brook trout enter the river to spawn.

Trout in the Rapid River feed on insects, minnows, crayfish, and fish eggs. Insects include mayflies, caddis, stoneflies, and terrestrials. The best hatches occur in May and June, with intermittent hatches throughout the summer and a brief resurgence in the fall. The predominant minnows are smelt, dace, and sculpin. While the latter are available year-round, smelt are present mostly during their spring spawning run, and primarily near the lake and pond. Trout gorge themselves on sucker eggs soon after the smelt run. While trout can be caught on streamers and dries, nymphing is usually the most productive method.

Fly-fishing the Rapid River is like stepping back in time. It is historically significant, rugged, remote, and, for the most part, undeveloped. It is also the finest wild native brook trout river in the country. Unfortunately, nonnative and highly invasive smallmouth bass have found their way into the Rapid River, putting the nation's premier native brook trout fishery at risk.

Rapidan River (VIRGINIA)

The Rapidan River is located in north-central Virginia, roughly three hours from Washington, DC. It is one of the finest, and most famous, wild native brook trout rivers in the country, and arguably the best in the East outside of Maine and New Hampshire.

The Rapidan River is the most famous trout stream in Virginia. It was ranked #38 in the Trout Unlimited book *America's 100 Best Trout Streams*. In 2000 the upper river was nominated for a Tier III Exceptional Waterway designation by the state EPA. Unfortunately, it was rejected due to administrative failures and opposition from landowners.

The name Rapidan is a combination of the words *rapids* and *Anne*, as in Queen Anne of England. It was originally called the Rapid Ann River. The area near the river was the scene of numerous battles during the Civil War. Historic Brandy Station, Chancellorsville, Ely's Ford, Kelly's Ford, and The Wilderness are located nearby. Confederate legends Robert E. Lee, J. E. B. Stuart, Wade Hampton, "Rooney" Lee, and "Grumble" Jones fought here. Thomas "Stonewall" Jackson died here.

President Herbert Hoover built a camp on the headwaters of the Rapidan River in 1929, in what is now Shenandoah National Park. Known as Rapidan Camp, the 164 acres included 13 rustic cabins and was located where two small streams, Mill Prong and Laurel Prong, merged to form the Rapidan River. The Hoovers entertained family, friends, Cabinet members, politicians, and movers-and-shakers, who hiked, rode horses, and, of course, fished.

The upper Rapidan River, one of the finest wild brook trout streams in the country outside of New England. Visited by the likes of Presidents Teddy and Franklin Roosevelt, it also has a rich history. TODD JANESKI PHOTO

The Rapidan River in early spring. Fishable long before most northern streams can be fished, the Rapidan offers fly fishers a way to get a jump on the brook trout season. TODD JANESKI PHOTO

Visitors to the camp over the years included Charles Lindbergh, Edsel Ford, Theodore Roosevelt Jr., Franklin D. Roosevelt, and Jimmy Carter.

The Rapidan River is 88 miles long and drains an area of roughly 250 square miles. It begins in Shenandoah National Park at the confluence of Mill Prong and Laurel Prong, just west of Doubletop Mountain. It is the largest tributary of the Rappahannock River, joining it just west of Fredericksburg.

The Rapidan River drains a section of the eastern slope of the Blue Ridge Mountains. In its headwaters it is a self-sustaining native brook trout fishery. Most of the habitat suitable for wild brook trout is located within Shenandoah National Park and Rapidan Wildlife Management Area.

Shenandoah National Park covers roughly 200,000 acres. It was authorized by Congress in 1926, started in 1930, and established in 1935. The park is linked to Great Smoky Mountains National Park by the famous Blue Ridge Parkway. It is bisected by the equally famous 105-mile Skyline Drive, a National Scenic Byway and National Historic Landmark. It is also home to just over 100 miles of the Appalachian Trail. The park is covered in detail later in this book.

Rapidan Wildlife Management Area covers approximately 10,325 acres. It lies at 1,400 to 3,840 feet above sea level. The area is made up of eight tracts of land along the east slope of the Blue Ridge Mountains, four of which border Shenandoah National Park for a total length of nearly 25 miles. It is managed by the Virginia Department of Game and Inland Fisheries. The area was once settled: Stone walls, foundations, and small cemeteries can still be seen.

The Rapidan flows through a mature mixed hardwood forest interspersed with dense stands of laurel. The river is flanked by rugged mountains to the west. The area is home to black bear, bobcat, cottontail rabbit, coyote, gray fox, opossum, raccoon, red fox, and white-tailed deer. There have been unsubstantiated reports of cougars as well. Over 200 species of birds inhabit the area at least part-time. Barred owls, red-tailed hawks, wild turkeys, and recently reintroduced peregrine falcons are year-round residents.

In 1995 the area around the Rapidan River experienced what was called a "500-year flood." A major thunderstorm hung over the Blue Ridge Mountains for several days, causing record flows on many streams and rivers. The area was hit hard again 14 months later by Hurricane Fran. While the upper Rapidan was spared, there was significant damage to the river, riparian area, roads, culverts, and bridges downstream.

The upper Rapidan is a beautiful river, or more appropriately, stream. It is a classic mountain freestone stream with a mix of pocketwater, runs, riffles, and small plunge pools. Downriver it opens up, with some pools up to 6 feet

A typical wild native brook trout from the upper Rapidan watershed. They are as handsome as any you will find.
DIANA MALLARD PHOTO

deep and the size of a room. There are small ledge drops as well, the pools below offering some of the best brook trout holding water on the river. Fish also hold close to the bank where undercuts and structure can be found.

The headwaters of the Rapidan River can be reached via a roughly 2-mile hike on Prong Trail and Mill Prong Horse Trail. The trail starts on Skyline Drive and brings you to Rapidan Camp. Both Mill Prong and Laurel Prong hold wild native brook trout. Just downstream is Big Rock Falls, a popular designation with anglers.

Brook trout numbers in the Rapidan River are strong. Fish average 6 to 8 inches, with fish up to 12 inches possible. The trout in the tributaries tend to run a bit smaller. They are referred to as "Northern strain," and are the same fish as those found in New York, New Jersey, Pennsylvania, and New England—and just as beautiful. Like many wild trout, the fish can be skittish, especially after the river has seen some pressure. An upstream approach and drab-colored clothing is recommended.

Hatches on the Rapidan River start in mid-March or early April. The first insects to hatch are Quill Gordons.

March Browns follow in April or May, and the river's namesake pattern, local legend Harry Murray's Mr. Rapidan, is a very effective imitation. Sulphurs appear in May and June. Caddis and stoneflies, especially Yellow Sallys, overlap the end of the mayfly hatches and continue through June. By late spring trout start focusing on ants, beetles, crickets, and inchworms.

The Rapidan River and its tributaries upstream of the Shenandoah National Park boundary and within Rapidan Wildlife Management Area are open to fishing year-round. They are managed for catch-and-release and restricted to single-hook, single-point fly fishing only, no bait allowed.

The Rapidan is one of the finest self-sustaining native brook trout streams in the East, and arguably the finest south of New England. It is also rich in history, including fly-fishing history. That much of the best fishing lies within the protected Shenandoah National Park and Rapidan Wildlife Management Area ensures that it will remain that way for generations to come.

Red Brook
(MASSACHUSETTS)

Red Brook is one of only a handful of streams in Massachusetts that are still home to wild native sea-run brook trout. It is the finest sea-run brook trout stream in the state, and arguably the best in the country outside of Maine. Red Brook is almost solely responsible for the renewed interest in sea-run brook trout, or salters, after years of being neglected. Sea-run brook trout are covered in detail later in the book.

Sea-run brook trout are diadromous, moving between freshwater and saltwater. Unlike anadromous fish such as Atlantic salmon that live in saltwater and enter freshwater only to spawn, sea-run brook trout live and spawn in freshwater but move into saltwater to feed and find thermal refuge. The fish in Red Brook spend the winter in the ocean and return to the stream in early spring.

At one time there were hundreds of streams along the northeastern Atlantic coast in the United States that were home to sea-run brook trout. They included the Agawam, Mashpee, Monument—now buried beneath the Cape Cod Canal—Santuit, and Quashnet Rivers, as well as Red Brook in Massachusetts. Massachusetts's sea-run brook trout fishery was popular and regionally known going back to the early 1800s.

While most early sea-run brook trout averaged a pound or so, which is noticeably larger than today's average, fish up to 10 pounds or larger were occasionally caught. The most famous sea-run brook trout was a 14.5-pound specimen caught in 1827 by Daniel Webster from the Carmans River on Long Island, New York.

Red Brook is located in Plymouth and Wareham, with a small portion of the stream in Bourne, in upper Cape Cod. In all cases it serves as a town boundary. It begins at White Island Pond and runs roughly 4.5 miles before emptying into the ocean at Buttermilk Bay. While it originates at a lake, Red Brook receives water from several springs along its way, helping it to remain cool even in the summer.

Like most sea-run brook trout fisheries in Massachusetts, Red Brook's sea-run brook trout had been badly

A typical sea-run brook trout from Red Brook on upper Cape Cod. Note the slightly washed-out colors indicative of a fish that was recently in saltwater. The fish fell for a small white and yellow streamer. BOB MALLARD PHOTO

Once you get above the head of tide, Red Brook is not an easy stream to fish. I have had the best success fishing downstream with small streamers while staying low to avoid detection. JOHN VACCA PHOTO

diminished. They suffered at the hands of agriculture—Cape Cod's signature crop, cranberries. The canopy and streamside vegetation were stripped away, and the stream was dammed and diverted into canals carved into a man-made aquatic field known as a cranberry bog. This destroyed critical habitat and warmed the water. Fertilizers, herbicides, and pesticides didn't help. Prior to that it had been mined for bog iron, an impure form of iron found in bogs or swamps. And, of course, there was angler exploitation.

The Lyman Reserve on Red Brook was a game changer and helped bring the sea-run brook trout population back from the brink. Established in 2001, this 210-acre parcel of land on the lower end of Red Brook was formerly a private fishing camp. The land was donated to the state by the family of conservationist and former fisheries commissioner for the state of Massachusetts, Theodore Lyman III. Several small dams were removed, giving the sea-run brook trout access to more stream. Banks were stabilized, and structure was added.

The sea-run brook trout in Red Brook are probably the most studied of their kind in the country. The Massachusetts Division of Fisheries and Wildlife, along with several nonprofits, have taken a special interest in the fishery, and it has reaped huge benefits. There are semipermanent solar-powered Passive Integrated Transponder, or PIT, tag

reading stations along the stream, and ongoing electrofishing surveys.

Driven by warming water temperatures in the spring, Red Brook's sea-run brook trout leave the ocean and head back to the stream at the same time their cousins in Acadia National Park are dropping out of the brooks and into the ocean for the same reason. It is at this time that they are easiest to catch. Once in the stream for a bit, they become much more difficult to catch, most likely due to the amount of fishing pressure the stream sees.

When the sea-run brook trout of Red Brook return to the stream, they are chunky and silvery, and still feeding primarily on minnows; small streamers, #12–#10, are your best bet. White and yellow seem to work best. As the fish reacclimate to the freshwater, they regain their normal coloration and start feeding on insects. But even then, they are more likely to chase a streamer than many other small-stream resident brook trout.

Other than the estuary and area immediately above the highway bridge, Red Brook is not an easy stream to fish. Dense brush pushes right up against the stream in most places, hanging over it in many. The canopy is low, making casting difficult. Large mats of aquatic vegetation line much of the streambed, and some areas are muddy. Roll-casts, bow-and-arrow casts, and short, efficient, precise casts are the rule if you want to catch fish.

Red Brook at the head of tide. Home to the best sea-run brook trout population south of Maine, Red Brook is a blueprint for effective salter management. BOB MALLARD PHOTO

Red Brook is open to fishing year-round. It is managed for catch-and-release, and tackle is restricted to artificial lures and flies only. Brook trout average 6 to 8 inches, but fish up to 12 inches or more are occasionally caught. Like most sea-run brook trout, the fish in Red Brook fight harder than similarly sized fish found in inland streams. Unlike the fish in many interior streams that feed heavily on insects, they are highly piscivorous and eager to chase small minnow imitations.

Red Brook is a small brook trout paradise in the last place you would expect to find it, busy and heavily developed Cape Cod. It is the blueprint for sea-run brook trout restoration and conservation, and proof that we are capable of undoing some of the damage we have done when we put our minds to it. It is a true success story, and the result of vision, generosity, and years of hard work by local sportsmen, conservationists, and state agencies.

Roach River (MAINE)

Located in central Maine, the Roach River is the second-largest tributary to Moosehead Lake, a water covered in this book. It enters Moosehead Lake on its east shore roughly halfway up the lake. It is one of the most important brook trout spawning streams on the lake, and possibly the most important.

The Roach River was part of a canoe route used by Native Americans to move between Maine's two largest river systems, the Penobscot and Kennebec. After European settlement it was used to float millions of board feet of lumber from surrounding woodlands into Moosehead Lake, then down the Kennebec River to mills in Madison and Skowhegan. Today it is used primarily for recreation.

The Roach River is surrounded by public land, as well as thousands of acres of privately owned land, some of which is managed for conservation. It begins at a series of ponds named for the river they feed: First, Second, Third, Fourth, Sixth, and Seventh Roach Ponds. Interestingly, no Fifth Roach Pond appears on current maps.

The headwaters of the Roach River were purchased by the Appalachian Mountain Club in 2009 as part of their Maine Woods Initiative. This nearly 30,000-acre parcel of land is open to public access and part of the largest and longest contiguous protected land in Maine, which also includes Baxter State Park, Debsconeag Lake Wilderness, Nahmakanta Public Reserved Lands, and Appalachian Mountain Club's 100-Mile Wilderness. In 2010, AMC designated nearly 5,000 acres of land encompassing Trout Pond, Third Roach Pond, Fourth Roach Pond, and the upper section of the Roach River as an ecological reserve.

For fishing purposes the Roach can be broken into three sections: upper, middle, and lower. The upper river runs from Third Roach Pond to Second Roach Pond, the middle from Second Roach Pond to First Roach Pond, and the lower from First Roach Pond to Moosehead Lake.

The upper Roach River is very lightly fished. This roughly 2-mile section looks more like a small stream than a river. It is home to wild brook trout in the 6- to 10-inch

A large lake-run brook trout from the Roach River in central Maine. Brook trout enter the river from Moosehead Lake in the fall to spawn. Note the eyes looking down toward the water, a sign of a live fish. EMILY BASTIAN PHOTO

range. During the summer the water gets low and warm, fish move into thermal refuge areas, and fishing drops off. It is managed under general law regulations. Access is gained via a network of logging roads located northeast of the outpost of Kokadjo.

The middle Roach River receives moderate pressure. It resembles a large stream or small river, with pools, riffles, and beaver dams. It is easily waded but too small to float. Anglers can expect brook trout in the 6- to 12-inch range. It is restricted to artificial lures and flies only, with a daily bag limit of two trout. Access is gained via the Smithtown Road northeast of Kokadjo.

The lower Roach River is by far the most popular section, and one of the most famous and heavily fished waters in the state. It flows west approximately 6.5 miles before terminating at Spencer Bay on Moosehead Lake. This section is critical spawning habitat for Moosehead Lake's brook trout, as well as landlocked salmon. Angling is restricted to fly fishing only and catch-and-release.

The land surrounding the lower Roach River is owned and managed by the Maine Department of Inland Fisheries and Wildlife, which also controls the dam. It is accessed via the Lily Bay Road out of Greenville. There is a parking lot on the left side just before you cross the river in Kokadjo. A trail on the north side of the river provides access to the first four pools: Dump, Corner, Warden's, and Lazy Tom. The rest of the river is accessed by unmarked and unmaintained dirt roads and paths.

The lower Roach River is primarily a wade fishery. While it can be floated at certain levels, and has been, it rarely is. The river is a rugged freestone stream averaging from 20 to 50 feet wide. It is high gradient with boulder-strewn runs, riffles, plunges, and pools along its entire length. Wading is difficult, and studded boots and a wading staff are recommended.

The banks along the lower Roach River are lined with alders and spruce, and the woods are dense and nearly impenetrable. There is evidence of its historic past all along its length including log cribs, remnants of a fish hatchery started in the 1930s but never completed, a few abandoned cabins, and piles of refuse left by hunters, trappers, and anglers when it was a much wilder place. The decades-old streamside dump at the aptly named Dump Pool was finally cleaned up in 2017.

In the early spring, usually mid-May, smelt enter the upper and lower ends of the lower Roach River from First Roach Pond and Moosehead Lake to spawn. They are followed by brook trout in search of an easy high-protein meal, including some very large ones. Fish concentrate on the upper and lower reaches, and the midsection can be slow. This is the perfect time to swing and strip a smelt imitation.

June brings hatches to the lower Roach River, giving anglers the opportunity to land large brook trout on dries, nymphs, and emergers. Mayflies, caddis, stoneflies, and midges are all present. During this time, fly fishers can expect brook trout in the 12- to 18-inch range. Late spring

Emily Bastian with a healthy wild brook trout caught from Split Rock Pool on the lower Roach River in late September. While fresh fish will take streamers, once they settle in your best bet is to nymph. LARRY BASTIAN PHOTO

Moose call the densely vegetated woods along the Roach River home. It is not unusual to have one cross the river above or below you while you are fishing. EMILY BASTIAN PHOTO

and fall bring ants, beetles, and other small terrestrials. Resident minnows, leeches, and crayfish are available throughout the season.

During July and August, fishing is unreliable and very weather and water dependent. The water is often low and the temperature high, and brook trout seek thermal refuge in deep pools, springs, and tributaries, and many drop back to the lakes. Heavy rain can bump up the flow, providing relief for the resident fish and drawing new, and sometimes large, fish from the lakes above and below.

What the lower Roach River is best known for, however, is its fall fishing. Starting in late August, large brook trout and salmon begin to stage at the mouth of the river. In early September the dam at First Roach Pond is opened, providing adequate flow to allow spawning brook trout from Moosehead Lake access to the river. Some fish drop down from First Roach Pond as well.

As temperatures cool, large brook trout move into the river and head toward their historic spawning grounds. They move under the cover of darkness and settle into pools and runs during the day; anglers converge on the river to intercept them as they work their way upriver. At this time brook trout up to 20 inches and 4 pounds are encountered. The average fish, however, is in the 12- to 16-inch range.

One of the things that makes the Roach River so special is its rugged, remote, undeveloped, and unspoiled nature. Many of the best-known pools such as Bateau, Spring, Slaughter, Ledge, and Moose are on the lower river and require a hike to reach. Wild native brook trout add to its allure, and the chance of encountering a trophy fish seals the deal.

Savage River (MARYLAND)

The Savage River is located in western Maryland. It is close to 30 miles long and a tributary of the North Branch Potomac River. The river was named after an eighteenth-century surveyor, John Savage.

More than half the river is located in Savage River State Forest, the largest land in the state forest and park system. Established in 1929, Savage River State Forest covers an area of roughly 54,000 acres. It was started with the state-sponsored purchase of roughly 9,350 acres of distressed clear-cut forest, which was added to a 2,000-acre parcel

A beautiful wild native brook trout from the upper Savage River in Maryland, caught on a Tenkara rod. I am seeing more Tenkara anglers on small streams each year. ADAM KLAGSBRUN PHOTO

A lean-and-mean wild brook trout from the lower Savage River. The large head indicates that the fish is a stunted adult. ZAK BART PHOTO

donated to the state by the Garrett brothers in 1906. The forest continued to grow as the result of subsequent purchases of large and small tracts of land. Savage River State Forest is home to beaver, black bear, coyote, muskrat, otter, and white-tailed deer, as well as ruffed grouse and wild turkey, and, of course, brook trout. Part of the forest—2,700-acre Big Savage Wildland—has been designated by the state as a wilderness area.

The Savage River is a popular whitewater paddling destination when water is available. The US Olympic Trials were hosted here, and it was the site of the 1989 International Canoe Federation Canoe Slalom World Championships, the first time the race was held in the United States.

Brook trout are the only freshwater salmonid native to Maryland. They have been greatly reduced, some say by over 60 percent, as a result of habitat degradation, nonnative fish, stocking, and angler exploitation. There is reported to be roughly 150 populations of brook trout remaining in the state, 80 percent of which are said to be "greatly reduced." Many of those remaining are found in the Savage River watershed.

The Savage River is the finest wild native brook trout river in Maryland, and arguably the best in the Mid-Atlantic. There are over 120 miles of river and streams that are home to the highest density of wild native brook trout in the state.

The Savage River is divided into two sections, above and below Savage River Reservoir. The upper section represents nearly three-quarters of the river and is a free-flowing freestone stream. Below the reservoir is a tailwater. Most of the river is remote and undeveloped, especially the upper section. The upper river is also rich in tributaries, many of which hold brook trout.

The wild native brook trout population in the upper Savage River watershed is one of the finest outside of New England. There are 10 major and several small tributaries, all of which hold brook trout. In total it is said to represent over 100 miles of interconnected water. Brook trout migrate throughout the system depending on water levels and temperature, utilizing the streams in the summer and dropping back to the river for the winter. The tributaries also serve as critical spawning habitat.

According to the Maryland Department of Natural Resources, not all brook trout in the upper Savage River are migratory. Some fish remain in the tributaries and move very little, despite there being nothing to prevent them from doing so. Others move around considerably.

Crabtree Creek, a tributary of the Savage River Reservoir. Catch-and-release regulations help protect wild brook trout populations. ZAK BART PHOTO

The upper Savage River suffered a decline in its brook trout fishery in the early 2000s, particularly where angler access was the easiest. This resulted in the creation of the Upper Savage River Brook Trout Special Management Area. Referred to as a Zero Creel Limit Area, most of the upper Savage River and its tributaries are catch-and-release for brook trout. Tackle is restricted to artificial flies and artificial lures, and it is open year-round to fishing.

Maryland Department of Natural Resources also implemented a long-term program to monitor the brook trout populations in the upper Savage River watershed. This will help gauge the impacts of angling pressure, drought, weather, climate change, and other factors.

Brook trout on the upper Savage River average from 6 to 10 inches, 12-inch fish are not uncommon, and fish up to 14 inches are caught. Interestingly, while the typical lifespan for brook trout in many Appalachian streams is two to three years, fish up to seven years old have been found in the upper Savage River.

Wild native brook trout, while mixed in with nonnative browns and rainbows, can also be caught from the lower Savage River. The tailwater below Savage River Reservoir offers ideal habitat for trout and is managed as a trophy fishery. A self-sustaining population of brook trout was confirmed by Maryland Department of Natural Resources in 1982, resulting in the suspension of stocking on 4 miles of river immediately below the dam in 1987, creating what is now a mixed-species wild trout fishery.

Wild trout densities in the Savage River tailwater are referred to as "abundant." It is estimated there are over 1,000 adult brook trout and brown trout per mile. This includes more than 35 brook trout greater than 9 inches. Referred to as a Trophy Trout Management Area, tackle is restricted to fly fishing only for the first roughly 1.25 miles below the dam, and the remaining 2.75 miles are restricted to artificial lures only. There is a 2-fish, 12-inch length limit on brook trout.

The forage base on the Savage River and its tributaries is rich and diverse, especially on the lower river, with mayflies, caddis, stoneflies, midges, terrestrials, and minnows all present. A relatively high pH level results in what would be considered strong hatches for a freestone stream.

Brook trout on the Savage River can be caught on dries, nymphs, emergers, buggers, and streamers. Match-the-hatch, terrestrials, and attractors all work. Buggers and streamers should be relatively small on the upper river (#12 to #10 range) and larger on the lower river (#8 to #4), and include sculpin and minnow patterns, and Black-Nose Dace and Mickey Finns on the upper river.

The Savage River is a beautiful river in a beautiful setting. It flows through a mature mixed-hardwood forest with dense rhododendron. It is recognized regionally for its quality brook trout fishing, and was listed by Trout Unlimited as one of "10 Special Places" and featured in their book *America's 100 Best Trout Streams*. The river and its tributaries produce some of the largest brook trout caught in the region, and it's well worth the time and effort to experience it.

Swift River (MASSACHUSETTS)

The Swift River is located in central Massachusetts just an hour and a half from Boston. It starts at the outlet of Quabbin Reservoir, a municipal water supply for greater Boston. It is the most popular fishery in Massachusetts and probably sees more anglers than any two rivers combined.

At over 25,000 acres with a maximum depth of more than 150 feet, Quabbin Reservoir is a large body of water. It was constructed in the late 1930s at the expense of several small towns. Old roads, stone walls, and other structures, including a church steeple, can be seen beneath the lake's surface.

The area around Quabbin is the largest tract of undeveloped and protected land in Massachusetts. Beaver, black bear, coyote, fisher, moose, otter, white-tailed deer, turkey, and loons call it home. There have also been cougar sightings, one of which was confirmed via DNA in the late 1990s. The area was used to reintroduce eagles, and they are now a common sight.

Historically the East and West Branch of the Swift River converged to form the mainstem. Today their confluence is underwater, and they empty into the reservoir miles apart. The West Branch is mostly freestone with some beaver ponds in its upper reaches. The East Branch is more like a meadow stream. Both branches are home to wild brook trout, especially in their headwaters.

Today the Swift River begins below Windsor Dam. Water exits the reservoir via two outlets, the "Bubbler," which comes from deep on the dam, and the spillway, which comes from the top of the dam. They meet at the aptly named Y Pool, one of the most fished spots in New England. The river ends at its confluence with the Ware River roughly 10 miles downstream.

A large male brook trout caught in the fall from the Swift River in central Massachusetts. The source of the river, Quabbin Reservoir, provides drinking water to much of metropolitan Boston. DIANA MALLARD PHOTO

A late fall brook trout from the Swift River. The males hang around a bit longer than the females after the spawning season. DIANA MALLARD PHOTO

The water released from the spillway is the same temperature as the lake surface—cold in the spring, cool in the fall, and warm in the summer. When it spills over, it brings with it smelt, landlocked salmon, and the occasional lake trout. The dam releases water between 38 and 55 degrees F depending on the time of year, with average flows in the 40 to 60 cfs range. Nowhere in New England does a river better fit the description of "tailwater," running cold and clear year-round. The river has the midge biomass one expects to find in a tailwater, but other than that, hatches are sparse and weak.

While best known as a stocked rainbow trout fishery, the Swift River also boasts a robust, and often overlooked and underappreciated, wild native brook trout population. While resident fish average 4 to 6 inches, trout in the 8- to 10-inch range are not uncommon, and fish up to 18 inches are caught. These brook trout are as beautiful as any you will encounter.

Below Windsor Dam the Swift River runs through 1,500-acre Herman Covey Wildlife Management Area. This is the most popular wade fishery in Massachusetts and home to the famous Y Pool. It is restricted to fly fishing only and catch-and-release, and like all Massachusetts waters, open to fishing year-round.

The Swift River is arguably the most challenging trout water in New England. Long leaders and light fluorocarbon tippet are the rule. Regulars use tippet down to 8X, rarely if ever anything above 6X. While the fish are not afraid of people, they are very picky about what they eat, and your terminal tackle can make or break your day.

Midges hatch year-round, and mayflies, caddis, and small stoneflies intermittently. While flies in the #20 to #30 range are usually your best bet, trout also feed on eggs and aquatic worms. During high water they feed on smelts flushed over the dam and will take streamers. Small terrestrials will take fish in the summer.

There is a long, slow, deep pool below the Route 9 bridge, at the end of which are the remnants of a stone mill dam. Brook trout averaging 6 inches, often in small schools, patrol this stretch, and while wading can be difficult due to deep water, the fish can be taken on dry flies.

From the old dam to Cady Lane, a distance of less than a mile, the river is mostly shallow riffles. While brook trout are there, they are outnumbered by stocked rainbows. There is a deep pool below the outflow of McLaughlin Fish Hatchery. Trout congregate to feed on pellets flushed from the hatchery, and it can erupt like a piranha feeding frenzy when the hatchery fish are fed.

The section between Route 9 and Cady Lane is managed under a seasonal catch-and-release regulation, and harvest is prohibited from July through December. At this time tackle is restricted to artificial lures and flies. It is

The Swift River is one of New England's most popular trout fisheries. While stocked nonnative rainbows and small wild brook trout are always present, the large wild native brook trout are here today and gone tomorrow.
DIANA MALLARD PHOTO

primarily a wade fishery, and hatches are similar to the upper river.

Below Cady Lane the Swift is slow, windy, and deep, and littered with logjams. The clear water, sand bottom, and dense weeds make it look like a large spring creek. Insect life is stronger and more diverse than it is upstream. Trout will also take buggers, streamers, and terrestrials. This is excellent trout habitat, and some of the largest trout in the river are found here. Wading is difficult, and it is best fished from a canoe or raft.

There is a small dam approximately 4 miles below Cady Lane, the roughly 1 mile of impounded water above it referred to as the Swift River Reservoir. Large brook trout can be found here. Public access is limited and wading difficult, making it one of the least fished sections of the river. It is best fished from a boat.

Roughly a half mile of river between the Swift River Reservoir dam and the head of a small impoundment is created by a second dam. Below this is approximately 3 miles of riffles and runs. The last 1.5 miles is mostly deep, slow pools that are difficult to fish. Access is limited, and it sees the least traffic of any stretch of the river.

While brook trout can be caught anywhere in the Swift River, they tend to be in certain places at specific times of year. In the spring they are in the upper river gorging on rainbow trout eggs. In the summer they are sipping insects in the slow water below Route 9. Come fall, fish in the 16- to 18-inch range move into the upper river to spawn. Otherwise they are downstream of Cady Lane. The best way to catch brook trout in the Swift River is to hunt them. This means walking the banks looking for their distinctive white-tipped fins. The smaller fish tend to surface feed more than the rainbows, so always move toward rising fish.

The wild native brook trout fishery in the Swift River is the finest in the state, and arguably the best in New England outside of Maine and the Dead Diamond River in New Hampshire. These fish deserve far more protection than they are getting, including a river-wide catch-and-release regulation and the seasonal closure of critical spawning areas.

Upper Connecticut River (NEW HAMPSHIRE)

The Connecticut River is New England's longest river at roughly 410 miles. It drains an area of approximately 11,250 square miles and includes nearly 150 tributaries, roughly 40 of which are considered major rivers. Its watershed reaches into five states: Maine, New Hampshire, Vermont, Massachusetts, and Connecticut; and one Canadian province, Quebec. The river serves as the entire 255-mile eastern border of Vermont.

The Connecticut River begins in northern New Hampshire just short of the Canadian border. It terminates at Long Island Sound where it contributes approximately 70 percent of the sound's freshwater. Its tidal area was named one of the Western Hemisphere's "40 Last Great Places" by The Nature Conservancy. In 1997 it was designated as an American Heritage River. In 2012 it was named the nation's first National Blueway.

The Upper Connecticut River Valley has a rich history. It was long home to the Western Abenaki (Sokoki) tribe, who later merged with members of other Algonquin tribes that were displaced by wars and famines. It was first settled under a land grant from King Philip, or Metacom, son of the famous Wampanoag sachem Massasoit.

In 1783 the Treaty of Paris was signed ending the Revolutionary War. It established an international boundary between the United States and Canada identified as the "northwestern most headwaters of the Connecticut River." Several streams—Halls Stream, Perry Stream, Indian Stream—and the Connecticut River fit the description, resulting in a boundary dispute that took decades to resolve.

The Upper Connecticut River was also the location of the independent Republic of Indian Stream. From 1832 to 1835 it was home to a few hundred citizens and had its own government and constitution. It was incorporated into Pittsburg in 1840. It was also said to be a favorite haunt of Tomhegan, perpetrator of the last Native American raid on European settlers in New England.

Beginning in the mid-1860s, the Connecticut River was used to drive logs from Third Connecticut Lake to the mills downriver. Trees were cut from the area around Perry Stream, Indian Stream, and Halls Stream as well. Several river drivers died trying to move logs through the dangerous Perry Falls in Pittsburg. These drives were stopped around 1915.

For years New Hampshire and Vermont disputed their right to the Connecticut River. It took a 1935 US Supreme Court case to settle the matter. The court identified the boundary as being the low-water mark on the Vermont side of the river, thus reaffirming a King George–era definition of the boundary. In some places that boundary is now submerged under impoundments created after the court case.

Of most interest to the brook trout angler is the so-called Upper Connecticut River. While there is no formal boundary, this generally refers to the section of river within

A good-sized stocked brook trout from the "trophy section" on the Upper Connecticut River. Much larger fish are caught here, some of which approach 20 inches. DIANA MALLARD PHOTO

A healthy wild brook trout from the Upper Connecticut River. While not as large as the stocked fish found downstream, the wild fish in the upper reaches are worthy of your attention. DIANA MALLARD PHOTO

As rugged and beautiful as a northern New England brook trout river gets, the Upper Connecticut River is not an easy place to wade. Felt or studded felt soles and a wading staff are advised. DIANA MALLARD PHOTO

Pittsburg, New Hampshire, a position I share. And while not its formal name, "Upper Connecticut" is commonly used to refer to this section of river and the valley it runs through. I had one of my first notable fly-fishing outings, a 30-fish day, in the Upper Connecticut Valley.

The source of the Connecticut River is tiny 1.8-acre Fourth Connecticut Lake. The lake is located in the town of Pittsburg at 2,660 feet above sea level and within 300 yards of the Canadian border. It is accessed via the Fourth Connecticut Lake Trail. The trail is a little over a half mile long and crosses back and forth between the United States and Canada on its way to the lake. The land surrounding the lake is owned by The Nature Conservancy.

In its headwaters the Connecticut River is interrupted by five lakes known as the Connecticut Lakes: First, Second, Third, and Fourth Connecticut Lakes, and Lake Francis. The sections between Second Connecticut Lake and First Connecticut Lake, and First Connecticut Lake and Lake Francis, are of most interest to fly fishers looking for brook trout.

There are approximately 2.5 miles of river between the dam at the outlet of Second Connecticut Lake and First Connecticut Lake. At roughly 15 to 20 feet wide with flows in the 60 to 90 cfs range, it looks more like a stream than a river. It is home to wild and stocked brook trout in the 6- to 12-inch range. Larger fish enter the lower end from First Connecticut Lake in the spring to feed on smelt, and in the fall to spawn. This section of river is a rugged freestone stream with riffles, runs, and pools. There is a small pond-like area where Dry Brook enters the river, which is easily accessed via the Cohos Trail. This section is restricted to fly fishing only, and it is catch-and-release from the dam down to the Magalloway Road Bridge.

There is roughly 2 miles of river, known as the "trophy section," between the dam at the outlet of First Connecticut Lake and the head of Lake Francis. This large freestone stream is 20 to 30 feet wide with flows in the 150 to 300 cfs range. The water remains cold most of the season due to the dam. Wading is relatively easy, and access is good due to conservation easements along much of its length. There is a mix of wild and stocked brook trout. Fish average 8 to 12 inches, with fish up to 18 inches possible. Large fish enter the lower end of the river in the spring to feed on smelts and again in the fall to spawn. It is restricted to fly fishing only with a 2-fish, 12-inch length limit.

The Upper Connecticut River is open to fishing from January through October 15. Hatches start in mid-May and run through the end of the season. There are mayflies, caddis, stoneflies, and midges present. Small spring stoneflies hatch first, followed by mayflies, caddis, and more stoneflies—Yellow Sallys and Golden Stones. Midges hatch in the early spring and fall, and caddis hatch all spring and into the summer. In addition to the typical Northeast spring hatches (Quill Gordons, Hendricksons, March Browns, and Sulphurs), Blue-Winged Olives hatch intermittently throughout the season. Terrestrials such as ants and beetles are an important food source in the summer. Streamers are best used in the spring and fall and when the river is high or off-color.

The Upper Connecticut River is located in a rugged and relatively unspoiled area. There are black bear, bobcat, coyote, moose, and white-tailed deer, as well as eagles and loons, and gray jays that will eat out of your hand. The tourist infrastructure is robust, especially when you consider where it is, with a wide variety of lodging options, restaurants, convenience stores, and gas stations. That it is located within a few hours' drive of Boston is actually quite amazing.

Upper Dam (MAINE)

Upper Dam, sometimes referred to as Upper Dam Pool, is arguably the most famous brook trout water in America, at least from a historical standpoint. It is a short but productive stretch of brook trout water located in historic Rangeley, Maine. What it lacks in size it makes up for in quality, with brook trout up to 20 inches caught. And while short in length, it is long in fly-fishing history, lore, and pedigree.

Upper Dam is best known as the home of legendary fly tier Carrie Stevens. Carrie Gertrude Stevens was born in 1882 and died in 1970. Stevens is best known for her famous Gray Ghost streamer, designed to imitate the abundant smelt found in the area. She was responsible for the creation of over 150 other patterns as well. *Field & Stream* magazine featured Ms. Stevens in 1924, which helped introduce her fly patterns to a national audience. A self-taught tier, her flies received national and international attention. Her signature fly is one of the few "traditional" patterns still sold in fly shops today.

Born Carrie Gertrude Wills, she married Wallace Clinton Stevens in 1905. In 1919 they moved to Upper Dam where Wallace worked as a fishing guide. This is where Stevens was first exposed to flies, fly tying, and fly fishing. Fascinated by the classic flies, she began to tie her own. In 1924 Stevens caught a brook trout at Upper Dam that weighed just short of 7 pounds; the fish took second place in the 1924 *Field & Stream* fishing contest. Her flies became staples at tying contests throughout New England, and she started receiving orders for her flies from around the country.

Carrie Stevens is credited with shortening streamers so that they extend only slightly beyond the hook, making them less likely to wrap around the shank. She preferred long-shank hooks and designed streamers that had a streamlined profile more like actual baitfish. She added shoulders to imitate gill plates. Her flies were easily recognized by her signature red band tied into the head. It is said that nearly half of all record fish caught from Upper Dam

The historic cabins at Upper Dam where Carrie Stevens invented the fabled Gray Ghost streamer. Upper Dam is arguably the most famous brook trout fishery in America. DIANA MALLARD PHOTO

Rangeley Region Celebrities

Cornelia "Fly Rod" Crosby was Maine's first registered guide. As a major promoter of the movement to register guides, Ms. Crosby was given the honor of receiving Maine's first guide license in 1897. She plied her trade in the Rangeley region, and pictures show her with brook trout as well as landlocked salmon. Crosby promoted Maine's outdoor sports at shows and wrote a column that appeared in many newspapers around the country. She is also reported to have shot the last legal caribou buck in Maine.

Famed fly tier Carrie Stevens caught a 6-pound, 13-ounce brook trout from Upper Dam near Rangeley, Maine, on July 1, 1924. Caught while testing her new Gray Ghost streamer, she entered the fish into a *Field & Stream* magazine contest, winning the second-place prize. Stevens's fly patterns are recognized throughout the region and country and include the Colonel Bates, Blue Devil, Golden Witch, Morning Glory, Pink Lady, Rangeley Favorite, Shang's Special, and Wizard. It is said that roughly half the record fish taken from the Upper Dam in the 1930s were caught on Stevens's patterns.

While not an angler, author Louise Dickinson Rich wrote her classic novel, *We Took to the Woods*, while staying at a remote cabin on the banks of the fabled Rapid River near Rangeley, Maine, the finest wild native brook trout river in the country. She makes numerous mentions of fishing, fly tying, and eating freshly caught "trout" in her 1942 book. One of the few pictures in the book shows a Maine Guide fishing from a rowboat on what looks to be the Rapid River.

Former president Dwight Eisenhower came to Rangeley, Maine, in June 1955 for a fly-fishing trip. While there he stayed at the Parmachenee Club on Parmachenee Lake, a high-quality native brook trout water. He also fished the Magalloway River, one of Maine's top two wild native brook trout rivers. A streamside plaque at Little Boy Falls on the upper Magalloway River marks one of the places Eisenhower fished.

While replaced under the guise of public safety, the new Upper Dam can never replace the historic wood structure that was one of the most famous fly-fishing landmarks in the United States. DIANA MALLARD PHOTO

in the 1930s were caught on Stevens's flies. The Stevens family cabin and a plaque dedicated to Carrie can be found at the site of the dam.

Historic Upper Dam House catered to fly fishers in the late 1800s and early 1900s. They came by a train that operated until the 1930s. The guest register includes the signature of Carrie Stevens.

Another famous resident of Upper Dam was White Nose Pete. This mythical brook trout was purported to live in the pool below Upper Dam. The legend of White Nose Pete began in the late 1890s. Anglers who lost flies to large fish regularly placed the blame on old Pete. He got his name from all the broken-off flies believed to be hanging from his mouth. The legend of White Nose Pete persisted into the 1940s, five times longer than the oldest brook trout on record.

A likeness of White Nose Pete's head was carved by Shang Wheeler, a well-known carver from Connecticut and regular Upper Dam angler. Wheeler took first place in the amateur division at the annual International Decoy Maker's Contest held at the National Sportsman's Show in New York City 12 years in a row. The carving was presented to Wallace Stevens, Carrie's husband. Wheeler also wrote a poem about the fish, "The Ode to White Nose Pete." Today White Nose Pete can be seen at the Rangeley Outdoor Sporting Heritage Museum in Oquossoc.

The fast water downstream of Upper Dam Pool can provide some of the best action in this short stretch of brook trout water. It fishes best at high flows. DIANA MALLARD PHOTO

Upper Dam is located at the outlet of Mooselookmeguntic Lake, a notable wild brook trout fishery. At 16,300 acres, Mooselookmeguntic Lake is the fourth-largest lake in Maine and the third-largest Principal Brook Trout Fishery in the state. The name is Abenaki for "moose feeding place," not the locally perpetuated myth that it had to do with a Native American who forgot to load his gun before taking aim at a moose.

Fabled Rangeley Lake empties into Cupsuptic Lake, part of Mooselookmeguntic Lake. The Cupsuptic and Kennebago Rivers, both featured waters in this book, flow into Cupsuptic Lake. Kennebago Lake, also a featured water, flows into the latter. Mooselookmeguntic empties into Upper Richardson Lake, which is connected to Lower Richardson Lake, the outlet of which, Middle Dam, is the beginning of the famous Rapid River, another featured water. The Rapid flows into Umbagog Lake, the termination of two other featured waters, the Magalloway and Dead Diamond Rivers.

While brook trout are native to Upper Dam, today it is primarily a stocked fishery. Fish average over a foot long, fish in the 14- to 16-inch range are common, and fish up to 20 inches are caught. Upper Dam fishes best in the spring and fall, as water temperatures can get warm in the summer, forcing the trout to seek refuge in the lake below.

Upper Dam is open to fishing from April through October, a month longer than most waters in the Rangeley area. Tackle is restricted to fly fishing only, and it is catch-and-release on brook trout. Motored boats are prohibited within 150 yards of the dam.

Brook trout in Upper Dam feed on insects, minnows, and fish eggs. Mayflies, caddis, stoneflies, and midges are all present. The best hatches occur in May and June and include Quill Gordons, Hendricksons, and a variety of caddis. Hatches continue intermittently throughout the summer with caddis and Golden Stones and pick up again in the fall with BWOs. Smelt are an important food source, and dace and sculpin are present as well. In the spring, suckers enter the tailrace to spawn—at this time trout can be caught on egg patterns.

Upper Dam offers a unique opportunity to fish for large brook trout in an area rich in fly-fishing history and lore. It is surrounded by quality wild brook trout water, the best in the country by most accounts. If you are ever in the Rangeley area, you owe it to yourself to take a side trip to Upper Dam. And while you are there, be sure to take a few casts with a Gray Ghost in honor of the venerable Carrie Stevens, and keep an eye out for White Nose Pete.

NONNATIVE WATERS

While there is nothing like wild native brook trout in a natural setting, not everyone has access to such, and even those who do can't always get there when they want to. As a result, some anglers have no choice but to fish for nonnative brook trout, and others do so because it's fun.

Some nonnative brook trout waters are stocked, and some are wild. Many nonnative, including stocked, waters offer outstanding fishing for brook trout. Some waters are stocked with adult fish, including so-called brood fish and other legal-to-harvest fish, and some with fry or fingerlings. Those stocked with fry and fingerlings have cleaner, more natural looking fish, as Mother Nature can weed out the weak.

The brook trout found in self-sustaining nonnative waters are often as beautiful as any other brook trout. I saw wild brook trout in a Wyoming stream that were as beautiful as any I have ever seen in Maine. And I caught stocked brook trout in a lake in Idaho that were some of the largest and hardest fighting I have ever encountered.

Brook trout are viewed as an invasive pest in the West, and when it comes to native cutthroat, they are. If you want to eat wild brook trout, these are the places to do it, as you are doing more good than harm.

A beautiful wild nonnative brook trout caught from a small stream in Bighorn National Forest in Wyoming. Brook trout adapt quite well—some would say too well—to the fertile waters of the Rocky Mountains.
DIANA MALLARD PHOTO

Blacktail Deer Lakes (WYOMING)

Known best for its geysers, bison, elk, grizzly bears, wolves, and native cutthroat trout, Yellowstone National Park is the last place most people think of when they think of brook trout. However, in a land where the cutthroat is king lies one of the finest small wild brook trout ponds I have ever fished: Blacktail Deer Lakes near Mammoth Hot Springs.

Yellowstone National Park was established in 1872 as the nation's first national park. The park covers 2,219,791 acres. It was designated an International Biosphere Reserve in 1976 and a World Heritage Site in 1978. One natural feature, Obsidian Cliff, and five buildings are designated National Historic Landmarks.

Native Americans frequented the area in and around Yellowstone National Park starting more than 11,000 years ago. Some called the area home while others came to hunt, and still others passed through on long-established trade routes such as the Bannock Trail. The Nez Perce under Chief Joseph came through the park in 1877 while being pursued by the US Army. Obsidian, a volcanic glass, from Obsidian Cliff was prized for making arrowheads,

some of which have been found as far away as the Mississippi Valley.

John Colter of Lewis and Clark Expedition fame is credited with being the first European to see the area that is now Yellowstone National Park. He passed through the area in 1807 while trapping, and his stories of the geothermal features were viewed as too far-fetched to be true. Considered delusions hatched in the mind of a delirious man, the area became known as Colter's Hell.

National parks are some of the most protected lands in America. Logging, mining, hunting, and trapping are prohibited. It is illegal to disturb natural features and artifacts or harass wildlife. Many backcountry roads are gated to vehicular access, and development is restricted. In 2017 Yellowstone National Park saw over 4,000,000 visitors, many of whom came to the park to take advantage of its world-class trout fishing.

Arctic grayling, mountain whitefish, and two subspecies of cutthroat—westslope and the namesake Yellowstone—are the only salmonids native to Yellowstone National Park. Snake River fine-spotted cutthroat, an aesthetically different but biologically similar form of Yellowstone cutthroat, are found in the headwaters of their namesake river.

Yellowstone National Park has a long history of fisheries management. In 1889 park manager Captain Frazier Augustus Boutelle approached the US Fish Commission in regard to stocking some of the fishless waters in the park, resulting in the first nonnative fish introductions in Yellowstone. This practice was continued until the mid-1950s, leading to the establishment of self-sustaining populations of nonnative rainbow trout, brown trout, lake trout, and brook trout.

Nonnative fish compete with native fish for food and space. They also prey on them, and nonnative rainbows hybridize with native cutthroats. In some cases nonnative fish such as lake trout have reduced the amount of forage available to native birds and animals as well. In many cases total eradication of nonnative fish is impossible. Often the best we can do is to reduce populations through scientific control methods and angling to lessen their impact. In some instances, chemical reclamation can be used to successfully remove nonnatives from the system. Yellowstone National Park has a pro-native policy and has eradicated many nonnative fish populations, including brook trout from upper Soda Butte Creek, and is working to reduce others.

A beautiful brook trout from Blacktail Deer Lakes in Yellowstone National Park. People we talked to at the scenic overlook said a grizzly bear and her cubs had passed by earlier in the day. DIANA MALLARD PHOTO

With a focus on native flora and fauna, Blacktail Deer Lakes are one of the few waters in Yellowstone National Park that are managed for nonnative brook trout. BOB MALLARD PHOTO

Most of the nonnative brook trout waters found in Yellowstone are located in the northwest corner of the park. While many waters contain brook trout, there are some that are primarily, and even exclusively, brook trout fisheries. My personal favorite is Blacktail Deer Lakes, located just off the road between Roosevelt and Mammoth, closer to the latter than the former.

Blacktail Deer Lakes is located in a meadow at 6,600 feet above sea level. There are two ponds connected by a short thoroughfare. They are spring fed, and you can see the bubbling of the springs in the smaller pond. At a combined 11 acres they are small bodies of water, and you can literally cast across the pond closest to the road. While the smaller pond is very shallow, the maximum depth in the larger pond is 26 feet, deep for a pond its size.

While you can fish Blacktail Deer Lakes from the shore, the surrounding land is very marshy. If you are not careful you can find yourself waist-deep in mud with no graceful way to extract yourself. On one outing I got so covered with mud I had to change and rinse off with bottled water roadside before I could get back into the truck. Because of this, a float tube is a good idea, as it will not only keep you clean but also give you access to fish you cannot reach from the shore.

The brook trout in Blacktail Deer Lakes are as beautiful as any I have ever seen. They average 12 inches, fish up to 14 inches are not uncommon, and trout up to 18 inches

are possible. Fish numbers are high as well, and it is not unusual to land six to eight fish in a few hours of fishing.

Blacktail Deer Lakes get mayfly and midge hatches. Most days there are fish surface feeding until the water chops up. I have encountered *Callibaetis* spinners that provided for some fast action. Damselflies are also present and can provide good fishing. I have had success fishing scud imitations, too. When all else fails, put on a sinking line and a small Woolly Bugger and probe the depths.

Nearby Blacktail Deer Creek is a solid wild brook trout fishery as well, with plentiful fish that average 6 to 8 inches and can reach up to 10 inches.

While Yellowstone is open to fishing from the Saturday of Memorial Day weekend through the first Sunday in November, Blacktail Deer Lakes do not open until July 3 to protect nesting trumpeter swans and sandhill cranes. You will need a permit to fish in the park, and only single-hook barbless flies are allowed.

As noted, Yellowstone National Park is not known as a brook trout destination, nor should it be. In most cases nonnative brook trout are detrimental to native cutthroat. This is not meant to be an endorsement of nonnative fish in locations where they are harming native fish; in fact, I completely support the park's efforts to eradicate nonnatives wherever it can be done successfully—including Blacktail Deer Lakes. But as long as they are there, I'll fish for them.

Boardman River
(MICHIGAN)

The Boardman River is located in the northwest portion of the Lower Peninsula of Michigan, about a half hour drive from Traverse City. Its headwaters are found near the towns of Kalkaska and South Boardman, west of historic Grayling. The river empties into the West Arm of Grand Traverse Bay on Lake Michigan in Traverse City. It is considered one of the finest wild brook trout rivers in Michigan, and some say the best.

The area around the Boardman River and its tributaries is home to a number of state-listed species including common loon and red-shouldered hawk (threatened), king rail and Kirtland's warbler (endangered, the latter is also a federally endangered species), and bald eagle and wood turtle (species of concern).

The Boardman River has a long and rich history. It was previously known as the Ottawa River, named for a Native American tribe that once called the area home. They used the river as a transportation route and a source for food. Native Americans camped at Squaw Point near where the river empties into Lake Michigan, where they fished and foraged. They camped on Boardman Lake in the winter to hunt. Renamed in honor of Captain Horace Boardman, who settled in the area in 1847 and was the first European to do so, the Boardman River was also used by European settlers to float logs to sawmills near modern-day Traverse City and harness the water to generate power for the mills and other industries.

Today the Boardman is a state-designated Natural River. Under rules established in 1980, certain types of development and use are restricted within 400 feet of the river and its tributaries to protect critical riparian areas.

The mainstem of the Boardman River is approximately 28 miles long. It begins at the confluence of its two branches, North and South, in an area known as The Forks. The Boardman River drains an area of roughly 295 square miles via approximately 130 miles of tributaries. It is a placid river, dropping only roughly 500 feet in elevation between its headwaters and its termination at Lake Michigan. It has a reported 35 named tributaries, including the two main branches.

A typical northern Michigan wild brook trout. Which brook trout populations in northern Michigan are and are not native is unclear and often challenged. BRIAN KOZMINSKI PHOTO

An upper Boardman River brook trout. Whether these fish are native to the river or not is a subject of debate. But they are wild, beautiful, and fun to catch. CHRIS DOYAL PHOTO

The North Branch Boardman River begins east of Kalkaska and flows southwest toward its junction with the South Branch Boardman River. The South Branch starts south of South Boardman and flows north before heading northwest and meeting the North Branch. The two branches merge roughly halfway between Kalkaska and Traverse City to form the mainstem of the Boardman River. The upper Boardman River is a medium-sized river, while the North and South branches are more like large streams. The water runs clear and cool, and the bottom is mostly gravel.

Kalkaska is home to a fountain with a giant brook trout statue in the middle. Officially known as the National Trout Memorial, it is referred to locally as the Fisherman's Shrine. It is said this is the third statue of a brook trout, Michigan's official state fish, to serve as the centerpiece for the fountain since 1966. Reported to be between 17 and 18 feet long (or actually tall), it is quite impressive. Kalkaska is also home to the annual National Trout Festival.

Whether the Boardman is or is not a native brook trout river is subject to debate, and it won't be settled anytime soon. While there are those who claim it is a native brook trout fishery, the majority opinion is that it is not, and that is my position until the tide shifts and it is proven otherwise.

The only species of salmonid absolutely known to be native to the Boardman River watershed is the now extirpated Arctic grayling, or Michigan grayling. Nonnative brown trout, rainbow trout, and brook trout were introduced to the river in the mid- to late 1800s and established self-sustaining populations. It is purported that brown trout were introduced before brook trout. There are also nonnative stocked steelhead, king, and coho salmon below Sabin Dam.

The Boardman River has provided outstanding fishing for wild brook trout for generations. Much of the watershed is designated as a Blue Ribbon Trout Stream by the Michigan Department of Natural Resources. This includes the first 18 miles of the mainstem, 10 miles of the North Branch, and 8 miles of the South Branch. This designation is given to rivers and streams that support high densities of wild trout, are conducive to fly casting and wading, and offer diverse insect life and excellent water quality.

The Boardman River is also the birthplace of the fabled Adams dry fly, arguably the most fished dry fly in history and still popular with anglers today. The fly was invented in 1922 by Leonard Halladay of nearby Mayfield, who named it in honor of his friend, C. F. Adams, a Boardman River regular. It gave birth to the Parachute Adams, likely the most fished dry fly today, and the Irresistible Adams, a high-floating version with a trimmed deer hair body.

Most of the brook trout found in the Boardman River system are located above Sabin Dam on the mainstem. Below here the river is influenced by Lake Michigan and is home to runs of nonnative steelhead and salmon, as well as a number of warmwater fish species. Both branches are home to wild native brook trout.

The highest brook trout densities on the Boardman River are found from the headwaters of the two branches down to Brown Bridge Pond on the mainstem. The largest fish are found near where the two branches meet, and near Ranch Rudolf, where state surveys say brook trout experience the best growth rates, reported to be over an

A public access site on the lower Boardman River below Forks State Forest Campground. Upper Michigan has some of the best angler access infrastructure I have ever seen. SHANE HADD PHOTO

inch more than the state average. Fish average from 6 to 8 inches, with larger fish caught.

Insect hatches on the Boardman River are diverse and strong and include mayflies, most notably Hendricksons, Brown and Gray Drakes, and *Hexagenia*, as well as caddis. Hatches start later than on many other rivers and streams in the area due to the cool water temperature. Terrestrials are available in the summer, and streamer fishing can be good when the water is high or off-color.

The best public access on the Boardman River is found in the upper river and two branches. While access becomes more difficult as you move downriver, there are places you can access the river, such as Ranch Rudolf, but you will have to work a bit to find them. The limited access helps keeps the pressure down, which protects the fish to at least some degree.

The Boardman River looks like a brook trout river. The brook trout are wild and look as "native" as any you will encounter. But they are apparently not, and while I am against displacing them with stocked steelhead and king and coho salmon due to their "wild" status, I would take the opposite position if it involved the restoration of native grayling. But until then, enjoy this wonderful wild brook trout fishery.

Boulder Mountain (UTAH)

Boulder Mountain is part of the Aquarius Plateau in south-central Utah. This nearly flat 70-square-mile, or roughly 45,000-acre, summit is said to be the highest forested plateau in North America, with elevations over 11,000 feet. Located in Dixie National Forest, it is commonly referred to as the Boulders. It would also be fair to call it "Brook Trout Mountain."

Aquarius Plateau is part of the Colorado Plateau. It is encircled by the town of Torrey to the north, Boulder and Escalante to the south, Widtsoe to the west, and Capitol Reef National Park to the east. The area lies almost entirely within the Dixie National Forest and is bisected by Scenic Byway 12.

Dixie National Forest covers roughly 1,900,000 acres and is the largest national forest in Utah. It is made up of four noncontiguous parcels. The highest point is 11,325-foot Blue Bell Knoll on Boulder Mountain. Originally called Dixie Forest Reserve, it was established in 1905, taken over by the US Forest Service in 1906, and became a national forest in 1907. In 1922, Sevier National Forest was added to it, and in 1944, Powell National Forest. It contains four formally designated wilderness areas: Ashdown Gorge (7,000 acres), Box-Death Hollow (24,750 acres), Cottonwood Forest (2,600 acres), and Pine Valley Mountain (50,000 acres).

Many of the lakes and ponds on Boulder Mountain lie between 8,000 and 11,000 feet above sea level. Most are fed by snowmelt and lack inlets or springs, and some have small dams that have increased their depths. The largest drainage is Boulder Creek, a tributary of the Escalante River. West Fork Boulder Creek and East Fork Boulder Creek are both trout streams, especially the former. The streams in the northern reaches drain into the Fremont River, while the streams in the west flow into the Sevier River.

Brook trout are not native to Utah, having been introduced to the state in the early 1900s. According to Utah Division of Wildlife Resources, they have been stocked in Boulder Mountain lakes, ponds, and streams since the mid-1940s. Early stockings were done via horseback using milk cans to transport fingerlings. By the mid-1950s, stocking was being done by truck. Today there is a mix of stocked and wild fish.

According to Utah Division of Wildlife Resources there are approximately 75 lakes and ponds on Boulder Mountain capable of supporting trout, many of which are home to brook trout. While things can change from one year to the next, waters that have historically been managed for brook trout include Bear Creek Pond, Bess Lake, Blind Lake, Blue Lake, Box Creek Reservoirs, Donkey Reservoir, East Lake, Flat Lake, Green Lake, Halfmoon Lake, Horseshoe Lake, Joe Lay Reservoir, Left Hand Reservoir, Lost Lake, Lower Barker Reservoir, Lower Browns Reservoir, McGath Lake, Oak Creek Reservoir, Pear Lake, Pleasant Lake, Purple Lake, Ridge Lake, Rim Lake, Round Lake, Scout Lake, Spectacle Lake, Surveyor's Lake, Tule Lake, and Yellow Lake.

Charlie Perry hooked up on a remote Boulder Mountain lake. Boulder Mountain is home to what is arguably the finest concentration of nonnative brook trout stillwaters in the country. CHARLIE PERRY PHOTO

While the lakes, ponds, and streams of Boulder Mountain may not look like brook trout water, they offer some of the finest nonnative brook trout fishing in the country. CHARLIE PERRY PHOTO

Many rivers and streams on Boulder Mountain hold brook trout as well. While not as large as the fish found in the lakes and ponds, they can be plentiful and fun to catch. The percentage of wild fish versus stocked fish is higher in the streams than in the lakes and ponds in most cases, due to a lack of spawning habitat in the latter. Like lakes and ponds, management can change from one year to the next. However, Boulder Creek, East Fork Boulder Creek, Oak Creek, Pine Creek, Pleasant Creek, and West Fork Boulder Creek have been managed for brook trout in the past.

Boulder Mountain has been popular with fly fishers for generations. It is well known for producing trophy-sized brook trout. The current Utah state record brook trout was caught from an undisclosed location on Boulder Mountain in the early 1970s. The fish weighed an impressive 7.5 pounds. While brook trout average 10 to 14 inches, fish in the 3-pound range are fairly common, and trout up to 5 pounds are caught. Fish numbers can be very high, including exploding to the point where they cause stunting.

Brook trout on Boulder Mountain feed on a variety of foods. Mayflies, caddis, and midges are present. *Callibaetis* and *Baetis* are the most common mayflies, and midge hatches can be especially strong in the spring and fall. There are dragonflies and damsels as well. In the summer terrestrials such as ants, beetles, and hoppers are available. Many of the lakes and ponds have one or more minnow species, and most ponds have leeches and scuds. Some waters have salamanders or frogs, and it is said that trout feed on the juveniles of both. Larger trout will take the occasional mouse.

Access to Boulder Mountain is via four-wheel drive. While some of the lakes and ponds can be reached by 4x4, ATV, or UTV, others require a hike of up to several miles. Some lakes and ponds can be waded, but a watercraft will help you reach more fish. While a canoe or kayak can work, the area is best fished from a float tube due to its remoteness and the small size of most of the waters.

Most years the roads are not passable until early May, and snow is often present well into the month. Fishing starts in the lower elevations first and works its way up the plateau as the month progresses. By late May things are in full swing, and they stay that way through October. Some feel that June, July, and October are the best time to target brook trout, with October the best time for large fish.

Boulder Mountain is a beautiful and remote place on public land. While it is the last place you would expect to find brook trout, it is a great place to fish for them. The stillwaters on the mountain are home to some of the largest pond-dwelling brook trout caught in the country. That these fish come from what are, for the most part, very small ponds makes it even more unique and special.

Henrys Lake (IDAHO)

Henrys Lake is located in southeastern Idaho near the Montana border. It is part of the headwaters of the fabled Henrys Fork, considered by many to be the finest trout river in America. Like its namesake river, the lake is considered one of the finest stillwater trout fisheries in the country.

The area surrounding Henrys Lake was home to Native Americans for hundreds of years. After the Battle of Camas Creek, the Nez Perce under Chief Joseph pushed through the area on their way to Yellowstone to escape the pursuing military. General Oliver O. Howard rested his troops for several days at the lake after a 26-day forced march.

Henrys Lake lies at nearly 6,500 feet above sea level and covers roughly 6,200 acres. While it is a natural lake, a small dam built in 1923 tripled its surface area. It is relatively shallow with an average depth of less than 15 feet and a maximum depth of just over 20. The lake supported a commercial fishery in the early 1900s; today it is home to a large hatchery.

Henrys Lake has a reputation as a trophy fishery. Trout over 5 pounds are not uncommon, and trout over 10 pounds are caught. One outfitter boasted that his customers landed 600 fish over 5 pounds in a single season during the mid-1990s. More than 35 of these measured over 28 inches.

There is cutthroat, cutthroat/rainbow hybrids, and brook trout in Henrys Lake. Cutthroat are the most common species, and hybrids the largest. In addition, some of the largest brook trout caught in Idaho come from here as well. The state record, a brook trout over 7 pounds and more than 23 inches in length, was taken here in 1978.

While working on my list of waters for this book, a friend asked me if Henrys Lake really deserved a spot. He asked me if it was truly a *viable* brook trout fishery, a place where brook trout could actually be *targeted*, and where you'd have a reasonable chance of catching one. While I knew brook trout were there, and some very large ones, these questions caught me by surprise, forcing me to backtrack a bit.

Sure, I had seen pictures of large brook trout caught from Henrys Lake, and I was aware of the state record. I had also read numerous books and articles that said Henrys Lake put up some very good brook trout. I had even caught

A typical Henrys Lake brook trout. While there are days you can't buy a brook trout, there are also times when they are oddly cooperative. Concentrate on stream mouths in late summer and fall for the most consistent brook trout fishing. DIANA MALLARD PHOTO

Above: The view from Henrys Lake. While not what you expect from a brook trout lake, it's not too hard to take. DIANA MALLARD PHOTO

Left: The author and guide Ryan Loftice with a Henrys Lake brook trout. Although there were *Callibaetis* emergers, adults, and spinners all around us, the fish was caught on a midge pupa after numerous fly changes. DIANA MALLARD PHOTO

a few, albeit accidentally, while fishing for cutthroats and hybrids. I also knew that brook trout were outnumbered by cutthroats and hybrids 10 to 1 or better.

As part of my *25 Best Towns Fly Fishing for Trout* book, I went to Island Park, a featured town, to collect some pictures. Early on the first morning we headed over to Henrys Lake, a featured water in the chapter on Island Park, to take pictures. On the way I asked my guide if there was a place on the lake where we had a good chance of catching a brook trout—he said there was.

Upon arriving at the lake, rather than heading over to Staley Springs as I had done in the past, we launched at a spot where a couple of feeder streams entered the lake. According to our guide the streams were used by brook trout for spawning. Being mid-August there was a chance that they were already staging to run the creeks. If I could catch one, it would help validate my decision to include Henrys Lake in this book.

Over the next three to four hours we landed seven brook trout and missed or lost many more. The fish were in the 16- to 18-inch range and, while mostly stocked, were healthy, large, hard-fighting, and beautiful. In fact, it represented some of the most productive stillwater fishing for brook trout I had ever experienced, and I have lived in New England my whole life, and Maine for over 15 years.

The brook trout in Henrys Lake are as smart as any you will encounter. Although fish were rising all around us, it took an hour to dial them in. With the surface littered in *Callibaetis*, we assumed this is what they were feeding on. After every combination of patterns and tactics we tried failed to produce the desired result, we shifted to midges and went from zeroes to heroes.

Henrys Lake is not only a *viable* brook trout fishery, it is a very good brook trout fishery. Not only can you *target* brook trout in Henrys Lake, but you can have some very good brook trout fishing on Henrys Lake. You not only have a reasonable chance of catching brook trout on Henrys Lake, but you have a very good chance of catching brook trout on Henrys Lake.

While brook trout can be caught at any time of year, the best time to fish for them is in the late summer and fall. Concentrate on areas where streams enter the lake, and sandy areas near springs where brook trout may be trying to spawn. Forage is diverse and robust and includes midges, mayflies, damselflies, scuds, leeches, and minnows. But trout in Henrys Lake rarely look up and are almost always best fished subsurface.

To be clear, cutthroats and hybrids significantly outnumber brook trout in Henrys Lake. While brook trout can be encountered anywhere on the lake, there are times and places that are better than others. Henrys Lake is a large body of water and prone to high winds that can appear out of nowhere, so you need to be careful. Access is somewhat limited, at least in regard to where you can put in. There is public access at Henrys Lake State Park, located on the south end of the lake, as well as at a few private businesses. Staley Springs on the northwest shore has long been popular with fly fishers, and Wild Rose Ranch on the north shore is popular as well.

Henrys Lake is just up the road from the fabled Railroad Ranch on the Henrys Fork, just south of the equally famous Madison River, and just west of West Yellowstone, Montana. Next time you are in the area, do yourself a favor and make a point to fish Henrys Lake; it is one of the finest stillwater trout fisheries in the country and a solid brook trout fishery.

Driftboats, big sky, and brook trout are not usually found together. But that's exactly what you will find at Henrys Lake. DIANA MALLARD PHOTO

Rio Corcovado
(ARGENTINA)

The Rio Corcovado, or Corcovado River, in southern Argentina is said to be the finest self-sustaining brook trout fishery in the world, albeit a nonnative one. While I hope to get there, it is the only water in this book I have not personally been to. But I have spoken with anglers who have been there, most of whom are well traveled, and they say it eclipses even the great rivers of Labrador and Quebec.

Patagonia is a region in southern South America that encompasses Argentina and Chile and includes the southern end of the Andes Mountains. It is bordered by two oceans, the Atlantic and Pacific. The Colorado and Barrancas Rivers make up the Argentine Patagonia border, while the northern border of Chilean Patagonia is Reloncaví Estuary.

Historically devoid of trout and salmon, Argentina began importing eggs in the early 1900s. Eggs from brook trout, lake trout, and landlocked (Atlantic) salmon came from Canada. Brown trout eggs came from Belgium, France, Germany, and Great Britain. Rainbow trout eggs came from Denmark, Germany, and the United States. And chinook, coho, and sockeye salmon came from the United States.

In the years leading up to 1970, the Centro de Salmonicultura hatchery in Bariloche raised multiple species of

Eric Renninger with a giant Argentine brook trout. The Rio Corcovado is one of the finest brook trout rivers in the world, and some would say the best. JUSTIN WITT, HEMISPHERES UNLIMITED PHOTO

Guide Justin Witt with a large Argentine brook trout caught from the Rio Corcovado, considered by many to be the finest nonnative brook trout river in the world. JUSTIN WITT PHOTO

trout and salmon for stocking in Patagonian waters. The fishery took off in the 1950s, with Tierra del Fuego becoming one of the most famous trout fishing destinations in the world and spawning what is now a multimillion-dollar outfitting and guiding industry.

The Rio Corcovado is a large "western-style" river. It begins at Lago General Vintter, or Vintter Lake, and runs more than 60 miles before entering Chile, where it becomes the Palena River. It ends at the Bay of Corcovado.

Acclaimed Canadian writer and conservationist Roderick Haig-Brown, author of a dozen or so fishing books, is credited with "discovering" Argentina's burgeoning trout fishery. He spent several months there during the winter of 1951–1952 and wrote about it in his 1954 book, *Fisherman's Winter*. Ten years later television host Mort Neff did an episode featuring Argentina in his *Michigan Outdoors* show.

While most brook trout introductions outside North America have not fared well, Argentina is an exception. Many lakes, ponds, rivers, and streams are now home to self-sustaining populations of brook trout. And while many destinations offer world-class fishing for brook trout, one stands above all, Rio Corcovado.

Written about by Karas in his book *Brook Trout*, the chapter on Argentina includes a picture of an 8-pound fish caught from Rio Corcovado, almost unheard of in the United States today, and a trophy even in Quebec or Labrador. Rio Corcovado is home to brown, rainbow, and brook trout, some of which reach 10 pounds. Trout average between 15 and 18 inches, fish in the 20 to 22 inch range are common, and trout larger than that are caught. Interesting, most Argentines refer to brook trout as simply *fontinalis*.

There are no browns in the upper river due to a steep canyon that prevents them from accessing this section of river. Only rainbows and brookies can be found in Vintter Lake and the upper river. Boats are not allowed on the upper river, or on the lake within a thousand meters of the mouth. Tackle is restricted to single-point barbless hooks.

The best fishing on Rio Corcovado is in the upper river. While brook trout can be caught at any time, the best time to catch trophy fish is the end of the season, March and April. Brook trout in Rio Corcovado are caught on streamers, nymphs, and large attractor dries. Rio Corcovado is a deep and boulder-strewn river, and best fished from a drift boat.

If trophy brook trout in an exotic and wild setting south of the equator is attractive to you, Rio Corcovado is the place to go. That it peaks when many North American waters are unfishable makes it even more attractive.

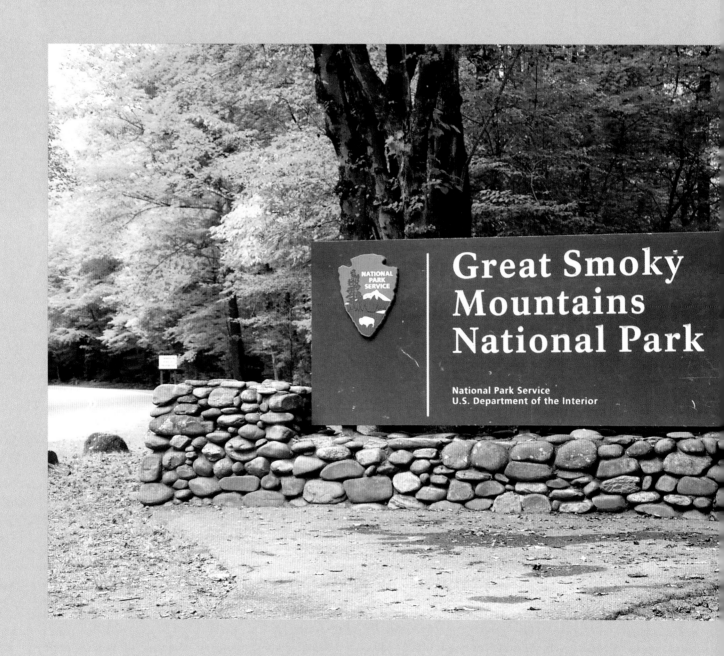

PUBLIC LANDS

Public lands are one of the nation's, and the world's, greatest treasures. They all but guarantee access for the masses in perpetuity. They are a gift that should be nurtured, expanded, and passed on through the generations. Most public lands have at least some level of tourism infrastructure including lodging, campgrounds, dining, food, gas, and supplies. If there are no services within the public land itself, there are almost always services outside the area to take advantage of the traffic.

Most of the public lands in the United States are home to lakes, ponds, rivers, and streams, many of which are inhabited by brook trout. Some of the brook trout are wild, some are stocked, some are native, and some nonnative. Public lands offer anglers one of the best, safest, most convenient, and most reliable ways to enjoy the nation's native brook trout waters. This includes federally and state-owned lands, which come in the form of national parks, national monuments, state parks, state public reserved lands, state wildlife management areas, and so on.

Great Smoky Mountains National Park in North Carolina and Tennessee is home to miles of wild native brook trout streams.
BOB MALLARD PHOTO

Acadia National Park (MAINE)

Acadia National Park is located in northern coastal Maine and is one of the most diverse, rugged, and dramatic natural settings in the state. Best known for its hiking, biking, and sightseeing, it is also home to brook trout, including several populations of rare sea-run brook trout.

The land around Acadia was home to Native Americans dating back to 4,000 BC. The first European to see the area was Samuel de Champlain, who in 1604 noted its rugged topography and offshore hazards, one of which "made a hole in our pinnace close to the keel." He said it looked like "seven or eight mountains one alongside the other," and named it Mount Desert Island.

What is now Acadia National Park was originally established as Sieur de Monts National Monument in 1916 by President Woodrow Wilson. It gained national park status in 1919, making it the first so-designated land east of the Mississippi River. Originally known as Lafayette National Park, it was renamed Acadia National Park in 1929.

Roughly 30,000 acres of Acadia National Park are located on Mount Desert Island, just over 2,725 acres are on Isle au Haut, and approximately 2,365 acres are on the Schoodic Peninsula. Acadia National Park sees roughly 3.5 million visitors a year, making it the seventh most visited national park in America behind Great Smoky Mountains, Grand Canyon, Zion, Rocky Mountain, Yosemite, and Yellowstone. At just over 47,000 acres it is the 47th largest park, or 12th smallest.

Acadia National Park is a unique landscape where the woods meet the ocean. It is home to seven peaks above 1,000 feet, many of which loom over rocky shores and

Acadia National Park in eastern Maine, where freshwater meets saltwater, the woods meet the ocean, deer feed within sight of seals, and brook trout rub fins with striped bass. BOB MALLARD PHOTO

Emily Bastian with a typical sea-run brook trout from a small stream in Acadia National Park. Lacking in estuary habitat, few if any salters have such an immediate transition between freshwater and saltwater as those found in Acadia. BOB MALLARD PHOTO

sandy beaches. Conifer trees hang over the shoreline, and white-tailed deer and harbor seals cross paths, as do brook trout and striped bass. At just over 1,500 feet Cadillac Mountain is the highest point in the park, as well as the highest within 25 miles of the coast from Nova Scotia to Texas. Named after French explorer Antoine Laumet de la Mothe, sieur de Cadillac, it is the first place in the United States touched by the sun each day from October to early March.

Sea-run brook trout are a diadromous form of fish, moving between freshwater and saltwater to feed and find thermal refuge. Living and spawning in freshwater, they are the opposite of sea-run, or anadromous, salmon that live in saltwater and only enter freshwater to spawn.

The sea-run brook trout of Mount Desert Island are unique due to the limited access to estuary habitat, which results in them spending proportionately more time in the ocean than most salters. In fact, they may be the most saltwater-dependent sea-run brook trout in the country.

Of note is Stanley Brook, a heavily studied and well-documented sea-run brook trout stream. Beginning in the hills and mountains on the southern end of Mount Desert Island, Stanley Brook flows south unbroken until terminating at a sandy beach on Seal Harbor, where a kiosk denotes its use by sea-run smelt, herring, and brook trout.

Other streams with sea-run brook trout include Jordan Stream, Otter Creek, and Little Harbor Brook. Whether other streams contain brook trout that utilize saltwater habitat is unclear. To learn more about these fascinating fish, refer to the "Sea-Run Brook Trout" chapter later in this book.

Hunters Brook is a small freestone stream that goes intermittent before entering the ocean in crashing surf through porous cobble. Cut off from the sea in all but extremely high tides and high stream flows, it is unclear to what degree the brook trout utilize saltwater habitat, and if they do, whether they can get back.

Brook trout can also be found in Asticou Brook, Breakneck Brook, Cannon Brook, Cromwell Brook, East and West Branches of Marshal Brook, Fire Pond Brook, Hadlock Brook, Kebo Brook, Kittredge Brook, Northeast Creek, Old Mill Brook, and Mill Stream on Schoodic Peninsula.

Water quality in Acadia is very good. Most lakes and ponds are extremely clear with gravel bottoms. Jordan Pond, a public water supply, is the deepest lake in Acadia at 150 feet and said to be one of the clearest lakes in Maine. While there are formal boat launches on many ponds, some require a carry and are best fished from a canoe or other small watercraft.

Thirteen lakes and ponds in and around Acadia are classified as Principal Fisheries for brook trout by the Maine Department of Inland Fisheries and Wildlife, one of which, Long Pond in Seal Harbor, is a self-sustaining State Heritage Fish water. Some of the better ones are Bubble, Halfmoon, Lakewood, Upper and Lower Breakneck, Upper Hadlock, Witch Hole Ponds, and Echo Lake.

Emily Bastian working a rising fish on Jordan Pond. A public water supply, and said to be the clearest lake in Maine, only nonmotorized boats are allowed, and wading is prohibited. BOB MALLARD PHOTO

Acadia National Park is home to roughly 40 species of mammals, including beavers that were reintroduced to the park in 1920 after being eradicated through trapping. If you explore a bit you will find beaver ponds, some of which are home to brook trout.

The brook trout in Acadia National Park's streams average just 6 inches. Fish up to 8 inches are caught, but it's rare to see a brook trout larger than that. Brook trout in the lakes and ponds average 8 to 12 inches, with larger fish taken.

Services are limited within Acadia National Park. It is, however, serviced by the tourist towns of Bar Harbor and Southwest Harbor on Mount Desert Island. Bar Harbor is one of the most bustling, albeit seasonally, and beautiful seaside towns in Maine.

While not known for its fishing in general, the brook trout fishing in and around Acadia National Park is better and more diverse than most realize, and greatly underutilized. Those who do fish the park are often quite satisfied with what they find.

Unfortunately, while the brook trout of Acadia National Park are heavily studied, they are poorly managed. Most lakes and ponds are stocked, and liberal regulations are in effect for most waters. This includes imposing general law tackle, bag, and length limits on almost all streams, including those that are home to rare sea-run brook trout.

The following excerpt comes from a response to an email I sent to then National Park Service director Jonathan Jarvis in 2016, where I questioned why Acadia's native brook trout, especially rare sea-run fish, were not receiving the same level of protection that similar fish were receiving in other national parks. The response shows that the problem lies in the multi-jurisdictional nature of the park:

Since 1995, the park has met with and expressed concern about fisheries management to IFW [Maine Department of Inland Fisheries and Wildlife]. During this twenty-year period, NPS [National Park Service] drafted several different Memoranda of Agreements. . . . While none of these draft versions were signed, the NPS believes that a signed Cooperative Agreement would clarify the respective management and regulatory authorities, goals and objectives, and the roles and responsibilities of the NPS and the State of Maine in conducting this collaborative fisheries conservation program. While the NPS and IFW have many areas of mutual interest in protecting fisheries resources, a constructive management framework remains to be agreed to and put into operation.

Adirondack Park
(NEW YORK)

Adirondack Park is located in Upstate New York. Created by the State of New York in 1892, the park was the brainchild of Verplanck Colvin, a surveyor, whose idea of preserving the land led to its creation. It encompasses most of the Adirondack Mountains, and part of the park is in New York's Forest Preserve. The park was designated a National Historic Landmark in 1963.

Adirondack Park is the largest protected wilderness area east of the Mississippi. It is bigger than several New England states, and larger than Glacier, Grand Canyon, Great Smoky Mountains, Yellowstone, and Yosemite National Parks combined. Unlike most parks, more than half the land is privately owned. At roughly 6 million acres, approximately 2.5 million acres are owned by New York State, and the rest by private landowners. One million acres are designated as wilderness. Adirondack Park contains over 100 small towns and villages, and numerous farms and businesses. Much of the land supports an active timber harvesting industry as well.

The roughly 2.5 million acres of state-owned land in Adirondack Park, Forest Preserve, is strictly managed. Designated as "forever wild," the land is protected under the state constitution "to preserve the exceptional scenic, recreational and ecological value." This land cannot be bought, sold, or transferred, and it is closed to logging.

The park, including the private inholdings, is regulated by the Adirondack Park Agency. Formed in 1971 by New York governor Nelson Rockefeller, Adirondack Park Agency is a government agency responsible for managing the park. It oversees development as well as activities within the park. The agency is headquartered in Ray Brook, New York.

A large brook trout from Adirondack Park, home to the best concentration of large wild native brook trout in the contiguous United States outside of Maine. The park is also home to the second-highest number of native brook trout ponds outside of Maine. JOHN SEGESTA PHOTO

A beautiful wild native brook trout caught using a Tenkara rod in a small stream in Adirondack Park. Note the traditional Tenkara net below the fish. ADAM KLAGSBRUN PHOTO

Adirondack Park is home to numerous mountains, including Mount Marcy, which at 5,343 feet is the highest point in New York. There are more than 2,000 miles of trails. The park is home to more than 50 species of mammals including black bear, bobcat, coyote, fisher, moose, otter, white-tailed deer, and beaver—and by default, beaver ponds.

The Adirondacks has a rich angling history dating back to the early 1800s. Starting in the 1820s, sportsmen flocked to the area to escape life and work in the urban and suburban Northeast to wet a line. Among them were fly fishers who came in search of wild native brook trout.

There are approximately 3,000 lakes and ponds and 30,000 miles of rivers and streams in Adirondack Park, many of which are home to native brook trout. It is said that the park is home to over 500 brook trout lakes and ponds.

Like other areas, however, Adirondack Park's brook trout have been greatly reduced. Acidification, habitat degradation, nonnative fish introductions, stocking, and angler exploitation have all taken their toll. According to one study, only 3 percent of historic brook trout waters in the Saranac Lakes Wild Forest in Adirondack Park are still home to such. As happened in many areas in the Northeast, the land in and around Adirondack Park was extensively logged. The once expansive forests of old-growth timber were fragmented and subject to clear-cutting and widespread deforestation. The Adirondacks were also a victim of acid rain. And it has not escaped the nonnative fish introduction plague either.

New York has established a unique acid precipitation control program that includes reducing power plant emissions as well as artificially "liming" many lakes and ponds. They have also prohibited the use of live fish as bait on most brook trout waters to try to stop nonnative fish introductions. Other waters have been reclaimed to remove nonnative fish.

Based on recent studies, there are a number of native strains of brook trout in Adirondack Park, including the Windfall and Little Tupper strains. These genetically pure fish escaped the onslaught of stocking for reasons that are not completely clear, but are most likely tied to poor genetic management at the hatchery, which left the stocked fish unable to reproduce. Others were isolated and not subject to stocking. While not genetically pure, there also are populations of brook trout that are self-sustaining. Others are maintained through stocking but offer good sport fisheries.

Areas known for their brook trout fishing include Lake George Wild Forest, Pharaoh Lake Wilderness, Siamese Ponds Wilderness, Silver Lake Wilderness, St. Regis Canoe Area, and West Canada Lake Wilderness. Many of the ponds in these areas require a hike to reach and offer remote fly fishing for native brook trout, many of which are wild.

Consider Bessie and Nellie Ponds in the St. Regis Canoe Area. These remote ponds are accessible by canoe only and home to self-sustaining brook trout. The roadside Bone and Grass Ponds have brook trout as well. Hour Pond, Peaked Mountain Pond, Puffer Pond, and Upper and Lower Siamese Ponds in the Siamese Ponds Wilderness are popular with anglers also. Black Pond serves as a brood stock pond for Windfall strain fish. Silver Lake in the Silver Lake Wilderness produced a state record brook trout of 22.5 inches and 6 pounds in 2013. Cranberry Lake in St. Lawrence County has long been considered one of the finest brook trout lakes in the state.

The highlight of Adirondack Park's moving-water offering is the fabled Ausable River system, specifically its two branches, East and West. The Ausable has long been considered one of the finest trout rivers in the East. Brook trout are present in its upper reaches, especially on the West Branch. Its two feeder streams, Marcy and South Meadow Brooks, hold brook trout also.

Many other streams hold brook trout as well. This includes Alder Brook, Ampersand Brook, Black Brook, Cold Brook, the Cold River, Little Black Brook, the North Branch Saranac River, Sumner Brook, and the West Branch Sacandaga River, but you may have to pick through some brown trout in some places to find them.

Like most places in native brook trout range, Adirondack Park is best fished in the spring and fall. While some rivers and streams hold up throughout the summer, lakes and ponds can be tough to fish as the brook trout go deep in search of thermal refuge. Consider mid-May through early July, and then again in mid-August until the season closes.

With a year-round population of over 125,000, approximately 200,000 seasonal residents, and countless visitors, Adirondack Park is a busy place. But due to the amount of backcountry, you can always get away from the crowds, and if you are willing to work hard enough, far away from them.

Other than Maine, no place in America is more synonymous with brook trout, and brook trout fishing, than the Adirondacks, much of which is now protected as part of Adirondack Park. It is also the only place outside of Maine with a significant inventory of brook trout lakes and ponds. While true trophy-sized fish are admittedly somewhat rare, respectable specimens, including fish up to 18 inches and 3 pounds are caught, and some larger than that. Other than Canada, the Great Lakes, and Maine, Adirondack Park probably puts up the biggest brook trout found anywhere else in their native range.

Allagash Wilderness Waterway (MAINE)

The Allagash Wilderness Waterway is in northern Pisca-taquis and Aroostook Counties in northern Maine. This 92-mile-long, 400- to 800-foot-wide corridor is owned by the state and acts as a protective buffer for a series of undeveloped wilderness lakes, ponds, rivers, and streams. The waterway is protected from development and logging, and is known nationally for its wilderness canoeing, camping, hunting, and, of course, fishing.

The word Allagash is of Penobscot Indian origin and means "bark stream," "hemlock bark," "bark camp," or "bark cabin lake." The area was inhabited by Algonquin Indians, whose lands extended from east of the Great Lakes into the Maritime region of Canada. Most of the occupants of the Allagash area were from the Maliseet and

Micmac, or M'kmaq, tribes, which were part of a group known as the Wabanaki.

The area was also visited by famed author and preservationist Henry David Thoreau, who came to the Allagash with Penobscot Indian guides Joe Aitteon, the son of the tribal governor, and Joe Polis in 1853 and 1857. He referred to it as "Allegash" and wrote about it in his 1864 classic *The Maine Woods*. They paddled, poled, and portaged their way along ancient canoe trails used by Wabanaki tribes for thousands of years into what was at the time unexplored wilderness and virgin forests.

In 1966 the people of Maine approved a $1.5 million bond for the protection of the Allagash watershed, which resulted in the creation of the Allagash Wilderness

Paddling Musquacook Deadwater in the Allagash Wilderness Waterway. A mix of river, streams, lakes, and ponds, the Allagash offers what is arguably the finest multiday wilderness brook trout fishing canoe trip in the country.
DAVE CONLEY PHOTO

Beautiful Allagash Falls on the lower Allagash River is the only thing between the Allagash Wilderness Waterway and nonnative and highly invasive muskies. If the muskies make it over the falls, the brook trout fishery will be lost.
DAVE CONLEY PHOTO

Waterway. The waterway received a National Wild and Scenic River designation in 1970, one of the first rivers to be so recognized. The water and land around it is managed by the federal Department of Agriculture, Conservation and Forestry's Division of Parks and Public Lands.

Historically, what is now the Allagash Wilderness Waterway was part of a single watershed, the St. John River. It included Allagash, Chamberlain, Churchill, Eagle, and Heron Lakes; Harvey Pond; Long, Telos, and Umsaskis Lakes; Little Round and three Round Ponds; Allagash Stream; and the Allagash River. The system was drained by the north-flowing Allagash River, which joins the St. John River in extreme northern Maine.

In the mid-1800s, two dams and a canal were built to reroute the flow of the headwaters of the Allagash to drive logs south to the mills in Bangor. Lock Dam was constructed on Chamberlain Lake to control the flows into Eagle Lake. Another dam was built at the top of Telos Lake. A canal, known as the Telos Cut, was dug between Telos Lake and Webster Lakes, a headwater of the East Branch Penobscot River. These ingenious man-made structures were used to divert water from the Allagash watershed into the Penobscot watershed.

The headwaters of the Allagash still flow into both the St. John River and Penobscot watersheds. Everything upstream of Eagle Lake drains into the Penobscot River via Webster Stream and the East Branch Penobscot River. Everything from Eagle Lake downstream flows into the St. John River via the Allagash River.

The Allagash River begins at the outlet of Churchill Lake. It is approximately 65 miles long, making it one of the longest wilderness rivers in the Northeast, and drains an area of just under 1,500 square miles. All but the last 5 miles are located within the Allagash Wilderness Waterway. Allagash Stream is within the waterway boundaries as well.

Portions of several streams lie within the Allagash Wilderness Waterway as well, including Chemquasabamticook Stream, Glazier Brook, Russell Brook, Snare Brook, Soper Brook, Thoroughfare Brook, and West Branch Allagash Stream.

Brook trout are native to the Allagash Wilderness Waterway and can be found in almost all lakes, ponds, and streams, as well as the river. The fish are wild; there is no stocking. Brook trout range from 6 to over 20 inches, with the smallest fish being found in the streams and the largest in the big lakes. The brook trout found in the river and small ponds fall somewhere between.

Allagash, Churchill, and Eagle Lakes have never been directly stocked or compromised by fish stocked in a connecting water. Telos, Umsaskis, and Webster Lakes and Round Pond have never been directly stocked, but may or may not have received stocked fish from a secondary source. Chamberlain Lake has not been stocked in over 50 years. The best lakes for brook trout are Eagle, Chamberlain, and Allagash.

Allagash Lake covers 4,260 acres. It has an average depth of 39 feet and a maximum depth of 89 feet. It is the largest never-stocked State Heritage Fish brook trout lake in Maine. Fish densities are high, and trout average between 10 and 12 inches, with fish approaching 18 inches possible. The brook trout in Allagash Lake are silvery, and while historically a bit skinny, seem to be improving regarding their length-to-weight ratio. Fishing is restricted to single-hook artificial lures only. There is a 2-fish, 12-inch minimum length limit, and only one fish can exceed 14 inches.

Eagle Lake is roughly 9,500 acres. It averages 34 feet deep with a maximum depth of 124 feet. Fish numbers are high. The average brook trout is 12 to 14 inches, with fish up to 20 inches caught. The brook trout are heavy-bodied and as beautiful as any brook trout you will ever see. There are no tackle restrictions, and the bag and length limits are the same as at Allagash Lake.

As for river fishing, while the entire Allagash River holds brook trout, the section immediately below Churchill Dam, known as Chase Rapids, is your best bet. Brook trout here average 10 to 12 inches, with fish up to 16 inches possible. Trout in streams average 6 to 8 inches. However, large fish from the lakes enter the streams in the spring to feed on smelts and sucker eggs, and in the fall to spawn.

The best fishing in the Allagash Wilderness Waterway is from late May through early July and late August through September. Midsummer fishing can be slow due to warm water. For those interested in stillwater fishing, or looking for large fish, while all the lakes and ponds hold brook trout, Chamberlain and Eagle Lakes tend to produce the largest fish.

Only canoes are allowed on Allagash Lake and Allagash Stream, and motors of any kind are prohibited. While there is no motor restriction, personal watercraft, hovercraft, airboats, racing boats, and pontoon boats are prohibited on Chamberlain and Telos Lakes. Waterskiing and similar activities are not allowed anywhere on the waterway.

Churchill Lake, Eagle Lake, Long Lake, Round Pond, and Umsaskis Lake, as well as the Allagash River, are restricted to canoes and kayaks only. Motors must be 10 horsepower or less, and inflatable boats and sails are not allowed. Canoes must be "sharp on both ends or sharp on one end and blunt at the other," the width at the widest point may not exceed 20 percent of the craft's overall length, and the transom cannot be wider than 26 inches. Kayak width may not exceed 25 percent of the overall length.

The Allagash Wilderness Waterway offers a unique opportunity to fish for wild native brook trout in a remote and unspoiled wilderness setting. While day-use is possible, it is best fished as part of a multiday trip. It takes between 7 and 10 days to canoe the entire length of the waterway, and there are over 80 formal campsites along its length.

There are ice caves at Allagash Lake, two abandoned locomotives at Eagle Lake, and numerous historic dams and buildings. The area is home to black bear, beaver, bobcat, coyote, lynx, moose, otter, and white-tailed deer. The lakes are home to loons, woodland ducks, and eagles.

Unfortunately, except for Allagash Lake, the Allagash Wilderness Waterway waters have not been included under Maine's State Heritage Fish law due to pressure from the bait lobby. The law was initiated by concerned sportsmen and prohibits the use of live fish as bait and stocking on lakes and ponds that meet a certain criterion, which most of the Allagash Waterway lakes do. Much of the Allagash Wilderness Waterway is open to fishing with live bait, putting some of the nation's last large, undeveloped native brook trout lakes at risk of being infected with invasive fish or diseases carried by fish from outside sources. In fact, nonnative sunfish were recently found in Churchill and Eagle Lakes.

Baxter State Park (MAINE)

axter State Park is located in north-central Maine, five hours north of Boston. It is the largest public land in Maine and one of the largest state-owned lands in the Northeast. The park was the work of Percival P. Baxter, governor of Maine from 1921 to 1924. An avid outdoorsman, he had fished the Maine woods since he was a child. Baxter started by purchasing nearly 6,000 acres of land in 1930, including Mount Katahdin. He donated the land to the state in 1931, with the requirement that it be "forever wild." Baxter continued to purchase land until 1962 and left a trust of nearly 7 million dollars to ensure that the park could be maintained without taxpayer money.

Subsequent purchases and gifts have increased the park's size to just under 210,000 acres. Roughly 75 percent of Baxter is managed as a wildlife sanctuary. Approximately 25 percent of the park is open to hunting and trapping except for moose, which are protected. About 30,000 acres in the northwest corner of the park are

managed as a Scientific Forest Management Area, where timber harvest is not only allowed but required.

Mount Katahdin, Maine's highest peak at 5,269 feet, is the northern terminus of the fabled Appalachian Trail and centerpiece of Baxter State Park. Author Henry David Thoreau wrote about it, referring to it as Ktaadn in his 1864 classic *The Maine Woods*.

Baxter stipulated that the sole governing authority of the park would be a group of three government officials. Known as the Baxter State Park Authority, it is made up of the acting attorney general, commissioner of Inland Fisheries and Wildlife, and director of the Maine Forest Service. There is a full-time director as well, and the park is funded through trusts, fees, and the timber sales.

There are more than 215 miles of trails, eight roadside campgrounds, two backcountry campgrounds, numerous backcountry campsites, and some cabins in Baxter State Park. There is no running water or electricity. Other than

John Vacca with a large brook trout caught on a Woolly Bugger from a remote hike-in pond in Baxter State Park. Brook trout over 20 inches are caught in the park. BOB MALLARD PHOTO

Nesowadnehunk Stream is one of Maine's few fly-fishing-only streams and a major draw for fly fishers coming to Baxter State Park. Miles of the stream are easily accessible from the Park Tote Road. DIANA MALLARD PHOTO

lodging and outhouses, there is very little infrastructure to support the approximately 80,000 people who visit the park each year. Access is controlled and restricted as well.

Do not let the name "Park" fool you. Baxter is managed primarily for the protection and preservation of the resource—tourism and recreation are secondary concerns. One of the park's stated objectives is to fund just 30 percent of its operating costs through user fees. The result is that while nearby Acadia National Park, one-quarter the size of Baxter, saw over 3.5 million visitors in 2017, Baxter saw fewer than 90,000.

Pets, chainsaws, and generators are prohibited in Baxter State Park. You cannot use electronic devices in a way that "impairs the enjoyment" of others. There is no rubbish disposal. Large groups are discouraged, restricted as to where they can camp, and prohibited from hiking together. There is no harassing wildlife, including intrusive photographing or filming. Scientific and commercial endeavors must be approved by the director in advance.

Baxter State Park favors Maine residents over people "from away." While residents can access the park for free, nonresidents pay a $15 per vehicle entry fee. Camping fees, however, are the same for both and range from $21 for a backcountry campsite to $135 for a six-person cabin. Overnight access to the park is best done in conjunction with a reservation; while same-day reservations are possible, the park can be shut down at any time due to traffic.

For some Baxter is too restrictive. For others it is exactly what they are looking for—a place to camp, hike, view wildlife, and fish without the drone of engines or noise from people more interested in partying than enjoying nature. The forest is some of the healthiest in Maine, and the scenery the most beautiful in the interior part of the state. It is reminiscent of a time when Maine's "working forests" worked and were not so overworked.

While the waters in Baxter are managed by the Department of Inland Fisheries and Wildlife, there is a unique-in-Maine park-wide ban on the use or possession of live fish as bait, done to prevent the spread of nonnative invasive minnows. Motorboats are allowed on the three largest lakes, restricted to 10 horsepower or less on two other lakes, and prohibited everywhere else.

Baxter is home to lakes, ponds, and streams that contain native brook trout. The three largest lakes are Grand Lake Matagamon, Webster Lake, and Nesowadnehunk Lake, the first two located partially in the park and a portion of the latter serving as a park boundary. The three largest lakes solely within the park are Katahdin Lake, Lower Togue Pond, and Wassataquoik Lake, also home to rare Arctic charr.

There are over 40 lakes and ponds in Baxter that hold brook trout. All but seven are self-sustaining, and over 30 are State Heritage Fish waters. Ten are fly fishing only: Celia, Daicey, Draper, Foss-Knowlton, Jackson, Kidney,

A remote backcountry campsite on Upper South Branch Pond, home to wild native brook trout. The park maintains canoes for use by anglers on many remote waters. EMILY BASTIAN PHOTO

Lily Pad, Nesowadnehunk—which at nearly 1,400 acres is the second-largest fly-fishing-only water in the state—Rocky, and Windy Pitch. While a few offer easy access, most require a hike. The most popular roadside ponds are Daicey, Draper, Kidney, Nesowadnehunk, and South Branch. Some of the more popular hike-in ponds are Foss-Knowlton, Jackson, Rocky, and Russell.

Most streams in Baxter are home to wild brook trout. The most popular is Nesowadnehunk Stream, pronounced "Sourdnahunk" or sometimes "soudyhunk," which is one of the few fly-fishing-only streams in Maine and the only one in the park. It begins at Nesowadnehunk Lake and terminates at the fabled West Branch of the Penobscot River. Trout Brook begins just north of Nesowadnehunk Lake and flows northeast to Grand Lake Matagamon. Remote Wassataquoik and Webster Streams are also worth trying.

While there is no park-specific permit, you will need a Maine fishing license to fish in Baxter. All waters are open to fishing from April through September. Ponds are typically ice-free by early to mid-May. Streams often run high until mid- to late May.

The park maintains an inventory of canoes on the ponds that are available for a fee on a first-come, first-served basis. Float tubes are always a good idea as canoes may not be available when you need them. You can also bring your own canoe into the park. Most of the streams are relatively small and easy to wade.

Baxter State Park is the centerpiece of the interior Maine forest, and one of the wildest places left in New England. It is home to bear, beaver, bobcat, coyote, deer, fisher, fox, marten, moose, and otter. Loons and woodland ducks inhabit its lakes and ponds, and eagles soar above, including the occasional golden eagle. The people of Maine owe a debt of gratitude to Percival Baxter for having the foresight and selflessness to preserve this beautiful place.

Cold Stream Forest (MAINE)

Cold Stream Forest in central Maine holds a special place in my heart and fishing memories. It is one of the first places I caught wild native brook trout, and the closest quality wild brook trout public land to my home. I can be there in roughly an hour and visit it often, including keeping a canoe at one pond for over 30 years.

Now that the nearby Dead Stream watershed has been infected with nonnative and highly invasive golden shiners, Cold Stream Forest in Johnson Mountain and Parlin Pond Townships near The Forks, Maine, has the best concentration of intact wild native brook trout ponds east of historic Rangeley and south of Moosehead Lake. It is also home to the finest brook trout stream in the region, its namesake Cold Stream, and one of the best brook trout rivers in the state, the upper Kennebec.

The area in and around The Forks has a rich sporting history. It was the stomping grounds of fictitious Maine Guide Dud Dean from the golden era of outdoor literature. Local Maine outdoor writing legend Gene Letourneau maintained a couple of remote camps in the area as well. The documentary *Dead River Rough Cut* was filmed just across Route 201 in the Enchanted area. It is also said that the last cougar killed in Maine came from the area.

Well-known for its whitewater rafting industry, The Forks region is also one of the finest wild native brook trout destinations in New England. In addition to Cold Stream Forest, there is high-quality wild brook trout water on private land open to public access in what is known locally as the Ten Thousand Acre Tract, as well as the Chase Stream, Dead Stream, Enchanted, Misery, Parlin, and Spencer areas.

Ted Williams and Emily Bastian on Cold Stream, one of the finest wild native brook trout streams in central Maine. Ted fished the area decades ago while attending school at Colby College and had not been back since.
BOB MALLARD PHOTO

Anglers fishing Lang Pond, one of seven State Heritage Fish waters in Cold Stream Forest. The pond is home to wild brook trout and has not been stocked in over 65 years. EMILY BASTIAN PHOTO

This 8,160-acre state-owned land was purchased in 2016 from the timber management company Weyerhaeuser for $7.34 million, with $1.5 million coming from Land for Maine's Future, $5.5 million from the federal Forest Legacy Program, and the rest from private funds. The land was gifted to the Maine Department of Agriculture, Conservation and Forestry and put into the state's Public Reserved Lands system.

Along with a buffer on either side of 15-mile Cold Stream and the land surrounding nine ponds, there is an important deer yard on the lower end of the property. Although not included in the purchase, the land around Cold Stream Pond, the headwaters of Cold Stream, is protected from development via an easement. While protected from development, the land will continue to be actively logged and open to hunting, trapping, and other forms of "traditional use," a requirement when Land for Maine's Future funds are involved.

The area is home to beaver, black bear, bobcat, "threatened" Canada lynx, coyote, fisher, mink, moose, muskrat, otter, pine marten, snowshoe hare, and white-tailed deer. There are eagles, gray jays, loons, ruffed and spruce grouse, and woodland ducks as well.

Cold Stream is a tributary of the Kennebec River, entering at the bottom end of what is known as the Kennebec Gorge. In addition to a resident population of fish, it is the primary spawning tributary for brook trout on the upper Kennebec, a population stressed by nonnative invasive smallmouth bass and extreme fluctuations in water level due to power generation, and the finest wild native brook trout river in the region.

Cold Stream is a classic freestone stream where tannic water flows over boulders, rocks, and gravel, under canopy, and through a dense forest. Beginning at Cold Stream Pond, it starts as a meandering meadow stream before crashing over a waterfall and turning into a burly freestone stream. In its lower reaches it is a gentle, flowing, sandy-bottom stream. There are three waterfalls, the one noted above, one just downstream, and another on the lower end, which isolate brook trout into four distinct populations.

Brook trout average 6 to 8 inches in Cold Stream, with fish up to 10 inches caught. The fish run slightly larger in the upper section than they do the middle, but numbers are higher in the middle. While numbers drop off a bit in the lower section, the average size bumps up a bit, and fish up to 16 inches are encountered, most likely run-ups from the Kennebec River.

The upper section of Cold Stream is best accessed from Lone Jack Campsite or a small bridge just above the upper falls. This section is best fished from a canoe. Access is limited and difficult from the upper falls downstream until the stream pushes up against the road. From there down to just below the Capitol Road, access is easy. Below here there is only one place a road meets the stream, and access is limited to those willing to hike.

The Kennebec River can be fished right off the mouth of Cold Stream at low water. You don't want to be anywhere near it at high water, a daily event scheduled for power

Middle Cold Stream, one of the finest wild brook trout streams in central Maine. BOB MALLARD PHOTO

generation and rafting, as the level bumps up from several hundred feet per second to 5,000 or more. You can access the upper Gorge from what is known as the Chase Stream Sluice as well. Brook trout up to 18 inches are caught from this section of river.

There are nine ponds in Cold Stream Forest: Big Berry, Campstove, Durgin, Fernald, Lang, Little Lang, Little Berry, Lone Jack, and Snake. Brook trout are present in all but Campstove and Fernald Ponds, and these once had fish and may still have remnant populations. The seven ponds with brook trout are self-sustaining and formally designated State Heritage Fish waters. Big Berry, Little Berry, and Snake Ponds were last stocked in 1916; Lang Pond was last stocked in 1941; and Durgin, Lone Jack, and Little Lang have never been stocked.

Lang, Little Lang, and Snake are hike-in ponds and best fished with float tubes. Big Berry, Lone Jack, and Little Berry are just a short walk from the road and can be fished from a carried-in canoe. The only pond that is roadside is Durgin, where you can easily slide a boat into the water.

Big Berry puts up the biggest fish, Lang puts up the most fish, and the other ponds fall somewhere in between. Durgin can be surprisingly good for a roadside pond, and while it gets a lot of camping pressure, fishing pressure can be oddly low. Little Berry and Lone Jack Ponds are similar, as are Little Lang and Snake Ponds.

Cold Stream Pond, just to the east of the public land, is a self-sustaining State Heritage Fish water last stocked in 1954, and a high-quality brook trout fishery. Misery and Upper Misery Ponds to the east are also self-sustaining State Heritage Fish waters. Chase Stream and Little Chase Stream Ponds hold brook trout as well; the former is a State Heritage Fish water last stocked in 1974, while the latter is stocked. Nearby Ten Thousand Acre Pond is a never-stocked State Heritage Fish water. Parlin Stream, to the west of Cold Stream Forest, can fish well at times for small wild brook trout and large stocked fish from the lake. Chase Stream to the east is home to wild brook trout, as are many of the smaller streams in the area.

Cold Stream Forest is outside the power grid and accessible by dirt road only. Cell coverage is limited, and there are no services. Campsites are available for free on a first-come, first-served basis. While most of the campsites are small and primitive, there is a large group site with fire pits, picnic tables, and outhouses near Lone Jack Pond.

Cold Stream Forest is a work-in-process. The management plan is being hashed out, and the details are not yet set in stone. Expect road, bridge, trail, and campsite improvements, as well as some level of new infrastructure, mostly formal outhouses. The proposed 100-foot no-cut buffer along the stream and ponds is not enough to protect the aesthetics and environmental health of the area; hopefully the powers that be will increase it.

Great Smoky Mountains National Park

(NORTH CAROLINA/ TENNESSEE)

Great Smoky Mountains National Park is located in western North Carolina and eastern Tennessee about an hour's ride from Asheville and Knoxville. Sometimes referred to as the Smoky Mountains or just the Smokies, the Great Smoky Mountains are part of the Blue Ridge Mountains, which are part of the Appalachian Mountains.

Authorized by Congress in 1926, Great Smoky Mountains National Park was established in 1934 and dedicated by President Franklin Delano Roosevelt in 1940. Financier and philanthropist John D. Rockefeller Jr. donated $5 million to the project; the rest came from the federal government and private citizens. It was the first national park partially paid for with federal money. Great Smoky Mountains is the most visited national park in America. It is also a World Heritage Site, International Biosphere Reserve, and part of the Southern Appalachian Biosphere Reserve. There are five historic districts in the park, and nine spots within the park are listed on the National Register of Historic Places.

Great Smoky Mountains National Park is connected to Shenandoah National Park, which is featured in this book, by the Blue Ridge Parkway, a federally designated national parkway. This roughly 470-mile road is the most visited site within the National Park System. The park is bordered by Cherokee and Pisgah National Forests, the latter of which is featured in the book, and unlike most national parks, there is no entry fee.

The area in and around Great Smoky Mountains National Park was the ancestral home of the Cherokee Nation. Europeans began settling the area in the late

The author's first Tennessee brook trout caught from a small headwater stream in Great Smoky Mountains National Park. The picture is being used by Native Fish Coalition on their Facebook page and website. DIANA MALLARD PHOTO

Walker Camp Prong on the Tennessee side of the park. The fish are wild and wary, requiring an upstream approach to effectively fish the stream. DIANA MALLARD PHOTO

eighteenth century. In 1830 President Andrew Jackson signed the Indian Removal Act, where Native Americans east of the Mississippi River were force-marched to what is now Oklahoma in what became known as the Trail of Tears. While most Cherokees left the area, some hid in what is now Great Smoky Mountains National Park, and their descendants still live in the area today.

At 522,419 acres, Great Smoky Mountains National Park is one of the largest public lands east of the Mississippi. It is nearly 95 percent forested, making it one of the largest deciduous forests in the United States. Roughly 35 percent is old-growth forest. Elevations range from 876 feet at the mouth of Abrams Creek to 6,643 feet at the summit of Clingmans Dome. There are 16 peaks over 6,000 feet.

The park has approximately 10,000 documented species of flora and fauna including roughly 100 trees, 1,800 plants, 200 birds, 65 mammals, 40 reptiles, 45 amphibians, and 50 fish. It is home to the densest black bear population in the eastern United States, and the most diverse salamander population outside of the tropics, including hellbenders, the largest salamander in the United States, capable of reaching nearly 30 inches. Some scientists believe there could be nearly 10 times as many undocumented species.

The park averages from 55 inches of rain per year in the valleys to 85 inches in the higher elevations, more than

anywhere in the United States except the Pacific Northwest and parts of Alaska and Hawaii. There are roughly 850 miles of trails, including 70 miles of the fabled Appalachian Trail. Some of the most popular attractions are Cades Cove, Clingmans Dome—the second-highest point in the East—Mountain Farm Museum, and The Chimney Tops. Carlos Campbell Overlook is named for a Knoxville, Tennessee, businessman who helped create the park.

Fishing, with an emphasis on fly fishing, is the third most popular activity in Great Smoky Mountains National Park after hiking and sightseeing. There are over 2,100 miles of stream in the park, over 700 of which hold trout. While the recreational value of fishing is understood and embraced by the park, its primary mission is to protect and preserve native flora, fauna, and environs, in this case brook trout and the streams they live in.

While rainbow trout are the most common species of trout found in the park, brook trout are the only species of salmonid that is native to the park. Brook trout were historically present in most streams above 2,000 feet elevation. Extensive logging in the early 1900s resulted in their extirpation in over 160 miles of stream, reducing their native range by roughly half. The introduction of nonnative trout contracted their range even further.

Between 1934 and 1974, Great Smoky Mountains National Park was heavily stocked. During this time nonnative rainbow trout and brown trout were introduced to park waters. Nonnative trout also migrated into the park from waters outside the park. Northern strains of brook trout were introduced as well, compromising the native Southern Appalachian strain. Stocking was discontinued in 1975 in favor of wild trout management, and current National Park Service policy restricts stocking to native fish restoration efforts only.

Some of the Great Smoky Mountains National Park's native brook trout populations are protected from invasive fish by natural waterfalls. It is believed that as many as a third of the park's remaining brook trout populations are protected by such barriers. Studies are being done to determine how high a waterfall needs to be to stop rainbow and brown trout from getting up and over it. This information could be used for future projects involving man-made barriers to protect brook trout from invasive fish.

The objective of the National Park Service is to increase the range of native brook trout wherever possible. Groups such as the American Fisheries Society, Great Smoky Mountains Natural History Association, and Land Between the Lakes have helped raise money to fund restoration efforts. Research is being done to determine if there is a distinct Southern Appalachian strain of brook trout in Great Smoky Mountains National Park. If true, restoration efforts will be even more intensive.

While many of the streams in Great Smoky Mountains National Park hold brook trout, some of the more popular are Alum Cave Creek, Big Creek, Bradley's Fork, Deep Creek, Eagle Creek, Forney Creek, Hazel Creek, Jakes Creek, Lynn Camp Prong, Noland Creek, Road Prong, Twentymile Creek, Upper Deep Creek, and Walker Camp Prong. Fish average 6 inches with fish up to 10 inches possible, and occasionally larger trout are caught.

Waters in Great Smoky Mountains National Park are open to fishing year-round. You may fish from a half hour before sunrise to a half hour after sunset. While there is no park-specific fishing license, you will need either a Tennessee or North Carolina fishing license.

Bait is not allowed, and tackle is restricted to single-hook artificial lures and flies only. Treble hooks are prohibited, and you cannot use more than two flies at a time. It is catch-and-release on all brook trout. Certain streams are closed to fishing to protect stressed brook trout populations. Others are closed to allow fish to repopulate post reclamation.

Great Smoky Mountains National Park is home to one of the largest concentrations of wild native brook trout living on protected lands in the country, some of which are pure Southern Appalachian strain. It is a national treasure and worth seeing if you are a brook trout aficionado.

Alum Cave Creek, a tributary of West Prong Little Pigeon River and home to small wild brook trout. The farther you walk, the tighter things get. DIANA MALLARD PHOTO

Green Mountain National Forest

(VERMONT)

Green Mountain National Forest is located in southwestern and west-central Vermont. It is made up of two noncontiguous sections, the largest of which starts at the southwest corner of the state and runs east roughly 15 miles along the Massachusetts border, and north along the New York border for approximately 40 miles. It surrounds the town of Manchester, the birthplace of Orvis and home of the American Museum of Fly Fishing. The smaller section lies north of Rutland and east of Middlebury.

There are 154 national forests in the United States, representing nearly 190 million acres of public lands. National forests are federally owned lands managed by the US Forest Service, which is part of the Department of Agriculture. Management varies considerably from one forest to the next and can include the conservation of flora and fauna as well as resource extraction, livestock grazing, and recreation.

Headquartered in Rutland, Vermont, Green Mountain National Forest is part of a unit that includes Finger Lakes National Forest in New York. Along with White Mountain National Forest in New Hampshire and Maine, it is one of only two such lands in New England.

Green Mountain National Forest was established in 1932. Like nearby White Mountain National Forest, the land had been heavily logged and damaged by fires and floods, both of which were a direct result of the former. It is just short of 410,000 acres, and by far the largest public land and contiguous forest in the state. The forest covers parts of Addison, Bennington, Rutland, Washington, Windham, and Windsor Counties.

There are eight formally designated wilderness areas, established between 1974 and 2006, in Green Mountain National Forest: Big Branch (6,725 acres), Breadloaf (24,924 acres), Bristol Cliffs (3,750 acres), George D. Aiken (4,800 acres), Glastenbury (22,539 acres), Joseph Battell (12,336 acres), Lye Brook (18,122 acres), and Peru Peak (7,823 acres). These areas are closed to mechanized traffic, including bicycles. It is also home to 36,400-acre

A beautiful wild native brook trout from a small headwater stream in Green Mountain National Forest, one of many such streams found throughout the forest. STEVE YEWCHUCK PHOTO

Cold, high-gradient freestone streams are found throughout Green Mountain National Forest. They offer ideal habitat for wild brook trout. BRIAN CADORET PHOTO

White Rocks National Recreation Area and its 2,600-foot cliffs.

Green Mountain National Forest is home to miles of hiking trails, including three nationally designated trails: the Appalachian Trail, Long Trail, and Robert Frost National Recreation Trail. There are three downhill ski areas—Mount Snow, Stratton, and Bromley—as well as seven cross-country ski areas. It also contains over 2,000 archaeological and historic sites.

There are beaver, black bear, coyote, moose, ruffed grouse, white-tailed deer, and wild turkey in Green Mountain National Forest. It is also home to wild native eastern brook trout. Like brook trout across most of their historic range, these fish have suffered from habitat degradation and the state-sponsored introduction of invasive fish, mostly rainbow trout and brown trout.

While brook trout can be found almost anywhere, most self-sustaining brook trout populations within Green Mountain National Forest are in the headwaters of small streams and rivers. Many of these are located above natural barriers such as small waterfalls that block access to nonnative fish. The farther you get away from the road, the fewer stocked and nonnative fish you will encounter.

Brook trout are also found in the nameless, often hidden, and ever-changing beaver ponds and flowages that dot the countryside. Some, albeit very few, small mountain ponds still hold wild brook trout as well.

The extensive trail network in the Green Mountain National Forest provides access to many of the area's brook trout rivers, streams, and ponds. Other waters can be accessed off Routes 9, 10, 11, 30, 100, and 125. Beaver ponds and flowages are best found using Google Earth, as they change from one year to the next.

Some of the places to consider are the headwaters of the Batten Kill, Deerfield River, Hoosic River, Mad River, Mettawee River, Neshobe River, New Haven River, Tweed River, West, and White River watersheds. Alder, Big Branch, Bingo, Brandon, Flood, Greendale, Griffith, Lye, Michigan, Mount Tabor, and Roaring Branch Brooks all hold brook trout as well. For stillwater fishing consider Beebe, Bourn, Branch, Hapgood, Little Rock, and Stratton Ponds.

Other than the stockers and an occasional holdover in one of the larger streams or rivers, most brook trout you encounter in Green Mountain National Forest streams will be in the 6- to 8-inch range, with a 10-inch fish considered large. Fish run a bit larger in ponds, including some beaver ponds, and can attain lengths of over 12 inches.

The fishing season in Green Mountain National Forest runs from the second Saturday in April through October. Hatches start in mid-May and end in the late fall. On most brook trout streams, hatches are not what would be referred to as diverse or robust. The somewhat sterile conditions

A typical small headwater stream brook trout caught in Green Mountain National Forest. In many streams a 6-inch fish is as large as you will find. COREY LAWSON PHOTO

and scoured streambeds found in these freestone ecosystems are not conducive to strong insect life. Hatches include mayflies, caddis, stoneflies, and midges. Beaver ponds, flowages, and natural ponds have these insects as well as damselflies and dragonflies. Summer brings terrestrials. Trout feed on leeches and small minnows as well, mostly sculpin, dace, and juvenile trout. After a rain, fish feed on earthworms that are washed into the stream.

The Green Mountain National Forest is a beautiful place. Like most national forests, it is one of the healthier forest ecosystems in the region, with minimal logging and limited development. Many of the roads into the interior of the forest have been blocked to vehicular traffic. The myriad small streams offer remote fishing for wild brook trout in a relatively unspoiled setting. Many of the streams stay cool enough throughout the summer to provide season-long angling.

When it comes to fly fishing for wild brook trout, Green Mountain National Forest is a diamond in the rough. Like most national forests, management of the fishery is the responsibility of the state. Wild brook trout in small-stream environments are very susceptible to angler exploitation. This depresses populations and results in calls for supplemental stocking, which provides temporary relief at the expense of the long-term health of the resource.

Vermont's stream-resident brook trout are the least protected in the East. Most waters are open to unrestricted bait. And while the aggregate limit on "trout" (brook, brown, and rainbow) is a highest-in-the-East 12 fish, only 6 can be nonnative browns and rainbows, but all 12 can be native brook trout. It's time the US Forest Service took a more active role in the conservation of this invaluable native fish resource and Vermont's official State Cold Water Fish.

Katahdin Woods and Waters National Monument (MAINE)

Deep in interior Maine can be found the Northeast's newest major public land, Katahdin Woods and Waters National Monument. The monument was created by President Obama in 2016 using powers granted him under the Antiquities Act. It is managed by the National Park Service. The land, along with an endowment to help fund initial operations, was gifted to the public by Elliotsville Plantation and the Quimby Family Foundation.

Katahdin Woods and Waters National Monument did not happen easily. In fact, it almost didn't happen at all. Owned by entrepreneur, preservationist, and philanthropist Roxanne Quimby, the land was originally offered to the federal government for use as a national park. This resulted in years of delays, challenges, unfounded claims of landgrabbing—and worse, by rural Maine residents who fear, dislike, or don't understand federal land ownership.

Quimby moved to Maine in 1975, bought some land, and built a cabin and outhouse. She befriended beekeeper Burt Shavitz and started selling beeswax candles at local fairs. The business, Burt's Bees, grew rapidly, with Quimby eventually buying out Shavitz. She sold her business to Clorox in the late 2000s, making Quimby a multimillionaire.

Quimby used her financial windfall to purchase over 120,000 acres of land in Maine. Much of this was offered to the federal government to be used as a national park in

A wild native brook trout caught from the East Branch Penobscot River, the centerpiece of Katahdin Woods and Waters National Monument. Much larger fish are present. EMILY BASTIAN PHOTO

the interior part of the state. After years of battling a local populace ingrained in the belief that multiple use is the only use, Quimby turned the project over to her son Lucas St. Clair.

To his credit, Lucas was able to gain the support of citizens and government officials, including a congressional delegation that fence-sat for years, afraid of upsetting rural voters. In the waning hours of the Obama administration, after years of looking as though it was never going to happen, the president acted, and the rest is history.

The 87,000-plus acres of land transferred to the US Department of the Interior by Quimby on August 23, 2016, was valued at $60 million. She also pledged $20 million in cash to fund operations. That Katahdin Woods and Waters National Monument was established on August 24, 2016, the day before the 100th anniversary of the National Park Service, seemed fitting.

Interestingly, Quimby didn't do anything that Percival Baxter didn't do. She purchased private land with her own money and donated it to the public. Like Baxter, she asked for concessions to ensure the land would be managed in a way that was conducive to her dream, a reasonable position that most of us would take if we were in her shoes. That Baxter is viewed as a hero by most Mainers, and Quimby not, is a shame.

At 87,563 acres, Katahdin Woods and Waters is the second-largest public land in Maine behind Baxter State Park. It is larger than Acadia National Park and Maine's portion of White Mountain National Forest combined. The land abuts Baxter State Park to the east and is part of what is now by far the largest contiguous tract of public land in the state.

Most of Katahdin Woods and Waters is west of the East Branch Penobscot River. There are several noncontiguous parcels of land east of the river as well. It is outside the power grid and undeveloped except for some small cabins. Access is via a network of unmarked dirt roads. It is intersected by the International Appalachian Trail, which connects the northern terminus of the Appalachian Trail with Canada.

Katahdin Woods and Waters offers views of majestic Mount Katahdin, the highest point in Maine and northern terminus of the fabled Appalachian Trail. It is home to bear, beaver, bobcat, coyote, deer, fisher, lynx, marten, moose, as well as eagles, ruffed and spruce grouse, loons, and woodland ducks.

Most importantly, Katahdin Woods and Waters is home to fish, including native brook trout. It is also home to federally endangered Atlantic salmon. There is very little stocking, and most of the brook trout you catch will be wild. The monument contains miles of rivers and streams and acres of lakes, ponds, and flowages, most of which are home to native brook trout.

The East Branch of the Penobscot, or East Branch, as it is referred to, is the cornerstone of the Katahdin Woods and Waters fly-fishing offering. It is one of the finest rivers in the state and offers quality angling for wild brook trout. It also sees the occasional Atlantic salmon. The East

Emily Bastian with a small wild brook trout caught from one of the many small streams within the monument. We caught close to 40 fish in just a couple of hours. BOB MALLARD PHOTO

Emily Bastian fishing a small State Heritage Fish pond in Katahdin Woods and Waters National Monument. There are five such waters within the monument. BOB MALLARD PHOTO

Branch begins at the outlet of Grand Lake Matagamon and flows approximately 50 miles before terminating at its confluence with its famous sibling, West Branch Penobscot, where they combine to form the fabled Penobscot River. It starts as a high-gradient freestone stream, with five major drops in the first 7 miles, several of which require portages, then flattens out. It is crossed by only a small footbridge between Matagamon and Whetstone, making it one of Maine's most remote rivers. There are primitive campsites, many of which can only be reached by boat.

The Seboeis River originates at Grand Lake Seboeis, northeast of Grand Lake Matagamon. It is smaller than the East Branch and offers quality fishing for brook trout in an unspoiled wilderness setting. Like the East Branch, it too sees the occasional Atlantic salmon, and is where I saw my last Atlantic salmon in the wild.

Wassataquoik Stream is one of Maine's finest wilderness brook trout streams, and one of the most remote streams in the Northeast. It begins at Wassataquoik Lake in Baxter, home to rare Arctic charr. It is also critical spawning habitat for endangered Atlantic salmon.

There are numerous small streams in the monument as well, almost all of which are home to native brook trout. Consider Big and Little Spring Brooks, Katahdin Brook, Sandbank Stream, Swift Brook, and Traveler Brook.

There are over 30 lakes and ponds within Katahdin Woods and Waters. Most are home to native brook trout, many of which are self-sustaining, some of which have never been stocked. Ranging from just a few acres to tens of acres, most of these waters are remote, and almost all are undeveloped. Consider Hathorn and Little Hathorn Ponds, Messer Pond, and Moose Pond, all of which are self-sustaining and State Heritage Fish waters, as well as Robar Pond.

Katahdin Woods and Waters National Monument is open to fishing from April 1 through September. Realistically, the season starts a month or so later due to weather and poor road conditions. Regulations vary from water to water and are subject to change.

While parts of Katahdin Woods and Waters are gated to vehicular traffic, some areas can be accessed by dirt road. Currently there is no fee to enter or camp in the monument. There are formal campsites and a few cabins, as well as boat launches and trails, some of which allow horses and bikes. But infrastructure is very limited, so plan accordingly.

While you will have to work harder to experience the fishing in Katahdin Woods and Waters than you do in other areas of the state, it's worth the effort as it allows you to experience something that is truly wild, remote, unspoiled, and uncrowded. For the dedicated explorer/fly fisher who wants to see what fishing in Maine used to be like, it offers one of the best opportunities to do so.

Katahdin Woods and Waters is a work in progress. The details as to how it will be run going forward have yet to be ironed out. The rules are different east of the East Branch than they are west of it, with the latter being managed as a wilderness area. What we do know is that a large swath of land has been protected in perpetuity from development and will be forever open to the public, and we have the Quimby family to thank for that.

Monongahela National Forest (WEST VIRGINIA)

Monongahela National Forest is located in eastern West Virginia. More than half its eastern boundary forms the border between West Virginia and Virginia, most of which abuts the George Washington National Forest. It encompasses roughly a third of the Allegheny Mountains, which are part of the Appalachian Mountains.

Monongahela National Forest covers an area of approximately 920,000 acres. It is the third-largest national forest east of the Mississippi after neighboring George Washington National Forest and Ottawa National Forest in Michigan. Two places in Monongahela, Craig Run East Fork Rockshelter and Laurel Run Rockshelter, are listed on the National Register of Historic Places.

Monongahela National Forest was started in 1915 via a 7,200-acre land purchase known as the Monongahela Purchase. It was formally designated Monongahela National Forest in 1920, and by the mid-1920s the size of the forest had risen to over 150,000 acres. Like many national forests, it had been heavily cut before it was purchased, and it took decades to restore its forests and streams.

Between the early 1930s and 1942 there were more than 20 Civilian Conservation Corps camps in Monongahela National Forest. The workers constructed roads and trails, managed the forest, and fought fires. In the 1940s the army used it for artillery practice for troops heading off to World War II, and shells are still occasionally found. Areas such as Seneca Rocks were used to train troops in climbing. Ironically, the area was used in 1980 and 2005 to host Rainbow Gathering, an anti-war event.

Monongahela National Forest is home to most of the highest peaks in West Virginia, including 4,863-foot Spruce Knob, the highest in the state. There are eight wilderness areas: Big Draft (5,147 acres), Cranberry (47,741 acres), Dolly Sods (17,776 acres), Laurel Fork North (6,055 acres), Laurel Fork South (5,784 acres), Otter Creek (20,706 acres), Roaring Plains West (6,794 acres),

Releasing a healthy brook trout caught from a small stream in Monongahela National Forest. While the area is prone to low water, the native brook trout have found a way to hold on. DAVID SANTEE PHOTO

A brook trout fins away in a typical Monongahela National Forest freestone stream. Note the shallow depth of the water. ANTHONY INTERNICOLA PHOTO

and Spice Run (6,037 acres). It is also home to Spruce Knob-Seneca Rocks National Recreation Area. There are roughly 320 acres of old-growth forest, the largest of which is 70-acre Fanny Bennett Hemlock Grove, a stand of eastern hemlock.

The national forest is home to black bear, beaver, bobcat, coyote, fisher, otter, red and gray fox, snowshoe hare, and white-tailed deer. During the 1930s deer numbers plummeted to a point where they were imported from Michigan to bolster the herd. Fisher were extirpated from the area for over 50 years, but were reintroduced in the late 1960s using animals from New Hampshire. There are rattlesnakes and copperheads as well. Approximately 230 species of birds live in the forest at least part-time, including grouse and wild turkey. It is home to roughly 75 species of trees.

Monongahela National Forest is a popular destination for tourists and recreationists. There are 23 campgrounds, 17 picnic areas, and over 500 miles of formal trails, the longest of which is 23-mile West Fork Railroad Trail. Monongahela sees roughly 3 million visitors a year. People come to camp, hike, rock climb, mountain bike, horseback ride, animal and bird watch, hunt, and, of course, fish.

There is reported to be over 600 miles of rivers and streams in Monongahela National Forest. Twelve waters in the national forest are being, or have been, considered for National Wild and Scenic River designation. Most of the streams are freestone in nature and very reliant on rain and snowmelt for their water. In the spring they experience

high water due to snowmelt; in the summer many suffer from low water due to a lack of rain.

More than 350 miles of rivers and streams in Monongahela National Forest are said to hold trout, and represent 50 percent of all trout streams in the state. Brook trout are the only trout native to Monongahela. It is believed that 90 percent of all wild brook trout streams in West Virginia are located within the national forest. Due to their small size, they are estimated to represent just 2 percent of the total stream miles in the state.

Monongahela National Forest is home to the headwaters of a number of major river systems: Cheat, Cranberry, Elk, Gauley, Greenbrier, Potomac, and Tygart—all of which hold brook trout. Many lesser-known streams such as Dry Fork and Gandy and Seneca Creeks hold brook trout as well, and these may be your best option for finding wild fish.

Most of the brook trout encountered run between 6 and 8 inches. While trout between 10 and 12 inches are caught, fish larger than that are rare, but not unheard of. There are both wild and stocked fish, and the farther you get away from the roads, the more wild fish you will find. In many cases natural barriers such as waterfalls prevent stocked and nonnative fish from gaining access to remote headwater streams.

By mid-May most rivers and streams in Monongahela National Forest have dropped enough to fish. While fish can be caught all season, the best fishing is usually between mid-May and late June. Fall fishing can be good as well but is very dependent on rain.

The sun sets over Seneca Creek, one of the larger streams in Monongahela National Forest. ZAK BART PHOTO

Brook trout in Monongahela National Forest feed primarily on insects. They also eat minnows, mostly sculpin and juvenile trout. Hatches start in April and run right into the fall and include mayflies, caddis, stoneflies, and midges. In the late spring and summer, trout feed on terrestrials such as ants, beetles, grasshoppers, and crickets.

West Virginia is a poor rural state. In fact, it's the third-poorest in the country behind Arkansas and Mississippi. It is home to coal, gas, and oil exploration. Monongahela National Forest is managed by the US Forest Service, not the National Park Service like nearby Shenandoah. This puts it at a much higher risk of resource exploitation than many other public lands. The latest threat to the area is fracking—toxic liquids used in the process have already been found in some of its waters.

In some ways West Virginia is a last frontier for wild brook trout. It lacks the fly-fishing infrastructure, shops, and guides that many other states have, making it hard to get accurate information. What we do know is that most of the wild brook trout habitat in the states lies within the borders of Monongahela National Forest. Finding it presents the biggest challenge, and that is part of what makes it so special.

Pisgah National Forest (NORTH CAROLINA)

Pisgah National Forest is located in western North Carolina. It consists of several segments, one of which lies just southwest of Asheville, one of the most popular destinations in the Southeast. Another is located just north and east of Black Mountain, a small but bustling community with a rich tourism history. The third starts on the eastern border of Great Smoky Mountains National Park and runs northeast along the Tennessee border.

Pisgah National Forest covers more than 510,000 acres and includes parts of the Blue Ridge Mountains and Great Balsam Mountains. It is rugged country with mountains over 6,000 feet above sea level, brawling freestone rivers and streams, cascading waterfalls, and heavily forested hills and valleys. There are hundreds of miles of trails and three designated wilderness areas: 11,786-acre Linville Gorge Wilderness, known as the Grand Canyon of North Carolina; 7,900-acre Middle Prong Wilderness; and 18,483-acre Shining Rock Wilderness.

Pisgah National Forest was established in 1916. It was one of the first national forests in the eastern United States, and parts of it included some of the first land purchases made by the US Forest Service under what was known as the Weeks Act. While already established in the West, this act gave Congress the authority to create national forests in the East. Boone National Forest was added to Pisgah in 1921, most of Unaka National Forest was added in 1936, and it was merged with the Croatan and Nantahala National Forests in 1954.

A remote, high-elevation, small native brook trout stream plummets hundreds of feet to the woods below in Pisgah National Forest. Upstream migration is blocked, and the resident brook trout are limited to barely a half mile of stream. DIANA MALLARD PHOTO

Modern American forestry has its roots in Pisgah National Forest. The Cradle of Forestry, located in the southern part of the forest, was home to the first forestry school in the United States. The brainchild of George Washington Vanderbilt II, creator of the famous Biltmore Estate, it operated in the late 1800s and early 1900s and played a major role in the creation of the US Forest Service.

Located entirely in North Carolina, Pisgah National Forest extends into 12 counties: Avery, Buncombe, Burke, Caldwell, Haywood, Henderson, Madison, McDowell, Mitchell, Transylvania, Watauga, and Yancey. It is under the jurisdiction of the US Forest Service, part of the US Department of Agriculture, and headquartered in Asheville with district offices in Pisgah Forest, Burnsville, and Nebo.

Two segments of Pisgah National Forest are bisected by the fabled Blue Ridge Parkway, the most visited site in the National Park System and a designated National Parkway. The parkway is roughly 470 miles long and links Great Smoky Mountains National Park with Shenandoah National Park. The world-famous Appalachian Trail borders much of the northern segment of the forest, with a small section crossing near Hot Springs.

Pisgah National Forest is home to over 46,500 acres of old-growth forest, much of which is located within Linville Gorge. Mount Mitchell, in Mount Mitchell State Park, lies just outside the national forest. At 6,684 feet it is the highest mountain east of the Mississippi River, and its summit can be reached via a road off the parkway.

Pisgah National Forest is well known for its hiking, backpacking, biking, and, of course, fishing. It is home to the headwaters of the Davidson River, the most famous trout fishery in North Carolina, as well as the headwaters of the Toe River. Bent Creek and Mills River, tributaries of the French Broad River, are also located in the forest, as are miles of lesser-known small streams that harbor healthy populations of wild native brook trout.

When it comes to brook trout in Pisgah National Forest, the small stream is king, and the smaller the better. Equally important is elevation, and in this case the higher the better. Most of the best brook trout habitat is located in headwater streams, and the farther up you go, the better it gets. Those that are off the beaten path and protected by natural barriers such as waterfalls offer the best chance of finding wild brook trout, and without competition from other fish.

The upper South Toe River northeast of Black Mountain drains the east slope of Mount Mitchell. This small, rugged freestone stream divides into even smaller streams as you move upriver, becoming all but impassable. The gradient is steep with pocketwater, glides, and small pools. While interspersed with wild rainbows and browns, the stream is home to a solid population of 4- to 6-inch wild brook trout, with the occasional larger fish. The farther upstream you go, the more brook trout you will encounter. Much of the stream is catch-and-release.

A stream I'm not comfortable naming—due to its small size and lack of protective regulations—off the Blue Ridge Parkway southwest of Asheville holds an isolated population of wild brook trout with no competing species. It begins at the confluence of three tiny streams too small to fish. From there it runs a mile or so before plummeting over a series of waterfalls and disappearing into the hollow below. From the edge of the falls you look down at the

A wild native brook trout from a small, remote headwater stream in Pisgah National Forest, my first from North Carolina. A short, light, glass fly rod was the perfect tool for the job. DIANA MALLARD PHOTO

The Blue Ridge Parkway offers great access to Pisgah National Forest's brook trout waters. It is also one of the most scenic roads I have ever driven. DIANA MALLARD PHOTO

tops of tall trees. The brook trout in this miniature ecosystem were as beautiful as any I have ever seen and ranged from 4 to 6 inches. While most of the fish were small, one fish, the lone occupant of the largest pool in the stream, went 8 inches.

While Pisgah National Forest is home to miles of wild brook trout streams, you have to work to find them. Local anglers protect these waters like miners guarding their claims. To find the best waters you will need to hire a guide or utilize topographic maps and a good pair of hiking boots. Look for waters that are located away from the road,

as they are less likely to have been compromised by nonnative fish. And look for contour lines on the map indicating steep drops that block nonnative fish from downstream.

Isolated populations of native trout such as those found in Pisgah National Forest are rare and unique. While the fish may be small, they can be amazingly picky, and flee at the first sign of intrusion into their little world. In some cases the fish you catch may be remnant pure-strain Southern Appalachian brook trout. And the dense laurel, moss-covered rocks, wildflowers, and salamanders make these streams some of the most beautiful places in the East.

Shenandoah National Park (VIRGINIA)

Shenandoah National Park is two and a half hours from bustling Washington, DC. It lies wholly within Virginia and encompasses part of the Blue Ridge Mountains. The park covers approximately 200,000 acres, roughly 80,000 of which, or almost 40 percent of the total, are designated as a wilderness area. The highest peak in the park is Hawksbill Mountain at just over 4,050 feet.

Shenandoah National Park was authorized by Congress in 1926. Work commenced in 1930 after an epic drought that resulted in significant crop loss in the area. The park was established in 1935. Prior to becoming a park the area was heavily farmed—you can still see remnants of old buildings in some places. The land was acquired by the State of Virginia via eminent domain and then deeded to the federal government for the creation of a national park.

While many families left the park voluntarily, some had to be forced out. Others simply refused to go and were allowed to remain in the park until they died of natural causes. The government also allowed elderly and disabled residents to stay until they passed. The last park resident to die was Annie Lee Bradley Shenk, who passed away in 1979 at the age of 92. Some of the park's earlier residents are buried at a cemetery near Hawksbill Mountain.

When the land was transferred from Virginia to the federal government, the state requested that African Americans be prohibited from accessing the park. The feds

Pete Evans fishing a small native brook trout freestone stream in Shenandoah National Park. Wet and green is the rule. KENNY NELSON PHOTO

Fishing in White Oak Canyon on White Oak Run. Best known for its hiking, waterfalls, and swimming holes, the stream also offers great fishing for wild native brook trout. TODD JANESKI PHOTO

protested, and they ended up agreeing to separate facilities for blacks and whites. Skyland Resort, Panorama Resort, and Swift Run Gap were restricted to whites only, while a separate facility for blacks was established at Lewis Mountain. The park did not become fully desegregated until 1950.

Shenandoah National Park is linked to Great Smoky Mountains National Park by the fabled Blue Ridge Parkway. It is bisected by the equally famous 105-mile Skyline Drive, a National Scenic Byway and National Historic Landmark. It is also home to just over 100 miles of the Appalachian Trail. The park's headquarters are located in Luray.

Home to black bear, bobcat, cottontail rabbit, coyote, gray fox, opossum, raccoon, red fox, and white-tailed deer, there have been reports, albeit unsubstantiated, of mountain lions in the more remote areas of Shenandoah National Park. There are also rattlesnakes and copperheads. Over 200 species of birds call the park home for at least part of the year. Roughly 30 are year-round residents including barred owls, red-tailed hawks, wild turkeys, and the recently reintroduced peregrine falcon. There are 32 species of fish, including brook trout.

Shenandoah National Park's Fisheries Management Plan has two objectives: "(1) to preserve and perpetuate native brook trout as a key component of the Park's aquatic ecosystems; and (2) to allow for recreational fishing on those Park streams that consistently produce adequate numbers of gamefish for maintaining population stability." This includes the removal of nonnative brown and rainbow trout from streams to lessen competition for food and space, predation, and potential hybridization.

Fly fishing is very popular in Shenandoah National Park, much of it done in pursuit of brook trout, the only trout that is native to the park. Stocking is limited, and most of the fish you encounter will be wild. The park's numerous waterfalls act as natural barriers against the proliferation of stocked and nonnative fish from the larger rivers outside the park, and the farther you push upstream, the less likely you are to encounter stocked or nonnative fish. In some cases you may be fishing for rare pure-strain brook trout.

Shenandoah National Park is home to approximately 90 small streams, most of which contain brook trout. This is the headwaters of the James, Potomac, Rapidan, Rappahannock, and Shenandoah river drainages. The Rapidan, featured in this book, was ranked #38 in the Trout Unlimited book *America's 100 Best Trout Streams*. Built in 1929 the restored Rapidan Camp located at its headwaters was a fishing retreat for President Herbert Hoover. Lesser-known waters such as the Conway River, Hughes River, Ivy Creek, Laurel Prong, Madison Run, Mill Prong, Rose River, Staunton Run, Thornton River, and White Oak Run are worth trying as well.

Brook trout in Shenandoah National Park run from 6 to 12 inches. They vary from 6 to 8 inches in headwater streams, 8 to 10 inches in larger streams, and 10 to 12 inches in the larger rivers. Brook trout up to 16 inches are possible.

Early spring brings hatches to the small streams and rivers of Shenandoah National Park. Quill Gordons can hatch as early as mid-March and last into April. As soon as they appear, brook trout will start actively feeding on the surface, hungry after a long hard winter. March Browns are the largest insect found on park waters and appear in April or May. A local favorite, Harry Murray's Mr. Rapidan, is a very effective imitation. Next are Sulphurs, which hatch in May and June. Caddis and stoneflies are present as well. By late spring trout start feeding on terrestrials such as ants, beetles, crickets, and inchworms.

Most headwater streams in Shenandoah National Park remain cold enough throughout the summer to support trout. Assuming there is enough water, they can offer season-long fishing. As a result of low clear water, and in some cases early season pressure, the brook trout can become particularly wary this time of year. Approaching the water from downstream, keeping a low profile, and wearing drab-colored clothing can mean the difference between success and failure.

Waters in Shenandoah National Park are open year-round to fishing. Only single-hook, single-point artificial lures are allowed; bait is strictly prohibited. The limit on brook trout is six fish with a 9-inch minimum length limit. Some waters are closed to fishing and others are restricted to catch-and-release. If you catch a brown trout, it is illegal to release it and it must be killed. Regulations change from year to year, and you will need to contact the park for a current list.

Many consider Shenandoah National Park home to the finest concentration of small wild brook trout streams in the Mid-Atlantic, a tough claim to refute. Growth rates are better than they are in many other places where brook trout are found. The approximately 500 miles of trails within the park offer access to many of its small streams. Angling traffic is generally light due to the remote nature of its streams and the fact that many of today's anglers are focused on big fish, regardless of species or origin, not small wild native fish.

Fly fishing for wild native brook trout in an undisturbed setting on public land is an all too rare experience. Shenandoah National Park is one of the few places you can still do so. That it is within a few hours' drive of several major cities is amazing. That the fish are beautiful wild native brook trout seals the deal.

White Mountain National Forest (NEW HAMPSHIRE/MAINE)

White Mountain National Forest is located in north-central New Hampshire and southwestern Maine, roughly two hours from Boston. It is arguably the most beautiful place in New England, and where I caught my first brook trout, and first fish on a fly. I spend more time fishing in this national forest than I do anywhere else except my home waters of Maine.

National forests are owned by the citizens of the United States. They are managed by the US Forest Service, part of the US Department of Agriculture. Management varies wildly from one to the next and can include land, water, and wildlife conservation, as well as logging, mining, livestock grazing, and recreation. As far as land management goes, White Mountain National Forest in New Hampshire and Maine is one of the better-managed national forests.

At 765,000 acres White Mountain National Forest is large by Northeast standards. Roughly 715,000 acres are located in New Hampshire and approximately 50,000 acres are in Maine. It was established in 1918 using land purchased from timber barons who took what they wanted and left a giant stump field behind. Since then it has evolved into what would be considered a relatively healthy woodland ecosystem.

White Mountain National Forest is nationally known for its hiking and skiing, both downhill and cross-country. It is serviced by the tourism towns of Gorham, Jackson, Lincoln, North Conway, and Twin Mountain in New Hampshire, as well as Bethel in Maine. The now defunct Old Man of the Mountain rock formation in Franconia Notch State Park is New Hampshire's official state emblem, the source of its state song, and the image on its state quarter.

A beautiful wild native brook trout from a tributary of the Beebe River in the southern end of the White Mountain National Forest. While the area is heavily stocked, wild fish can be found in most headwater streams.
DAVE PUSHEE PHOTO

The author's wife with a brook trout caught in a small river in White Mountain National Forest. It's not often she gets out from behind the camera to fish, so when she does she makes it count. BOB MALLARD PHOTO

White Mountain National Forest includes five formally designated wilderness areas: Dry River Wilderness (27,600 acres), Great Gulf Wilderness (5,650 acres), Pemigewasset Wilderness (46,000 acres), Sandwich Range Wilderness (35,000 acres), and Wild River Wilderness (61,400 acres). It is home to Mount Washington, the highest point in New England at 6,288 feet. The forest surrounds 6,000-acre Crawford Notch State Park and 6,700-acre Franconia Notch State Park. The famous Appalachian Trail runs through the national forest, as does the fabled Kancamagus Highway.

White Mountain National Forest is home to miles of streams and rivers and numerous lakes and ponds, many of which contain brook trout. This includes the headwaters of the Ammonoosuc, Israel, Moose, Pemigewasset, and Saco Rivers and their branches. Rivers such as the Cold, Dry, Ellis, Gale, Little, Lost, Mad, Peabody, Sawyer, Swift, Wild, Wildcat, and Zealand are entirely, or almost entirely, within the forest boundaries. While many of these rivers are stocked with brook trout, most hold wild brook trout in their upper reaches, and some throughout much of their length.

Lesser-known, but equally or more important, are the miles of small streams that contain populations of wild native brook trout, including Applebee, Cascade, Crawford, Deception, Downes, Drake, Eastman, Evans, Haystack, Mill, Oliverian, Nineteenmile, Sabbaday, and Smarts Brooks. Many others, some of which do not even appear on maps, contain wild brook trout as well. There are also numerous and ever-changing beaver ponds and flowages that contain wild brook trout.

Most rivers and streams in White Mountain National Forest are freestone. They originate high in the mountains and have steep gradients in the upper sections, then flatten out as they enter the valleys. They increase in size as they pick up tributaries. These streams are very susceptible to runoff from snowmelt and rain, and can go from mere trickles to raging torrents in just minutes. The streambeds are made up of granite boulders, fieldstone, gravel, or sand and change from one section to the next. Most are at least partially shaded, and many have a full canopy.

Some of the streams found in the southern extremities of White Mountain National Forest are meadow-like in appearance. They get their water from underground springs or lakes and ponds. These streams are less affected by runoff and tend to be fishable earlier than the high-gradient freestone streams.

There are numerous brook trout ponds in White Mountain National Forest. Profile Lake, which while technically in Franconia State Park, is a favorite of White Mountain anglers. So is Saco Lake, the headwaters of the Saco River. Both are stocked waters managed for fly fishing only. Basin Pond is a small stocked pond in a beautiful setting. Hike-in ponds, most of which are aerial stocked, include Black Pond, East Pond, Upper and Lower Greeley Ponds, Lonesome Lake, Mountain Pond, Sawyer and Little Sawyer Ponds, and Zealand Pond. Falls Pond is an easy walk from the Kancamagus Highway.

Two of just three formally designated Wild Trout Management ponds in New Hampshire, Ethan Pond and Shoal Pond, are located in White Mountain National Forest. They are not stocked, and are restricted to artificial lures and flies only and managed for catch-and-release.

Like most Northeast ponds, the typical White Mountain lake or pond has a mud bottom and slightly off-color water. Some, such as Sawyer, are clear with a sand bottom. In most cases the forest pushes right up to the shoreline, making some sort of watercraft necessary to fly-fish them effectively. These ponds remain locked under ice from December through early to mid-May.

The trail network in White Mountain National Forest is extensive and provides easy access to many of the remote streams and ponds. Other waters can be easily reached from Routes 2, 3, 16, 93, 112—the Kancamagus Highway—113, and 302. There are backcountry huts, lean-tos, and campgrounds maintained by the Appalachian Mountain Club (AMC) and US Forest Service that can be used to fish the more remote waters. Roadside campgrounds, cabins, and motels are plentiful as well.

Hatches start late and end early in White Mountain National Forest. They are not what you would call diverse or robust; the often-sterile water and scoured riverbeds are

Emily Bastian fishing a remote section of a small river in White Mountain National Forest. There's wild fish in the Wild River. BOB MALLARD PHOTO

not conducive to strong hatches. Spring and fall hatches include mayflies, caddis, stoneflies, and midges. The ponds get damselfly and dragonfly hatches in the summer. Summer also brings terrestrials. Fish feed on leeches and small minnows as well—primarily sculpin, dace, and juvenile trout. After rain, fish feed on worms washed into the stream.

White Mountain National Forest is one of my favorite places to fish. I consider it the most beautiful place in the Northeast. It is also one of the healthier forest ecosystems in the Northeast, with very little logging and development. Many of the roads into the interior have been blocked to vehicular traffic. Most importantly, many of the streams and rivers stay cool enough throughout the summer to provide reliable fishing.

Unfortunately, New Hampshire Fish & Game has failed to designate any river or stream in the White Mountain National Forest as a Wild Trout Management water. It is also stocking over wild native brook trout by rule, not exception, and managing most rivers and streams under general law regulations. This has placed a high level of stress on the wild native fish populations and kept many waters from reaching their potential.

When it comes to fly fishing for brook trout, White Mountain National Forest is a diamond in the rough. Managed for put-and-take fishing, the easily accessible rivers and streams are stocked to offset a level of harvest that is not conducive to maintaining wild fisheries. The Forest Service has taken a hands-off approach, leaving the state to manage the fishery. It's time it took a more active role in the conservation of this invaluable native fish resource and New Hampshire's official State Freshwater Fish.

OTHER
FISHERIES

There are some places, areas, types of waters, types of fish, and so forth that, while worthy of mention in regard to their brook trout fishing, just don't fit anywhere else in the book. They are not necessarily native or nonnative, a specific named water, a public land, or even a defined geographic area.

Some are geographic areas but not public lands, some are a type of lifeform found in a part of the country, some are a type of water found throughout native brook trout range, some are formal wild trout programs with waters spread across a broad geographic area, and in one case each a type of business and a town.

These other fisheries are, however, important to the brook trout angler and worthy of inclusion, and their omission would be a disservice to the reader.

Nothing says "brook trout" like a small New England freestone stream, especially in the fall. DIANA MALLARD PHOTO

Appalachian Trail

The Appalachian Trail runs from central Maine to northern Georgia. While known worldwide for its hiking and thru-hikers, it could just as easily be called the Appalachian Brook Trout Trail. Throughout much of its length, the AT, as it is known, is within a mile or less of a lake, pond, river, or stream that is home to brook trout. From beginning to end it runs along, crosses, and comes within striking distance of a whole lot of brook trout water.

The Appalachian Trail is approximately 2,200 miles long. Its highest point is Clingmans Dome in Tennessee, which at 6,643 feet is the third-highest point east of the Mississippi, and its lowest point is Bear Mountain State Park in New York at just 124 feet above sea level. It is a federally designated national scenic trail.

The Appalachian Trail was the brainchild of a forester named Benton MacKaye. He documented his idea in 1921, and his plan was made public in 1922 by Raymond H. Torrey of the *New York Evening Post*. The headline read, "A Great Trail from Maine to Georgia!"—and the rest is history. The first segment of the Appalachian Trail was completed in 1923 and ran from Bear Mountain to Arden, New York. In 1925 the Appalachian Trail Conference, now known as the Appalachian Trail Conservancy, was created to oversee the project. The Connecticut segment was mapped out between 1929 and 1933, and by 1937 the trail was extended to Sugarloaf Mountain in Maine.

The northern terminus of the Appalachian Trail is Mount Katahdin, the highest point in Maine, in Baxter State Park, and its southern terminus is Springer Mountain in Georgia. The southern end was originally Mount Oglethorpe, located roughly 14 miles northeast of Springer Mountain, but was moved in the late 1950s due to encroaching development.

One of many backcountry ponds within striking distance of the Appalachian Trail in New Hampshire. We landed several brook trout over 12 inches, including one that went 15 inches. DIANA MALLARD PHOTO

Fording a remote stream near the Appalachian Trail in New Hampshire. We caught close to a hundred wild native brook trout in two days. EMILY BASTIAN PHOTO

Baxter State Park is home to myriad native brook trout populations and is featured in this book. The Little Amicalola Creek drainage located just southwest of Springer Mountain is said to hold the southernmost population of native brook trout in the world. So as far as brook trout go, the Appalachian Trail begins and ends with a bang.

Along with Maine and Georgia, the Appalachian Trail passes through New Hampshire, Vermont, Massachusetts, Connecticut, New York, New Jersey, Pennsylvania, Maryland, West Virginia, Virginia, Tennessee, and North Carolina. There are 500 miles of trail in Virginia, 281 in Maine, 229 in Pennsylvania, 161 in New Hampshire, 150 in Vermont, 90 in Massachusetts, 88 in New York and North Carolina, 75 in Georgia, 72 in New Jersey, 71 in Tennessee, 52 in Connecticut, 41 in Maryland, and 4 in West Virginia.

Roughly 99 percent of the Appalachian Trail is on public land. This includes Baxter State Park, White Mountain National Forest, Green Mountain National Forest, Delaware Water Gap National Recreation Area, Shenandoah National Park, George Washington National Forest, Jefferson National Forest, Cherokee National Forest, Pisgah National Forest, Great Smoky Mountains National Park, and Chattahoochee National Forest.

The Appalachian Trail is home to thousands of species of plants and animals, over 2,000 of which are classified as rare, threatened, or endangered. There is old-growth forest at Sages Ravine on the Massachusetts-Connecticut border, the Hopper near Mount Greylock in Massachusetts, and The Hermitage near Gulf Hagas in Maine. It is home to bear, beaver, bobcat, coyote, deer, elk, fisher, lynx, moose, otter, and wild boar, with reports of mountain lion. There are eagles, grouse, loons, and wild turkeys. Rattlesnakes and copperheads are present as well.

There are more than 250 campsites and shelters along the Appalachian Trail. This includes tent sites, platforms, lean-tos, cabins, and lodges. Facilities are never more than a day hike apart, and most are near a water source. Facilities usually include some sort of toilet, and many have bear-proof food storage containers. The Appalachian Mountain Club (AMC) maintains eight remote huts in New Hampshire's White Mountains, which offer lodging and meals. There are also full-service facilities that can be reached by vehicle.

Some of the towns that provide easy access to sections of the Appalachian Trail that offer good brook trout fishing are Millinocket, Greenville, and Rangeley in Maine; North Conway and Lincoln in New Hampshire; Manchester in Vermont; Front Royal and Waynesboro in Virginia; Erwin and Gatlinburg in Tennessee; Hot Springs and Cherokee in North Carolina; and Blue Ridge and Helen in Georgia.

The author relaxing after fishing for wild native brook trout nearly 2,000 miles from home yet still on the Appalachian Trail in Great Smoky Mountains National Park. DIANA MALLARD PHOTO

The Appalachian Trail sees a lot of traffic. Those who hike the entire length in a single season are referred to as thru-hikers. Most start in Georgia and work north to Maine to allow for enough time to complete the journey. Others complete the length over a period of years and are called section-hikers. There are also those who day hike or do overnights, too. What is oddly missing from the mix is anglers, and that is part of the allure. While some of the better-known waters close to the road get pressure, many others see very few anglers.

Brook trout are native to the entire Appalachian Trail corridor. While some of the high-elevation ponds were barren of fish, and other waters too warm for brook trout, many waters held native populations. Some waters are stocked, some have been stocked in the past, and others may have received stocked fish from another source. However, some have never been stocked and are home to genetically pure fish, including rare Southern Appalachian strain brook trout.

Most of the best brook trout river and stream fishing along the Appalachian Trail is found in Maine, New Hampshire, Virginia, Tennessee, North Carolina, and Georgia. While most are not well known, the Kennebec River in Maine and the Rapidan River in Virginia are nationally known brook trout fisheries and featured in this book. Others such as the West Branch Pleasant River and Bemis Brook in Maine and the Ellis River in New Hampshire are regionally known for their brook trout fishing.

The best brook trout stillwaters on the Appalachian Trail are found in Maine and New Hampshire. Speck Pond in Grafton Notch in Maine is the highest-elevation brook trout pond in the state. Ethan Pond in Crawford Notch State Park is one of just three formally designated Wild Trout Management ponds in New Hampshire. Pierce Pond in Maine is covered in this book. Rainbow Lake and Bald Mountain Pond in Maine have brook trout as well as rare Arctic charr.

While many are not aware of it, the Appalachian Trail is a great place to fly-fish for brook trout. The infrastructure is better than you might expect and includes well-maintained and well-marked trails, as well as a variety of lodging options. There are also gateway towns you can stay in. The waters can be fished on a day-use basis or as part of a multiday trip. What is most amazing is that it gets as little fishing pressure as it does.

Beaver Ponds

With the exception of small freestone streams, no type of aquatic habitat is more identified with brook trout than beaver ponds. In areas such as interior Maine, they are more important to the brook trout angler than freestone streams, which are often nearly unfishable due to downed timber and dense streamside vegetation.

The image of brook trout sipping insects off the surface of a dead-tree-dotted beaver pond is burned into the minds of many anglers. Located anywhere brook trout and beavers coexist, regardless of the origin of either, these unique aquatic micro-environments can be found throughout most of native brook trout range, as well as in much of the rest of the country.

The North American beaver, *Castor canadensis*, is native to much of the United States and Canada. The second-largest rodent in the world after the South American capybara, they are semiaquatic, herbivorous, and primarily, but not exclusively, nocturnal. Known for their dams, lodges, and canals, beavers are nature's "engineers," altering their habitat more than any other animal.

Once numbering over 60 million, North America's beaver population is said to be just one-tenth that today. The precipitous decline can be attributed to extensive hunting and trapping for fur, perfume, medicine, and to prevent beavers from damaging trees and flooding roads and property. Their fur is prized for use in hats, including the iconic cowboy hat. Today beavers have repopulated much of their historic range, even rebounding to nuisance status in some areas.

Beavers are known for their oversized incisors and paddle-shaped tails. Their hind feet are webbed; their front feet are not. Their eyes, ears, and nostrils are sealed to facilitate their semiaquatic lifestyle. They have a thick layer of fat that keeps them warm even in the coldest of weather. Their coat is made up of a mix of long, coarse guard hair and short, fine hair. They secrete oil that helps waterproof their fur.

Adult beavers can weigh over 50 pounds, with females being as large as males, an anomaly in the animal world. They can live almost 25 years. Beavers are herbivores and eat mostly wood, including alder, ash, aspen, beech, birch,

There are hundreds of beaver ponds in Maine, some of which never see an angler. Note the dark color of the fish resulting from life in heavily tannic water. DIANA MALLARD PHOTO

The author working a rising brook trout among the standing dead trees in a small New Hampshire beaver pond. While older beaver ponds are often muddy due to silt buildup, newer ones often have hard bottoms and can sometimes be waded. DIANA MALLARD PHOTO

cherry, cottonwood, maple, oak, and willow, and occasionally pine and spruce. They also eat aquatic vegetation such as cattails, pondweed, sedges, and water lilies. They do not eat fish, and that's good news for brook trout.

Beavers are very territorial and well known for their startling tail slaps when they feel that they, their kits, or their lodge or dam are threatened. This warns other beavers in the area, which may come to investigate. More determined individuals can ruin your fishing by circling around, muddying the water, slapping their tails incessantly, and otherwise doing their best to put the fish down. Beavers are strong swimmers and can stay underwater for up to 15 minutes. Some will move defiantly toward you only to go under when they are unnervingly close, leaving you to wonder where they will reappear and what they will do when they do.

While rare, beavers can and do bite humans. When they do they can inflict serious injuries, including life-threatening bleeding. Beavers are also known to carry rabies, which can trigger aggressive behavior. I found a report from 2013 of a 60-year-old fisherman in Europe who died when a beaver severed an artery in his leg. Beaver attacks have been reported in Nova Scotia, Pennsylvania, and Virginia as well, and a beaver in Massachusetts bit a raft, putting a hole in it.

Having evolved over thousands of years, the relationship between beavers and brook trout is complex and often misunderstood. Their immediate impact on brook trout can be positive or negative but is often temporary. Sometimes, however, the impacts span generations and change from one year to the next.

So-called beaver ponds are created when beavers dam up streams. They make dams out of rocks, mud, and branches, cutting entire trees down with their teeth to get the latter. The ponds created by these dams serve as locations for their homes, aptly named beaver houses or lodges, as well as protective refuge.

Beaver dams run from a few feet long to hundreds of feet. The longest documented beaver dam is in Wood Buffalo National Park in Alberta, Canada, and measures roughly 2,800 feet long. The dam was built sometime after 1975 according to satellite photographs and was the result of linking two older dams. Google Earth images show that new dams are being built that could increase its length even more. A beaver dam of nearly 2,150 feet long, almost 15 feet high, and over 20 feet thick was documented in Three Forks, Montana.

When beavers are actively maintaining a dam, it gets longer and higher, backing up more water behind it. Breaches in dams are sensed by the beavers due to changes in water level and are addressed as soon as they feel safe doing so, usually after dark. However, as soon as beavers stop maintaining a dam, it begins to deteriorate. High water flows over the dam, eroding it, and dropping the water level of the pond.

Whether a beaver pond lasts months, years, or even decades has a lot to do with local weather patterns and the area's ability to absorb runoff from rain and snowmelt. In high-gradient areas with heavy runoff and limited buffering capacity, many beaver dams get washed out in the spring. In low-gradient areas, areas with limited snowpack, and those with an ability to absorb runoff, they can last for decades.

The positive impacts beavers have on brook trout include creating critical deep-water habitat and thermal refuge used during periods of drought and warm weather. I have seen times when practically every brook trout in a section of stream had moved into a beaver pond to escape low or warm water. They create winter refuge in streams that would otherwise freeze nearly solid as well.

While not all beaver ponds contain brook trout (if the stream does not, the pond will not), those that do allow brook trout to attain sizes and densities not normally seen in small-stream habitat. And while they can silt up and submerge brook trout spawning habitat under stagnant water, they provide important woody debris needed for spawning downstream and create rearing habitat for juvenile fish.

Beaver ponds can also increase nutrients and enhance forage, especially insects. They help reduce flooding, decrease erosion, and increase stream flow during dry periods by storing water and raising groundwater tables. They are also said to help remove sediments and pollutants such as herbicides and pesticides from waterways.

Beavers can negatively affect brook trout as well, albeit usually temporarily. Beaver dams can block fish passage, isolate populations, cause siltation, and increase predation by mammal and avian predators. As they dry up they can become dangerously, and even fatally, warm. While some problem dams last for only a few years, some, especially those in low-gradient areas, can remain in place for decades. And while blamed for giardiasis, or the dreaded "beaver fever," the parasite that causes the malady, *Giardia lamblia*, is carried by birds, humans, and other animals as well as beavers.

Beaver ponds are considered by many anglers to be the Holy Grail of brook trout fishing. Finding a previously undiscovered beaver pond full of outsized brook trout is like winning the lottery. Once discovered, the location of a beaver pond is guarded like Jack Daniels guards its bourbon recipe. Writing a book about brook trout and not talking about beaver ponds would be like writing about baseball parks and not talking about Yankee Stadium.

From an angling standpoint, beavers can create some of the finest backcountry fly fishing you will ever encounter. I have caught brook trout up to 16 inches in tiny beaver ponds on streams that rarely produced fish over 6 inches. I have caught dozens of small brookies in a section of stream that prior to impounding would have yielded just a few fish. For years my home water was a meadow stream with a series of small beaver ponds in its headwaters. Some of the dams were decades old, and others came and went from one year to the next. The farther you pushed upstream, the better the fishing got. The biggest brook trout I ever caught there was 14 inches and taken from a pool-sized rectangular pond created by three converging beaver dams.

I once stopped to fish a roadside beaver pond that had been blocked to vehicular traffic for a couple of years, the gate being opened just days before. Its roadside location

A typical well-fed beaver pond brook trout. Note the doughnut-style float tube in the background; it's a great way to fish deeper water and places with a muddy bottom. DIANA MALLARD PHOTO

resulted in a high level of angler exploitation, limiting it to just freshly stocked fish and a few small wild fish. I caught 10 beautifully colored, deep-bellied 12-inch brook trout, a testimony to how fertile, yet easily exploited, these waters can be.

Fishing beaver ponds is not easy. They are often hard to find and hard to get into when you do. The area surrounding beaver ponds is often wet, rutted, and littered with hummocks, brush, and other things that make getting around difficult. The standing dead trees and submerged logs and branches present a challenge to the fly fisher, as they are a major source of snags. And rarely do you have enough room to get a good backcast.

Most beaver ponds are either too muddy or too deep to wade. Casting from the shore is difficult and limiting. The best way to fish beaver ponds is with a doughnut-style float tube. Add waders and rubber lug–sole boots sans fins, and off you go walking when you can and kicking when you can't. Due to the size of these waters, you can't get blown off course and unable to kick your way back.

When I was young we found most beaver ponds by accident, usually while hiking, hunting, or canoeing. While we used topographic maps to identify likely spots, we were wrong more often than we were right. Today's fly fisher has the benefit of tools like Google Earth that can be used to scan the countryside looking for these brook trout utopias.

Using data culled from these maps and a handheld GPS, waters that would have been difficult to find just a decade or so ago are easy to find today.

Beaver ponds can appear out of nowhere and disappear just as quickly. They are at their best a year or two after being formed, and most do not hold up for long due to angler exploitation or Mother Nature. By the time a visible trail is cut to a beaver pond, it is usually too late, at least for fishing.

Beaver ponds are beautiful and bountiful. They are rich in aquatic, mammalian, and avian life. They are home to fish, frogs, salamanders, turtles, waterfowl, wading birds, muskrat, otter, mink, and beaver, and visited by moose, deer, and bear. Beaver ponds are small, quiet, and a great way to enjoy a day of fishing for brook trout.

Beaver ponds have a certain mystique to them. The fish are often larger than those found in natural ponds of similar size. Unfortunately, as part of a stream, beaver ponds rarely have the benefit of protective regulations. This makes them easy to exploit, and when that happens it affects everything involved, including us, as once the trout are gone they can take years to repopulate. Knowing that what you just found is most likely temporary, there is a sense of urgency that keeps bringing you back to a beaver pond with brook trout, recognizing that while it is great today, it most likely won't last forever.

Coaster Brook Trout

The current world-record brook trout was a coaster caught from the Nipigon River in Ontario. Coasters are a potamodromous form of brook trout that spend part of their life in the waters of the upper Great Lakes. Once plentiful and widespread, coaster numbers have been greatly reduced as a result of dams, angler exploitation, logging, and the introduction of nonnative fish. Many populations have been lost.

Coasters got their name from their propensity for cruising the coastline of the lakes. They are sometimes referred to as "nearshore" fish due to the fact that they do not venture too far from the shore. They are also known as "salmon trout" and "rock trout," the former due to their size, the latter because they were often caught in areas where rocks had slid into the lake from shoreline cliffs.

Coasters were historically found in Lake Huron, Lake Michigan, and Lake Superior. They are said to have utilized over 50 streams along the Michigan, Minnesota, and Wisconsin shore of Lake Superior alone. The highest concentrations, and largest fish, were found on the north shore of Superior. Coasters have been extirpated from Lake Huron and Lake Michigan, and while efforts are under way to restore them, they are now extant in Lake Superior only.

Most of Lake Superior's approximately 2,725 miles of shoreline and tributary streams once supported fishable populations of coasters. It is said that spawning runs occur in only three or four streams in the United States side of the lake today. They are known to spawn in Salmon Trout River in the Upper Peninsula of Michigan, and Big and Little Siskiwit Rivers on Isle Royale.

In Canada, coasters historically occurred in approximately 60 Lake Superior tributaries. It is said that spawning runs remain in just a few Canadian streams today. There are also coasters in Lake Nipigon, but they too are reported to have declined by up to 75 percent compared to the early 1900s. Most of the fish caught in Canada come from Nipigon Bay. They spawn in the Cypress, Little Cypress, and Jackpine Rivers, as well as Dublin Creek.

Few fish have been studied as much as coasters. Federal agencies from Canada and the United States and several state and provincial agencies have done exhaustive studies on coasters. While much is known about their habits and habitat, there are still many mysteries as to what coasters do and why. The biggest unknown is whether it is a genetic trigger or simply opportunity that makes these fish take advantage of the inshore large-lake habitat.

A large coaster from the Canadian side of Lake Superior. Coasters are one of the most studied lifeforms of brook trout in the world. NICHOLAS LAFERRIERE PHOTO

145

Not all brook trout born in Lake Superior tributaries, or even those in the same tributary, venture out into the lake to become coasters. In some cases fish leave the stream and head for the lake a year or two after they are born. In other cases, including siblings of fish that left the stream for the lake, they remain in the stream their entire life. Why this happens is not completely understood. Some coasters demonstrate adfluvial behavior, migrating between Lake Superior and tributaries to spawn. Others are reported to be lacustrine, spending their entire lives, including spawning, in the lake.

Coasters reach sexual maturity at a later age and live longer than most other forms of brook trout. They grow large feeding on the abundant baitfish found in Lake Superior. Coasters also have a longer growing season, and an easier life, than brook trout that remain in their natal streams.

While in the lake coasters can develop an almost silvery color similar to that of salters, their East Coast cousin. This unique coloration is most likely a result of habitat and forage. When they enter the rivers and streams, or shallows, in the fall to spawn, they develop a coloration like that of any other brook trout.

Coasters spawn in September and October. They utilize the same type of spawning habitat as other brook trout. Those that utilize streams for spawning stage at the mouths of tributaries until the conditions are right for their upstream migration. Many experts feel that a combination of water temperature and flow rate triggers this movement.

World-renowned for their large size, anglers came from all over to ply the waters of Superior in search of the brook trout of a lifetime. Coasters were to the Great Lakes region what salters were to the Atlantic coast. They came during spawning season when the fish were easy to target. Angling was practically unregulated, and fish said to average over 4 pounds were harvested by the hundreds by recreational anglers. They were also targeted by commercial fisherman.

By the mid-1800s coaster numbers began to plummet. Habitat degradation resulting from logging, agriculture, and development, as well as blocked fish passage caused by dams aided the decline. Making matters worse was increased competition from introduced species such as lamprey eels. Industrial and municipal pollution contributed as well. By the mid-1900s the population had been reduced to what was referred to as remnant.

Like most highly piscivorous fish, coasters tend to look like predators, especially the males.
NICHOLAS LAFERRIERE PHOTO

As coaster numbers dropped, pressure was put on state fish and game departments to stock fish. During the 1900s, millions of brook trout were stocked in Lake Superior and its tributaries. While these fish provided some level of put-and-take angling, they did not result in the restoration of self-sustaining populations. This led to the stocking of more hardy fish such as brown trout and rainbow trout, which only made the situation worse.

Today agencies in the United States and Canada are working to restore coasters. The goal is to restore them to as many streams as possible. Efforts include restricting harvest, restoring habitat, and removing impediments to upstream migrations such as dams, culverts, and even beaver dams.

While stocking was once the emphasis of restoration efforts, focus has shifted to habitat in recent years. Stream habitat is the primary limiting factor: If coasters can't get into the streams to spawn, or find suitable spawning habitat once there, it has a negative effect on the overall population. And their progeny must be able to make it back to the lake after hatching.

We are also protecting the coasters themselves. There is a 1-fish, 20-inch minimum length limit on coasters in Minnesota, and a 22-inch minimum length limit in Canada. Wisconsin established an experimental no-kill brook trout regulation on Graveyard Creek, Whittlesey Creek, and the Bark River, as well as a 1-fish, 20-inch minimum size limit on Lake Superior.

While most coasters caught are in the 1- to 3-pound range, fish approaching 10 pounds are always possible. As fish that spend much of their lives in a lake, coasters rely heavily on minnows for forage. As a result they are best targeted with streamers that represent baitfish, and relatively large ones. Coasters will also feed on the surface during a hatch. They can be caught with heavy trout or light salmon tackle. Sinking and sinking tip lines are a good idea, as coasters often feed subsurface.

Isle Royale National Park may be the best place to catch coaster brook trout. The fish here are protected by strict catch-and-release regulations. They are also believed to be native, meaning they were never fully extirpated. Another

Unlike salters, which can be pale in color, coaster brook trout are as beautiful as any brook trout you will find.
NICHOLAS LAFERRIERE PHOTO

option is the Salmon Trout River in Michigan. The Hurricane River in Pictured Rocks National Lakeshore in Michigan is also worth trying. Other waters where you could encounter coasters are Fish Creek, Sioux River, Pikes Creek, Cranberry River, and Flag River. The Bark River, Graveyard Creek, and Whittlesey Creek are also purported to hold coasters; all are managed for catch-and-release.

Lake Superior and the surrounding area is a spectacularly beautiful place. In some places the lake resembles Yellowstone Lake, the largest alpine lake in the country. In others it looks like the Pacific Northwest or the coast of Maine. Its rugged cliffs, rock islands, forest-lined shores, and sand beaches make you think you are somewhere far more exotic than where you actually are. That there are wild native brook trout measured in pounds makes it all the more special, and worth preserving.

Freestone Streams

Small freestone streams are what most people envision when they think of brook trout. In many parts of the country, they are the only places left where wild native brook trout are still extant. Their namesake water type, there are more miles of brook-trout-holding freestone "brooks" than there are all other water types put together.

The term *freestone stream* denotes a type of habitat—not just aesthetically, but biologically, too. There are streams with freestone-like physical characteristics that are spring creeks, or limestone creeks as they are called in the East, or even tailwaters. What I am talking about here are the small natural, free-flowing, boulder-strewn headwaters that get their water primarily from rain and snowmelt, with a small amount of groundwater influence.

Freestone streams can be streams, brooks, creeks, and even rivers, and there is no formal definition of what

constitutes what. While streams, brooks, and creeks are often smaller than rivers, this is not always the case. There are many rivers that are smaller than some streams, especially in their headwaters. And what would normally be called a stream in one part of the country would be called a river in another. In the Rocky Mountains most freestone streams are called creeks. In New Hampshire and Vermont most are called brooks, and in Maine, streams or brooks. And the while the term *creek* is usually only applied to coastal streams in New England, it is applied to interior waters in Pennsylvania, New York, and parts of Appalachia.

Freestone streams are by definition seasonally adjusted. They get their water from an inconsistent and somewhat unpredictable supply. In the summer and fall most freestone streams get warm and low, only changing after

Emily Bastian sitting down to change her fly on a small, remote freestone stream in north-central New Hampshire. Maybe it's the uniformity of the fish that allows you to relax a bit more when fishing small streams, or maybe it's just the surroundings. BOB MALLARD PHOTO

An impassable waterfall on a freestone stream in New Hampshire. Having fished the stream for 40 years, I thought I had seen every inch of it until I came upon this. The rugged topography is part of what makes freestone streams so special. BOB MALLARD PHOTO

rainfall and then only temporarily. Unless influenced by a high percent of groundwater, freestone streams do not cool down again until late summer. And even then they are often still low and will remain so until spring runoff.

The streambed in freestone streams is made up of loose gravel, rocks, and boulders. The rocks and boulders are smoothed and rounded by eons of movement and water flowing over them. They create micro-currents, promote oxygen, and provide refuge for brook trout. While often without the long in-stream vegetation found in meadow streams and rivers, freestone streams do have moss-like and other rock-anchored short vegetation.

The pH levels in freestone streams can bounce up and down with changes in flow caused by rain and snowmelt. This is because streams take on the chemical characteristics of what they flow over and what flows into them. The slightly acidic, often infertile, but highly oxygenated water creates a unique environment where only certain species can prosper, brook trout being one of them.

While generally cool enough to sustain brook trout year-round in their upper reaches, freestone streams tend to widen, lose their canopy, and warm in their lower reaches. The denuded rocky streambeds are often only partially covered in water during summer months, causing warming

due to exposure to the sun and heating of the rocks. This causes brook trout to push their way upstream in search of thermal refuge.

As brook trout move into narrower, shallower water, they become more vulnerable to angler exploitation. And while avian predation may lessen due to canopy that makes it harder for them to work, other types of predation, mostly smaller mammals, increases. Forage can become less available as well due to infertile conditions and increased trout biomass. But the loss of aquatic insects is somewhat offset by an increase in terrestrials.

Small freestone streams are what many devout brook trout fishers fish most often. They require more energy to fish than most other types of water, as you often must walk to get to them and, once there, cover a lot of ground to find fish. Small-stream anglers rarely mention their favorite waters by name and probably fish alone more than any other type of angler.

Freestone streams, at least the small ones most frequented by brook trout fishers, rarely produce large fish. From a pure fishing standpoint, they are more about quantity than quality. The fish are rarely difficult to catch as they can be recklessly opportunistic, slashing at the same fly multiple times before getting hooked. Long casts,

Jeff Moore fishing a small hike-in freestone stream in the White Mountain National Forest in New Hampshire. Note the summer abundance of vegetation. BOB MALLARD PHOTO

delicate presentations, mending, and match-the-hatch or life-stage are rarely necessary.

I learned about wild brook trout on freestone streams, and they are some of my favorite places to fish even today. In fact, by early summer they become my primary destination. The surrounding environs are rugged, remote, and beautiful. The fishing is active and aerobic, and physically and mentally rewarding. And the fish are beautiful, like miniature versions of their large cousins found in Labrador, Quebec, and parts of Maine.

Short casts, roll-casts, bow-and-arrow casts, and dapping are the rule, and small targets and low tight canopy the biggest challenge. It's not unusual to cover a mile or more of water, and doing so one step at a time while traversing back and forth across the stream takes far longer than many think. I like to fish from one vehicle to another because I can cover more water and not have to backtrack.

The key to truly enjoying small freestone stream fishing is to gear down to the size of the water and fish you will encounter. Short, light-line, slow-action rods are best, including glass, bamboo, and graphite, which by today's standards would be considered old fashioned. Tenkara rods have developed a following on small freestone streams as well.

Don't be afraid to explore when fishing small freestone streams. Check the temperature of each tributary, as there are times when brook trout push up into these tiny rivulets seeking thermal refuge. If it is noticeably cooler, walk in a bit to see if there are any fish in it. Walk far enough and you may discover a previously undetected beaver pond, even on a stream you know well.

These tiny ribbons of cold and usually clear water running through what is often dense forest are ecologically unique and, while somewhat lacking in aquatic biodiversity, home to "specialists" like brook trout. They also serve as corridors and water sources for other woodland fauna such as deer, moose, bear, coyote, fisher, and raccoon. The surrounding woodlands are home to grouse, turkeys, owls, hawks, woodpeckers, and songbirds.

Small freestone streams have a certain charm to them. Unlike more challenging and temperamental types of water, I rarely get skunked on small freestone streams, and there are times I catch so many fish I lose count. At the end of the day I feel fulfilled, alive, and a good kind of tired, a feeling you only get from having done something strenuous. For me, small-stream fishing is what keeps me fit, a form of exercise without giving up fishing time to get it.

Most importantly, small freestone streams are places you can go and spend a day fly fishing for wild native brook trout in a natural setting without seeing another soul, unless that soul came with you. They are places you can share with people you trust to treat the resource as you do, taking nothing out but memories and leaving nothing behind but boot tracks.

Labrador

Canada has far more, and much bigger, wild native brook trout than the United States. This is partly due to the amount of area conducive to brook trout, and partly due to the fact that it is far less developed. While I could write about several provinces and numerous specific waters, most people reading this book will never get there. Instead I thought I'd write about the most famous brook trout destination in the world, Labrador.

Labrador is the mainland section of the Canadian province of Newfoundland and Labrador. It is separated from the island of Newfoundland by the Strait of Belle Isle and is the largest and northernmost section in the Atlantic coast region of Canada. It is bordered by the Canadian province of Quebec and the Atlantic Ocean. While Labrador represents over 70 percent of the Newfoundland and Labrador

province geographically, it has less than 10 percent of the population. The area is home to the Northern Inuit of Nunatsiavut, the Southern Inuit-Métis of Nunatukavut, and the Innu tribes.

Labrador is also home to the Canadian Forces Base Goose Bay air force base. This base, code-named Alkali at the time, was an important airport in the early stages of World War II. Canadian, US, and British air forces all had war planes here. It was also the site of the first US nuclear weapons in Canada.

Labrador is known world-wide for its giant brook trout, with fish over 10 pounds caught. It is home to the highest concentration of trophy wild native brook trout on earth. Nowhere does the fly fisher have a better chance of catching the fish of a lifetime than in Labrador. Places

Tom Boyd with a 7.5-pound brookie from the Penalty Box hole on the Minipi River. The Minipi system is arguably the finest native brook trout watershed in the world. TOM BOYD PHOTO

like Andre Lake, Atikonak Lake, Awesome Lake, Quartzite River, Comeback River, Eagle River, Flowers River, Igloo Lake, McKenzie River, the Minipi region, and Osprey Lake put up brook trout measured in pounds, not inches.

I first went to Labrador 15 or so years ago. We stayed at Little Minipi Lodge, a small spartan camp deep in the backcountry. While flying in from Goose Bay, I was captivated by the large swaths of barren tundra and seemingly endless water, much of which was nameless. Every direction you looked was undeveloped as far as the eye could see. There were no signs of life anywhere beyond the occasional floatplane off in the distance.

When we landed and I took a quick walk around to stretch my legs, I was fascinated with the dense, stunted, and nearly impenetrable spruce forest with moss up to my knees, the result of never having been logged. If you walked out of sight of the trail and turned around a few times, it was difficult to ascertain which way was out. The flat landscape was sans visible landmarks, and one could easily get lost and maybe never find his or her way out.

While we flew over miles of game trails and saw several moose from the air, there was an amazing and odd lack of wildlife, and other than small birds and a pine marten that hung around camp eating scraps of food from the kitchen and whatever the guests threw for it, all I saw was one caribou track on a small spit of sand along a lake. One evening I heard wolves howling in the distance, but that was it.

After unloading my gear and moving into our room, I approached the guides to see if anyone was willing to take me out, as Sunday was turnover day and the fishing didn't start until Monday. One of the guides agreed to do so, probably bored with helping guests move into their rooms, and off we went in what I felt was a dangerously undersized square-stern canoe for the conditions. Donned in a rubber rain suit and hip boots and armed with a spool of 12-pound-test Maxima tippet, my guide motored along the edge of the downstream lake looking for rising fish. As the guide stared out like a pirate captain looking for a ship to rob, he suddenly shut down the motor and drifted into a flat cove, where I saw a disturbance on the water followed by a rather large fish taking a Green Drake off the surface. It resurfaced 6 feet farther away and then again 6 feet beyond that. I stood in the canoe, stripped out some line, and dropped a fly in the direction the fish was heading and 6 feet beyond where it last surfaced. Seconds later, and within less than an hour of arrival, I landed the largest brook trout of my life, a fish weighing 5.5 pounds.

Over the course of the next five days, while the numbers were low, roughly two to five fish a day, the fish we did catch were big. In fact, based on a tally the last night we were there, they averaged an amazing 5 pounds. My largest brook trout was over 7 pounds and caught on a dry fly, and two fish caught by the group broke 8 pounds, including one I pointed out to our guide and let my friend cast to.

A mouse-eating Labrador brook trout from the Minipi River. Labrador brook trout get big on a diet that includes small rodents. TOM BOYD PHOTO

A male brook trout from Labrador in its fall spawning glory. As fish go, it doesn't get much more impressive than a fall brook trout. TOM BOYD PHOTO

The fish came oddly easy in the lakes if you could get a fly where it needed to be. On the river, however, the fish were picky and not easy to fool.

We fished large lakes, concentrating mostly on small coves, as well as thoroughfares, and made a couple of trips down to the river, the name of which escapes me, which required an hour boat ride followed by a 20-minute walk. The guides packed lunches and let each other know where they were going and when they planned to return to lessen the likelihood of having someone out overnight due to engine failure. They were great outdoorsmen, but somewhat disinterested anglers.

The biting bugs—blackflies—were by far the worst I have ever seen, and I live in Maine. We lived in mesh bug jackets, and I cut a hole in the facemask of mine so I could smoke a cigar, which kept things to a dull roar. The landscape was interesting and unique, but by no means breathtaking. But the brook trout were incredible and beautiful, and a sad reminder of what Maine once had but lost.

Anyone who fashions themselves a brook trout aficionado needs to go to Labrador, even if it is just once. The fish are huge and beautiful, and the surroundings are undisturbed and wild. The fish are also wild, and genetically pure. And there are no stocked fish or nonnative fish to sort through. Nonresidents must hire a guide, and the best way to fish Labrador is out of a lodge. Labrador is the perfect brook trout ecosystem, and a living laboratory for brook trout management, as most camps have a strict catch-and-release policy.

Maine Fly-Fishing-Only Brook Trout Lakes and Ponds

There are roughly 1,200 lakes and ponds in Maine classified as Principal Fisheries for brook trout by the Department of Inland Fisheries and Wildlife, meaning you have a good chance of catching brook trout there. Approximately 200 of these are restricted to fly fishing only, which in Maine means casting—trolling is not allowed. Flies must be single-hook and single-point, and only two flies can be used at a time. This represents the largest inventory of fly-fishing-only stillwaters east of the Mississippi, and possibly in the country.

While Maine's fly-fishing-only lakes and ponds make up roughly 17 percent of the Principal Brook Trout Fisheries, they represent just 3 percent of the total acreage. The average size is roughly 60 acres, with approximately 50 percent less than 25 acres. Roughly 28 percent are between 25 and 50 acres, 11 percent between 51 and 100 acres, 7 percent between 101 and 250 acres, 2 percent between 251 and 500 acres, one between 501 and 1,000 acres, and two larger than 1,000 acres. Moose Bog is the smallest at less than an acre; the largest is Kennebago Lake at 1,700 acres, said to be the largest fly-fishing-only water east of the Mississippi.

Somerset County, in the south-central part of the state, where I live, and Piscataquis County, in the north-central part of the state, have the most fly-fishing-only brook trout lakes and ponds at roughly 60 each, or just over 60 percent

A healthy wild native brook trout from a northern Maine fly-fishing-only pond. The fish was taken on a local pattern— Big Trout Only, or BTO—fished slow and right on the bottom. JOHN VACCA PHOTO

Island Pond in the Deboullie region in northern Maine is a never-stocked State Heritage Fish water and about as far north as you can go without a passport. DIANA MALLARD PHOTO

of the total. Franklin County, in the western part of the state, has roughly 40 waters; Aroostook and Oxford Counties have 13 and 18, respectively; Hancock, Penobscot, and Washington Counties have one each; and eight counties, all of which are in the southern part of the state, have none.

Roughly 70 of Maine's fly-fishing-only brook trout lakes and ponds have never been stocked directly or indirectly, so the trout are genetically pure. Approximately 25 have never been stocked directly, but may or may not have received stocked fish from a secondary source. While stocked in the past, roughly 75 are no longer being stocked. Of these, approximately 40 have not been stocked in 50 years or more. Roughly 35 are currently being stocked.

From a regulatory standpoint, approximately 25 of Maine's fly-fishing-only brook trout lakes and ponds are managed under what are referred to as "trophy" regulations. They are roughly evenly split between catch-and-release and 1-fish, 18 inches. Another roughly 20 are managed under "experimental" regulations, with a slot limit that prohibits the harvest of fish over 12 inches. Roughly 80 are managed under what are called "quality" regulations, typically a 2-fish limit and a slot limit that allows only one large fish to be harvested. The rest are general law.

Approximately 40 of Maine's fly-fishing-only brook trout lakes and ponds are classified as "Remote" by the Land Use Planning Commission. This means that logging, development, and motorized access are restricted to some degree within a half mile of these waters. Roads cannot be built within 1,000 feet of the water, and roads that are built within the half-mile protection zone must be blocked to vehicular access.

Lakes and ponds in Maine greater than 10 acres are open to the public for the purpose of certain types of recreation, including fishing, under what is called the Great Ponds Act. The law guarantees overland and fly-in access in support of said pursuits.

The majority of Maine's fly-fishing-only brook trout lakes and ponds are in the western, central, and northern parts of the state. While many are on private land managed for logging, others are on public land such as Baxter State Park, Katahdin Woods and Waters National Monument, and Maine Public Reserved Lands; land owned by conservation groups such as The Nature Conservancy and Appalachian Mountain Club; and land owned by individuals such as media mogul John Malone.

Maine's lake- and pond-dwelling brook trout can reach 20 inches or more in length. Most, however, are between 8 and 12 inches. Brook trout over 12 inches are not uncommon, fish over 16 inches are not rare, and trout larger than that are always possible.

Most of Maine's fly-fishing-only brook trout lakes and ponds are open to fishing from April through September. Many stocked waters are open through November, with

The author casting to a rising brook trout on a fly-fishing-only pond in central Maine, one of roughly 200 such waters in the state. CECIL GRAY PHOTO

a catch-and-release restriction in place starting in October. Practically speaking, the fishing season starts in early to mid-May due to snow, ice on the lakes, and poor road conditions.

Hatches on Maine's brook trout lakes and ponds start soon after ice-out, which runs from late April to mid-May depending on where you are, and continue right into the fall. Mayflies, caddis, and midges are all present. The giant Green Drake hatch, a favorite of local anglers and actually a *Hexagenia*, starts in late June or early July and runs for a couple of weeks. Flying ants and beetles are available spring and fall, and dragonflies and damsels are available in the summer. Throughout the season trout feed on leeches, minnows, and, where available, crayfish.

You will need a watercraft to fish Maine's fly-fishing-only brook trout lakes and ponds effectively. Float tubes, pontoon boats, rafts, canoes, kayaks, and small boats can all be used. While most waters require a hike—ranging from minutes to hours—to reach the water, some have drive-in boat launches, and the presence of such and distance from the road will dictate what type of boat is most practical.

Most of Maine's fly-fishing-only brook trout lakes and ponds are located off a network of unmarked, and often unmaintained, dirt roads. They are outside the power grid, and gasoline, food, retail, lodging, restaurants, hospitals, and other services we often take for granted are usually miles, and even hours, away. Cell service is spotty or non-existent. While this can present a logistical problem for some, many waters are located near sporting camps that offer lodging, meals, guides, boat rentals, and floatplane service. Some have satellite connections for those who need access to the outside world. This is the most practical way for many to enjoy this resource.

Maine's fly-fishing-only brook trout ponds are a national treasure, especially the self-sustaining ones. Its fly-fishing-only lakes and ponds offer a rare and unique opportunity to catch native pond-dwelling brook trout, many of which are wild and some of which are genetically pure, on a fly, and with no one around but other fly fishers and wildlife. That they exist within a few hours' drive of Boston and a short flight from New York City is a bonus.

Maine Remote Brook Trout Lakes and Ponds

There are approximately 175 lakes and ponds in Maine that are classified as "Remote" by the Land Use Planning Commission. This means that the nearest road was at least 1,000 feet away at the time of review. More importantly, at least to those reading this book, it also means the water is capable of providing a coldwater fishery. Roughly 149, for a total of over 4,160 acres, of Maine's Remote lakes and ponds are also classified as Principal Fisheries for brook trout by the Department of Inland Fisheries and Wildlife, meaning you have a good chance of catching brook trout there.

Under the Land Use Planning Commission's Recreational Protection Subdistrict laws governing Maine's Remote ponds, logging, development, and motorized access are restricted, but not prohibited, within a half mile of these waters. Roads cannot be built within 1,000 feet of the water, and roads that are built within the half-mile protection zone must be blocked to vehicular access. Only hike-in and fly-in access is allowed.

While Maine's Remote lakes and ponds make up roughly 13 percent of the Principal Brook Trout Fisheries, they represent just 1 percent of the total acreage. The average size is roughly 28 acres, with approximately 63 percent less than 25 acres. Roughly 25 percent are between 25 and 50 acres, 8 percent between 51 and 100 acres, 3 percent between 101 and 250 acres, and only one is larger than 250 acres. The smallest, at 2 acres, is an unnamed pond in Holeb Township; the largest, Gardner Lake in Aroostook County, is 288 acres and home to rare Arctic charr.

Piscataquis County, in the north-central part of the state, has the most Remote brook trout lakes and ponds with roughly 70, or just over 40 percent of the total. Approximately 45, or roughly 30 percent, are in Somerset County, where I live, in the south-central part of the

Brook trout in Maine's Remote ponds average less than a foot long, though larger fish are taken. This is due to the small size of most of these waters. DIANA MALLARD PHOTO

Lou Beckwith float tubing one of the larger Remote ponds in Maine. Float tubes are the best way to fish these waters, as hiking in a canoe or kayak is often impractical. DIANA MALLARD PHOTO

state. Aroostook, Franklin, Hancock, Oxford, Penobscot, and Washington Counties have fewer than 10 each, and 8 counties in the southern part of the state have none.

Roughly 80 of Maine's Remote brook trout ponds have never been stocked directly or indirectly and contain genetically pure fish. Approximately 10 have never been stocked directly, but may or may not have received stocked fish from a tributary source. Roughly 30 have been stocked in the past but are no longer stocked. Of these, approximately 15 have not been stocked in 50 or more years. Roughly 30 are stocked.

From a regulatory standpoint, approximately 40 of Maine's Remote brook trout lakes and ponds are restricted to fly fishing only, another roughly 40 are artificial lures only, and 75 or so are open to the use of bait. Approximately 10 are managed under what are referred to as "trophy" regulations, and more or less evenly split between catch-and-release and 1-fish, 18 inches. Roughly 55 are managed under what are called "quality" regulations, typically a 2-fish limit and a slot limit that allows only one large fish to be harvested, and the remaining 80 or so have a 5-fish, 6-inch limit.

Lakes and ponds in Maine greater than 10 acres are open to the public for the purpose of certain types of recreation, including fishing, under what is called the Great Ponds Act. The law guarantees overland and fly-in access

in support of said pursuits. Not all Remote brook trout lakes and ponds in Maine are Great Ponds.

The majority of Maine's Remote brook trout lakes and ponds are in the western, central, and northern part of the state. While many are on private land managed for logging, others are on public land such as Baxter State Park, Katahdin Woods and Waters National Monument, and Maine Public Reserved Lands; land owned by conservation groups such as The Nature Conservancy and Appalachian Mountain Club; and land owned by individuals such as media mogul John Malone.

While rare, Maine's Remote lake- and pond-dwelling brook trout can reach up to 20 inches. Most, however, are between 6 and 10 inches. Brook trout over 10 inches are not uncommon, fish over 12 inches are not rare, and trout larger than that are always possible.

Most of Maine's brook trout lakes and ponds are open to fishing from April through September. Many stocked waters are open through November, with a catch-and-release restriction in place starting in October. Practically speaking, the fishing season starts in mid-May due to snow on the trails, ice on the lakes, and poor road conditions.

Hatches on Maine's brook trout lakes and ponds start soon after ice-out, which runs from late April to mid-May depending on where you are, and continue right into the fall. Mayflies, caddis, and midges are all present. The giant Green Drake hatch, a favorite of local anglers and actually a *Hexagenia*, starts in late June or early July and runs for a couple of weeks. Flying ants and beetles are available spring and fall, and dragonflies and damsels are available in the summer. Throughout the season trout feed on leeches and minnows.

You will need a watercraft to fish Maine's Remote brook trout lakes and ponds effectively. Float tubes, pontoon boats, and small rafts are your best bet due to the waters' remote nature and the fact that most require a hike of 15 minutes or more to reach the water.

Maine's Remote brook trout lakes and ponds are located off a network of unmarked, and often unmaintained, dirt roads. They are outside the power grid, and gasoline, food, retail, lodging, restaurants, hospitals, cell coverage, and other services are unavailable, so you must plan accordingly.

Maine's Remote brook trout lakes and ponds offer a rare and unique opportunity to catch native pond-dwelling trout in a remote and unspoiled setting. That they exist at all in a part of the world where we have tamed much of our wilderness is quite amazing.

Casey Mealy and the author walking into a Remote pond on land owned by the Appalachian Mountain Club in central Maine. After walking on an abandoned road for a bit, you turn onto a small trail before reaching the water. DIANA MALLARD PHOTO

Maine Sporting Camps

Maine is the stronghold for wild native brook trout in the United States. This includes being home to 90 percent of the remaining wild native pond-dwelling brook trout, 90 percent of the wild native sea-run brook trout, and most of the large lake and large river wild native brook trout.

There are over 1,500 lakes and ponds in Maine that are home to brook trout, over 600 of which are self-sustaining. There are hundreds of miles of river that are home to wild native brook trout as well, including the Allagash, Cupsuptic, Dead, Dennys, Kennebec, Kennebago, Magalloway, Moose, Rangeley, Rapid, and Roach. And there are countless miles of self-sustaining native brook trout streams.

A large rural state, a significant portion of Maine is located in the Unincorporated Townships. This swath of undeveloped and uninhabited land is for the most part without retail, grocery, food, gas, automotive, and other services. If you need it, you will have to bring it, and if you run out, you will have to go find it, and this can take hours. Lodging is limited, and campsites are primitive and rarely near potable water or bathrooms. Cell coverage is spotty or nonexistent.

Making matters even more difficult is the fact that most of Maine's best brook trout water is located off dirt roads that are often unmarked, and in some cases unmaintained. Roads are being built all the time in support of logging; many are temporary and only passable in the winter; and others become impassable due to washouts, deliberate blockage, or deteriorated culverts and bridges. Maps are often inaccurate, and most automobile GPSs don't know where they are. Even handheld GPSs are not always reliable, as you often find yourself heading off the end of a road into blank screen.

The main lodge at Libby Camps on Millinocket Lake, one of the oldest and best-known sporting camps in Maine. Located in the fabled Allagash Region, it is within striking distance of some of the best brook trout fishing in the state. BOB MALLARD PHOTO

Bradford Camps on Munsungan Lake offers lakeside cabins on a large State Heritage Fish water. BOB MALLARD PHOTO

The dining room at Libby Camps is typical of that found at most Maine sporting camps—rustic but quite comfortable. BOB MALLARD PHOTO

"Sports," as guests are referred to in Maine, arrive at Bradford Camps by float plane. BOB MALLARD PHOTO

For those unfamiliar with the area, not comfortable exploring unknown areas, without a vehicle capable of backcountry travel, without sufficient camping gear, or in need of creature comforts or contact with the outside world, your options are limited and, with the exception of traditional sporting camps, often nonexistent.

Maine is home to some of the last traditional sporting camps in the East, the others being found mostly in New York's Adirondack region. These businesses played a significant role in the state's outdoor heritage, and many have been in existence for generations, sometimes remaining within the same family. They have been catering to sportsmen, especially fly fishers, for decades, some dating back over a century. Today they cater to ecotourists as well, out of necessity as much as choice.

Most Maine sporting camps are located outside the power grid and accessible by dirt road only. They can be found as far south and west as Rangeley, as far east as Downeast, and as far north as the Canadian border. They offer lodging, meals, guiding, boat rentals, and fly-in services. These businesses offer a unique experience found in very few places in the contiguous United States.

While once numbered in the hundreds, it is said that Maine now has fewer than 50 sporting camps. Declining fishing, the loss of the northern Maine deer herd, and changes in recreational preferences have negatively affected them. Widespread mechanized logging hasn't helped, and neither have increased operating costs.

Maine's sporting camps have experienced significant changes over the last decade or so. Camp Phoenix and Grace Pond Camps went "condo." Little Lyford and Medawisla Camps were bought by the Appalachian Mountain Club and are now being managed for ecotourism. Others were sold to private citizens, and some simply closed. But many sporting camps remain open to the public and continue to cater to fly fishers.

Maine's fly-fishing-friendly, and fish-friendly, brook trout–centric sporting camps include Bradford Camps, Chandler Lake Camps and Lodge, Cobb's Pierce Pond Camps, Grant's Kennebago Camps, Lakewood Camps, Libby Camps, and Little Lyford Lodge & Cabins. If you want to fish the Maine backcountry and are not sure how to do it, give this uniquely Maine experience a try.

Maine State Heritage Fish Waters

Unlike most wild trout programs, Maine's State Heritage Fish program is a law, not a policy. Enacted in 2005 the law was originally applied to never-stocked brook trout lakes and ponds. It was amended in 2007 to include rare Arctic charr, and again in 2009 to add some water-specific exceptions. The next amendment came in 2014 when lakes and ponds that had not been stocked in 25 years or more were added, more than doubling the number of protected waters. It is amended annually to add new waters.

This groundbreaking pro-native fish law has four components: species covered, inclusion criteria, prohibited acts, and a list of waters. Critical language includes, "The commissioner shall adopt by rule a list of state heritage fish waters composed of lakes and ponds that . . . have never been stocked according to any reliable records . . . and waters that according to reliable records have not been stocked for at least 25 years," and "The commissioner may not stock or issue a permit to stock fish in a lake or pond listed as a state heritage fish water. . . . A person may not use live fish as bait or possess live fish to be used as bait on a lake or pond listed as a state heritage fish water."

Maine's State Heritage Fish law is the most widely applied wild trout program in the country affecting over 575 waters. To put this in perspective, neighboring New Hampshire has just 16 formally designated Wild Trout Management waters.

Maine's State Heritage Fish waters are the largest inventory of wild native trout stillwaters in the country. According to Vermont Fish & Wildlife: "Most of Vermont's brook trout pond fisheries are supported entirely by stocking . . . a few are not stocked at all." Per New York Department of Environmental Conservation: "The vast majority of our brook trout ponds are stocked. Ponds totally sustained by natural reproduction probably total less than 50." Outside of Maine, New Hampshire, Vermont, and New York, there are very few self-sustaining native brook trout lakes and ponds.

Maine's State Heritage Fish lakes and ponds represent a total of over 80,000 acres and range from under an acre to over 13,000 acres, the largest of which is Mooselookmeguntic Lake in historic Rangeley. The largest never-stocked water is 4,200-acre Allagash Lake, part of the headwaters of the fabled Allagash Wilderness Waterway.

A large brook trout caught from a State Heritage Fish pond in central Maine. A terrestrial did the trick. Nothing brings big brook trout to the surface like ants and beetles. CECIL GRAY PHOTO

State Heritage Fish water Galilee Pond. Located in T15 R9 WELS, it is only 15 miles from the Canadian border.
DIANA MALLARD PHOTO

Piscataquis County has the most State Heritage Fish waters with roughly 245. Approximately 145 are located in Somerset County. Aroostook County has roughly 85, Franklin County approximately 45, Oxford County roughly 25, Penobscot and Hancock roughly 15 each, Washington and York Counties fewer than 10, and the rest have none.

Over 325 of Maine's State Heritage Fish waters and close to 21,500 acres (approximately 55 percent of the waters and roughly 10 percent of the acreage) have never been stocked. This represents the largest inventory of genetically pure pond-dwelling native salmonids in the contiguous United States. Twelve percent of the waters and 15 percent of the acreage may or may not have received stocked fish from a secondary source. Roughly 30 percent of the waters and 75 percent of the acreage have been stocked but not in 25 years or more.

Of the previously stocked waters, nearly 40 percent of the previously stocked lakes and ponds representing roughly 60 percent of the total acreage have not been stocked in 25 to 49 years. Just over 45 percent of the waters and roughly 35 percent of the acreage have not been stocked in 50 to 74 years. The remaining 15 percent of the waters and just over 5 percent of the acreage have not been stocked in 75 years or more.

Close to 30 percent of Maine's State Heritage Fish waters and nearly 15 percent of the acreage are restricted to fly fishing only, the largest of which is 1,700-acre Kennebago Lake, said to be the largest fly-fishing-only water east of the Mississippi. Roughly 20 percent of the waters and 25 percent of the acreage are restricted to artificial lures only. The remaining 50 percent of the waters and over 60 percent of the acreage are open to worms and dead bait, but not live minnows.

Approximately 4 percent of Maine's State Heritage Fish waters and 3 percent of the acreage are managed under what are referred to as "trophy" regulations, with 60 percent of the waters and 45 percent of the acreage managed for catch-and-release, and the rest a 1-fish, 18-inch rule. Roughly 35 percent of the waters and 60 percent of the acreage are managed under what are called "quality" regulations, typically a 2-fish limit and a slot limit that allows only one large fish to be harvested. The remaining 5 percent are managed under "experimental" regulations or exceptions, the latter of which usually involve tribal lands.

Roughly 110 of Maine's State Heritage Fish waters are classified as "Remote" by Maine's Land Use Planning Commission. Nearly 70 percent of these and 60 percent of the acreage have never been stocked. To learn more about this, refer to the "Maine Remote Brook Trout Lakes and Ponds" chapter.

All lakes and ponds in Maine greater than 10 acres are open to the public for the purpose of certain types of recreation, including fishing, under what is called the Great Ponds Act. The law guarantees overland and fly-in access in support of said pursuits.

The majority of Maine's State Heritage Fish lakes and ponds are in the western, central, and northern part of the state. While many are on private land managed by North Maine Woods, others are on public land such as Baxter State Park, Katahdin Woods and Waters National Monument, and Maine Public Reserved Lands and land owned by conservation groups such as The Nature Conservancy and Appalachian Mountain Club.

Maine's pond-dwelling brook trout can reach 20 inches or more in length. Most, however, are between 8 and 12 inches. Brook trout over 12 inches are not uncommon, fish over 16 inches are not rare, and trout larger than that are always possible.

Maine's State Heritage Fish lakes and ponds are open to fishing from April through September. Practically speaking, the fishing season starts in early to mid-May due to snow, ice on the lakes, and poor road conditions.

Hatches on Maine's State Heritage Fish waters start soon after ice-out, usually early to mid-May depending on where you are, and continue right into the fall. Mayflies, caddis, and midges are all present. The giant Green Drake hatch, actually a *Hexagenia*, starts in late June or early July. Flying ants and beetles are available spring and fall, and dragonflies and damsels are available in the summer. Throughout the season trout feed on leeches, minnows, and, where available, crayfish.

You will need a watercraft to fish Maine's State Heritage Fish lakes and ponds effectively. Float tubes, pontoon boats, rafts, canoes, kayaks, small boats, and motorboats can all be used. While most waters require a hike—ranging from minutes to hours—to reach the water, some have drive-in boat launches, and the distance from the road and presence of launches will dictate what type of boat is most practical.

Most of Maine's State Heritage Fish waters are located off a network of unmarked, and often unmaintained, dirt roads. They are outside the power grid, and supplies and services are usually miles, and even hours, away. Cell service is spotty or nonexistent. While this can present a logistical problem for some, many waters are near sporting camps that offer lodging, meals, guides, boat rentals, and floatplane service. This is the most practical way for many to enjoy this resource.

At a time when nonnative, stocked, hybrid, and genetically altered fish are commonplace, and in a sport where moving water is king, Maine's State Heritage Fish lakes and ponds are a rare and unique resource. They offer anglers an opportunity to catch wild pond-dwelling native brook trout on a fly. Thanks to the efforts of those who have supported the law, these waters should remain viable for generations to come.

Unfortunately, the protections provided by Maine's State Heritage Fish law have not been extended to all

A remote State Heritage Fish water in Somerset County with a history of producing large fish. Note the formal State Heritage Fish sign on the tree. EMILY BASTIAN PHOTO

The author on a State Heritage Fish pond in central Maine. BEN BRUNT PHOTO

applicable waters. Politics, turf, and personal preferences have trumped trout, keeping such important wild native brook trout waters as the Allagash Lakes off the list. Small vulnerable waters surveyed by Audubon/Trout Unlimited volunteers are not being added as was promised as well, and for political not biological reasons.

While the rules used to create the initial list of waters were clear and concise, those for adding new waters are ambiguous and need to be changed to reflect what was used to establish the original lists: "The commissioner may adopt rules to amend the list established under subsection 1 to add a lake or pond if that lake or pond meets criteria established by the commissioner for classifying a lake or pond as a state heritage fish water."

Another concern is that the rules for removing waters from the State Heritage Fish list have been weakened under what was a well-intended but ill-advised compromise between advocates and the Maine Department of Inland Fisheries and Wildlife. If they get their way, Inland Fisheries and Wildlife may redefine what a lake and pond is, putting numerous waters at risk of removal.

A recent volunteer effort initiatcd by Native Fish Coalition to place signs at State Heritage Fish waters has been hampered by a refusal on the part of the Bureau of Parks and Lands and Baxter State Park to allow signs to be posted on their land. That the Maine Department of Inland Fisheries and Wildlife cosponsored the project and Maine Outdoor Heritage Fund helped pay for it seems to be of no concern. Hopefully this will be addressed in the future.

The protections provided Maine's State Heritage Fish lakes and ponds have not been extended to their tributaries. In fact, the program does not include any moving water and is applicable to lakes and ponds only. This is a major and dangerous oversight that may or may not be addressed before this book comes out.

The loopholes in Maine's State Heritage Fish law need to be addressed. To do this, all groups with a vested interest—Sportsman's Alliance of Maine, Maine Audubon, The Nature Conservancy, Appalachian Mountain Club, Trout Unlimited, and Native Fish Coalition—will need to get behind legislative initiatives to amend the law.

Maine Trophy Brook Trout Lakes and Ponds

Of Maine's roughly 1,200 lakes and ponds classified as Principal Brook Trout Fisheries by the Maine Department of Inland Fisheries and Wildlife, approximately 45 are managed under what are referred to as "Trophy" regulations. These regulations provide the highest level of protection afforded lakes and ponds in Maine, and waters where they are applied tend to offer the most consistent fishing for large brook trout in the state.

Maine's Trophy brook trout lakes and ponds represent a total of over 11,500 acres and range from under 3 acres to roughly 7,850 acres. The largest, Umbagog Lake on the Maine–New Hampshire border, is nearly twelve times bigger than the next largest, 675-acre West Carry Pond. Take the five biggest waters away and the average is just 35 acres.

Piscataquis County has the most Trophy brook trout lakes and ponds with roughly 20. Somerset, Aroostook, Franklin, and Oxford Counties have seven, six, four, and three, respectively. The rest are in Hancock, Lincoln, and York Counties.

Roughly 12 of Maine's Trophy brook trout lakes and ponds and close to 1,170 acres (approximately 30 percent of the waters and roughly 10 percent of the acreage) have never been stocked. Ten percent of the waters and 2 percent of the acreage may or may not have received stocked fish from a secondary source. Roughly 30 percent of the waters and 85 percent of the acreage have been stocked but not in 25 years or more. Approximately 25 percent of the waters and 3 percent of the acreage are stocked.

Nearly 25 of Maine's Trophy brook trout lakes and ponds are also formally designated State Heritage Fish waters. Half of these have never been stocked. To learn more about this, refer to the "Maine State Heritage Fish Waters" chapter.

Of the previously stocked Trophy brook trout waters, nearly 50 percent of the lakes and ponds and roughly 3 percent of the total acreage have not been stocked in 25 to 49 years. Approximately 35 percent of the waters and roughly 17 percent of the acreage have not been stocked in 50 to 74 years. The remaining 15 percent of the waters and nearly 80 percent of the acreage have not been stocked in 75 years or more.

Roughly 60 percent of Maine's Trophy brook trout lakes and ponds and approximately 80 percent of the acreage are managed under a 1-fish, 18-inch rule. The remaining 40 percent of waters and 20 percent of acreage are catch-and-release.

More than 50 percent of Maine's Trophy brook trout lakes and ponds and close to 10 percent of the acreage are restricted to fly fishing only, the largest of which is 510-acre Pond in the River, part of the fabled Rapid River. Roughly 45 percent of the waters and 15 percent of the

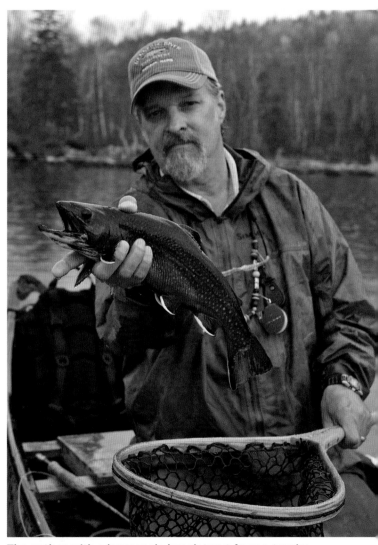

The author with a large male brook trout from a trophy pond in Maine. Good habitat, a lack of competing species, and regulations that protect large fish make these waters what they are. Take any one of these factors away and they would not be what they are.
CECIL GRAY PHOTO

acreage are restricted to artificial lures only. The remaining 5 percent of the waters and close to 75 percent of the acreage are open bait, with all but 5 percent of that open to live bait. The reason for the high amount of acreage open to live bait is Umbagog Lake.

Roughly 10 of Maine's Trophy brook trout lakes and ponds are classified as Remote by Maine's Land Use Planning Commission. Nearly 30 percent of the waters and acreage have never been stocked. To learn more about this, refer to the "Maine Remote Brook Trout Lakes and Ponds" chapter.

All lakes and ponds in Maine greater than 10 acres are open to the public for the purpose of certain types of recreation, including fishing, under what is called the Great Ponds Act. The law guarantees overland and fly-in access in support of said pursuits.

The majority of Maine's Trophy brook trout lakes and ponds are in the western, central, and northern part of the state. While many are on private land managed by North Maine Woods, others are on public land such as Baxter State Park, Katahdin Woods and Waters National Monument, and Maine Public Reserved Lands and land owned by conservation groups such as The Nature Conservancy and Appalachian Mountain Club.

Maine's pond-dwelling brook trout can reach 20 inches or more in length. Most, however, are between 8 and 12 inches. Brook trout over 12 inches are not uncommon, fish over 16 inches are not rare, and trout larger than that are always possible, especially in the Trophy brook trout lakes and ponds.

Maine's Trophy brook trout lakes and ponds are open to fishing from April through September. Many stocked waters are open through November, with a catch and release restriction in place starting in October. Realistically, the fishing season starts in early to mid-May due to snow, ice on the lakes, and poor road conditions.

Hatches on Maine's Trophy brook trout lakes and ponds start soon after ice-out, usually early to mid-May depending on where you are, and continue right into the fall. Mayflies, caddis, and midges are all present. The giant Green Drake hatch, actually a *Hexagenia*, starts in late June or early July. Flying ants and beetles are available spring and fall, and dragonflies and damsels are available in the summer. Throughout the season trout feed on leeches, minnows, and, where available, crayfish.

You will need a watercraft to fish Maine's Trophy brook trout lakes and ponds effectively. Float tubes, pontoon boats, rafts, canoes, kayaks, small boats, and motorboats can all

Tim Beckwith float tubing Black Pond in the Deboullie region, purported to be the source of the state record wild brook trout. An 18-inch minimum length limit protects larger fish. DIANA MALLARD PHOTO

The author fishing a Trophy brook trout pond in central Maine in the fall. Ants, beetles, midges, and bright streamers are your best bet. CECIL GRAY PHOTO

be used. While most waters require a hike—ranging from minutes to hours—to reach the water, some have drive-in boat launches, and the distance from the road and presence of launches will dictate what type of boat is most practical.

Most of Maine's Trophy brook trout lakes and ponds are located off a network of unmarked, and often unmaintained, dirt roads. They are outside the power grid, and supplies and services are usually miles, and even hours, away. Cell service is spotty or nonexistent. While this can present a logistical problem for some, many waters are near sporting camps that offer lodging, meals, guides, boat rentals, and floatplane service. This is the most practical way for many to enjoy this resource.

Maine's Trophy brook trout lakes and ponds offer anglers their best shot at catching a large native, and usually wild, brook trout in a stillwater environment on a cast fly. While other waters may have larger fish, they rarely have as many large fish.

New Hampshire Wild Trout Management Waters

New Hampshire's Wild Trout Management program is the most progressive "wild trout" program in New England. It was started in the early 2000s, with waters being added in 2003, 2005, and 2006. Although not specifically limited to brook trout, it has been applied only to waters where brook trout are the primary salmonid species.

New Hampshire's Wild Trout Management program has science-based inclusion criteria: A water must be shown to support wild trout biomass equal to or in excess of 13 pounds per acre. Lakes, ponds, rivers, and streams are eligible, and it has been applied to both ponds and streams.

Waters that receive a Wild Trout Management designation are managed under a standard set of rules, and there is no stocking. Tackle is restricted to single-hook barbless artificial lures and flies only, and they are catch-and-release. Ponds are open to fishing from the fourth Saturday in April through Labor Day. Streams are open from January 1 through Labor Day. Both are closed to fishing in the fall to protect spawning fish.

To put this in perspective, neighboring Vermont and Massachusetts, as well as Rhode Island, Connecticut, and many other states within native brook trout range, have no formal wild trout program. Maine's State Heritage Fish program is limited to lakes and ponds, has an arbitrary 25-years-since-last-stocking requirement, and only prohibits stocking and the use of live fish as bait.

There are 16 waters in New Hampshire with a formal Wild Trout Management designation. Thirteen are streams

A beautiful wild brook trout from a southern New Hampshire Wild Trout Management stream. The program works, and it should be expanded not curtailed. BOB MALLARD PHOTO

Most Wild Trout Management streams in New Hampshire are small in size but big in ecological, recreational, and social value. DIANA MALLARD PHOTO

and three are ponds. The streams represent some of the only small brook trout streams in New England managed for catch-and-release, as well as having a bait prohibition. The ponds are some of the only catch-and-release wild native brook trout stillwaters outside of Maine.

There is one Wild Trout Management water in Cheshire County, nine in Coos, four in Hillsborough, and two in Grafton. Two are in the suburb of Hollis, just over the Massachusetts border and abutting busy Nashua. Three are in the unorganized township Second College Grant, land granted to Dartmouth College in the early 1800s. The rest are in Bethlehem, Carroll, Chesterfield, Colebrook, Columbia, Hillsborough, Lincoln, Odell, Sharon, Stratford, and Wentworth Location.

One of the most interesting things about New Hampshire's Wild Trout Management waters is their geographic distribution. Five are in the southernmost quarter of the state, none in the next quarter, three in the next quarter, and eight in the northernmost quarter. Four are actually located in the southernmost eighth of the state, and only one is in the northernmost eighth.

The Wild Trout Management streams in southern New Hampshire are low gradient. They are often nearly impenetrable due to dense vegetation and muddy banks, and some sections are accessible by canoe only. As you move north they become more like the picturesque freestone streams New Hampshire is known for.

Two of the three Wild Trout Management ponds, Ethan and Shoal, are remote high-elevation waters at approximately 2,800 feet above sea level. The other, Little Greenough Pond, is located at roughly 1,400 feet above sea level. The former two require a strenuous hike to reach; the latter is located off a dirt road with just a short walk to the water.

Ethan Pond looks like a natural mountain pond, Shoal Pond resembles a beaver pond, and Little Greenough Pond looks like a Maine brook trout pond. All three are shallow, with less than 10 feet of water, and average depths of significantly less. While fish tend to run small in the first two, 4 to 6 inches, fish over a foot are caught in the latter.

Another interesting observation is where New Hampshire's Wild Trout Management waters are *not*: the White Mountains region and Pittsburg, arguably the two most popular brook trout destinations in the state, and in the case of the former, home to the largest concentration of self-sustaining brook trout waters in the state. There are none in the Lakes or Sunapee regions either.

The reality is that the areas noted above have streams that contain wild trout. Unfortunately, these waters have yet to receive Wild Trout Management designation. In fact, the formal list of Wild Trout Management streams represents just a small portion of the wild brook trout streams in New Hampshire. The actual number is probably closer to 100.

A small native brook trout from a Wild Trout Management stream in northern New Hampshire. There are just 13 such waters in the state. BOB MALLARD PHOTO

The Dead Diamond watershed in the northeastern part of the state is an example. It has three streams designated as Wild Trout Management waters, and a few, including the mainstem, that should be. Another one is Nash Stream, in the northern part of the state: Located on state-owned 40,000-acre Nash Stream Forest, it has two tributaries so designated.

As for ponds, like streams, the formal list is just part of the story. While much better represented than streams in regard to the percent of applicable waters that are so classified, there are some ponds that meet the Wild Trout Management criteria but have not been designated as such. Others could be if managed differently.

According to New Hampshire Fish & Game, its objective is to identify more waters where natural reproduction of brook trout occurs and determine if they support wild trout populations at densities that warrant Wild Trout Management designation. Unfortunately, liberal regulations could be negatively affecting the biomass in many waters, and stocking on others. And in cases like the Wildcat River, the water does support densities of wild trout that would warrant designation, but the department has not acted.

Sadly, although referred to as "ongoing," there have been no additions to the Wild Trout Management program since 2006. Worse is that there have been statements made by the fish and game department that imply the protections could be weakened and waters could be removed, and even some mention of the possibility of future stocking.

Signage associated with these important wild native trout waters has fallen into disrepair or disappeared. A recent proposal by the New Hampshire chapter of Native Fish Coalition to put up new signs was shot down by New Hampshire Fish & Game for reasons that would indicate the program could be in trouble.

The wild native brook trout potential in New Hampshire is huge. Its mountains are home to countless streams that remain cool throughout the summer and offer ideal habitat for brook trout. There are also remote ponds in the backcountry that have suitable habitat for wild brook trout, most of which are located in protected areas such as the White Mountain National Forest.

Like many such programs, the potential of New Hampshire's Wild Trout Management program has been lessened by its limited and somewhat random implementation. There are only 16 waters statewide, and while the program is referred to as ongoing, the department has not added a water in more than a decade. Meanwhile, New Jersey has over 200 so-designated waters. To imply that New Jersey has more wild brook trout streams than New Hampshire doesn't even pass the straight-face test. But unlike many states, at least there is a target to aim for, though getting folks to do so is the challenge.

Unfortunately, based on recent correspondences with New Hampshire Fish & Game, it may be moving to weaken the protections, remove waters from the list, or, worse, walk away from the Wild Trout Management program altogether.

New Jersey Wild Brook Trout Streams

The words "New Jersey" and "wild brook trout" don't exactly roll off your tongue. The same can be said about "progressive wild trout management" and "New Jersey"; they just don't sound like they go together. But they should, and they do.

When work would take me to New Jersey, not an unusual occurrence in the software and telecom game, I occasionally stayed over to get some fishing in, as was always the case while on the road. While there I fished a number of named, and nameless, streams, and while many contained stocked and nonnative trout, some were home to small wild native brook trout as beautiful as any I had seen anywhere.

New Jersey is a small, heavily populated state. The 47th-smallest state in the country, it has the 11th-highest population at over 9 million people, more than Maine, New Hampshire, Vermont, Rhode Island, and West Virginia combined. New Jersey's population density is the highest in the nation at more than 1,200 people per square mile.

Brook trout are native to New Jersey. They are New Jersey's official state fish, having been declared as such in 1991 and signed into law in 1992. Geographically, the state isn't what you expect when you think wild brook trout habitat. The highest point in the state is just 1,800 feet above sea level, and its mean elevation just 250 feet.

While their numbers have declined considerably due to development, pollution, nonnative fish introductions, stocking, and angler exploitation, New Jersey's wild native brook trout have managed to hold on. They have dodged a lot of bullets over the years and found a way to survive against all odds, proving once again how resilient wild native fish can be.

New Jersey's wild native brook trout are found in small headwater streams in the hills of the northern part of the state. Many are tributaries to popular stocked rivers, home to nonnative browns and rainbows. While some nonnative trout are found in these small streams, which established self-sustaining populations in some cases, many are home to primarily brook trout. Most of New Jersey's wild native brook trout spend their entire life within small streams, occasionally dropping down to larger rivers when the water

A beautiful wild native brook trout from a small New Jersey trout stream. That's right, New Jersey. BOB MALLARD PHOTO

gets too low or they outgrow their habitat. They eke out a living in what are relatively sterile waters with somewhat marginal forage.

There are approximately 200 streams in New Jersey that are said to be home to "wild" trout. Half or more are believed to contain at least some level of native brook trout. They are located in eight counties: Bergen, Camden, Hunterdon, Morris, Passaic, Somerset, Sussex, and Warren.

With two wild trout programs applicable to brook trout, and a large section of land managed as a Brook Trout Conservation Zone, New Jersey has more formally designated "wild trout" streams than New Hampshire, which, as mentioned in the previous chapter, doesn't even pass the straight-face test.

There are no brook trout in the New Jersey hatchery system, which although due to a disease outbreak is good news for wild native brook trout. Between 2005 and 2010 alone, stocking was discontinued on eight streams that were home to wild trout.

New Jersey Division of Fish & Wildlife has been making incremental improvements regarding how they manage the state's wild native brook trout resources for over 20 years. In 1997 they imposed a statewide 7-inch minimum length limit on "trout." The limit was bumped up to 9 inches in 2008. The current bag limit fluctuates between four and six fish depending on the time of year.

The most significant and important change, however, was the creation of a Brook Trout Conservation Zone in 2018. This large swath of land is home to most of New Jersey's remaining wild native brook trout populations and extends from I-287 and Route 202 to the Delaware River and the New Jersey–New York state line, an area of over 2,000 square miles.

Brook trout stocking is prohibited in the Brook Trout Conservation Zone. A genetics study done in 2007 indicates that some of New Jersey's brook trout may be descendants of fish that colonized the area as the glaciers retreated. Suspending stocking prevents genetic swamping and protects strains that have evolved to survive in a specific set of conditions and are more likely to be able to adapt to future changes as well.

New Jersey's Brook Trout Conservation Zone is open to fishing year-round. All brook trout caught in this area must be released immediately and unharmed. Tackle is restricted to artificial lures and flies only. The possession or use of bait, in any form, is strictly prohibited.

Established in 1990 the Wild Trout Stream program protects fish outside the Brook Trout Conservation Zone. These streams are not stocked, and many are home to wild native brook trout. There are two subcategories of Wild Trout Streams: Native Brook Trout Streams and Wild Trout Streams (mixed species).

Native Brook Trout Streams are almost exclusively inhabited by wild native brook trout. There are just over 10 so-designated waters, and others could be added after they are reclaimed and the nonnative trout removed. While native brook trout are protected by a catch-and-release restriction, there is no bag or length limit for nonnative

A Tenkara-caught wild brook trout from a small stream in northwestern New Jersey. Using centuries-old Japanese fishing techniques within striking distance of modern New York City. ADAM KLAGSBRUN PHOTO

A typical north-central New Jersey brook trout stream in the fall. We caught several small wild fish on nymphs that day. DIANA MALLARD PHOTO

trout to encourage harvest. Tackle is restricted to artificial lures and flies only, and barbless hooks.

Wild Trout Streams have multiple species of trout, including brook trout in many cases. There are just over 15 so-designated waters, but it is difficult to ascertain which have native brook trout and which do not. Native brook trout are protected by a catch-and-release restriction, and there is a 2-fish, 9-inch limit on nonnative brown trout and rainbow trout. Tackle is restricted to artificial lures and flies only, and barbless hooks.

New Jersey has really stepped up in regard to how they manage their wild native brook trout. It would be fair, and I believe accurate, to say that New Jersey has the most progressive wild trout management in the East. That the first place in the East to demonstrate truly progressive wild native brook trout management is the last place you'd expect, speaks volumes as to the vision and commitment to wild native brook trout of those in charge of the resource.

Pennsylvania Wilderness Trout Streams

Pennsylvania has approximately 86,000 miles of stream. According to the Pennsylvania Fish & Boat Commission, roughly 3,400 streams, for a total of over 12,800 miles, hold trout. Of these, more than 1,700 streams for a total of nearly 9,375 miles have been documented to contain wild trout. Wild trout are assumed to be present in another 1,702 streams for a total of just over 3,300 miles due to the fact they are located upstream of documented wild trout populations.

Of the 12,800 or so miles of stream in Pennsylvania that are reported to contain wild trout, a very small amount, less than 0.5 percent, holds wild brook trout. According to data obtained from the Pennsylvania Fish & Boat Commission, just 360 miles of stream is home to wild brook trout, most of which is in the Delaware, Genesee, Ohio, Potomac, and Susquehanna River watersheds.

Brook trout are native to Pennsylvania, but their habitat has been greatly reduced since European settlement. Development, road building, agriculture, logging, mining, pollution, invasive fish, stocking, and angler exploitation have all contributed to the decline. In many cases the state-sponsored introduction of nonnative brown trout, and to a

Tyler Groves with a small wild brook trout from Potter County, Pennsylvania. While gone from most large streams and rivers in the state, wild native brook trout can still be found in headwater streams. BRADEN BISH PHOTO

A beautiful Pennsylvania wild brook trout stream. Known best for its limestone creeks and nonnative brown trout, Pennsylvania has miles of small freestone streams that are home to native brook trout. JED HAMBERGER PHOTO

lesser degree rainbow trout, displaced native brook trout. Most of the remaining wild brook trout populations in Pennsylvania are found in headwater freestone streams and, in some cases, limestone creeks.

Most wild brook trout streams in Pennsylvania are classified as Wilderness Trout Streams. This designation is applied to waters that offer a wild trout fishing experience in a natural and unspoiled setting. The program was established in 1969, its goal to protect and promote wild trout fishcries.

Pennsylvania's Wilderness Trout Streams represent some of the best streams in the state from a water quality standpoint. All qualify for an "exceptional value" classification, which offers the highest level of protection provided by the Department of Environmental Protection.

According to the Pennsylvania Fish & Boat Commission, there are just over 100 sections of stream in the state that have received a Wilderness Trout Stream designation, nearly 98 percent of which are said to hold wild native brook trout. Of these, roughly 75 contain only brook trout and no other nonnative salmonids. Another roughly 20 have a mix of native brook and nonnative brown trout.

While somewhat concentrated in the north-central and east-central part of the state, Pennsylvania's Wilderness Trout Streams can be found in 30 counties. There is at least one in Adams, Cambria, Cameron, Carbon, Centre, Clarion, Clearfield, Clinton, Columbia, Elk, Fayette, Forest, Franklin, Jefferson, Lebanon, Luzerne, Lycoming, McKean, Monroe, Perry, Potter, Schuylkill, Somerset, Sullivan, Tioga, Union, Venango, Warren, Westmoreland, and Wyoming Counties. Centre has the most with 12; Clinton and Monroe are next with 10.

Many of Pennsylvania's Wilderness Trout Streams are classified as Class A, Class B, and Class C Wild Trout streams. This means that they meet a specific set of criteria in regard to wild trout densities and represent the strongest wild trout populations in the state.

In the case of Class A waters, the biomass metrics vary by species. They are lower for brook trout than brown trout due to their relative size. The metrics for brook trout are 26.7 pounds per acre total, and 0.089 pound per acre of fish less than 5.9 inches. Brook trout must also represent at least 75 percent of the total wild trout biomass. In waters where brook trout represent less than 75 percent of the

A wild native brook trout from Potter County, Pennsylvania. There are hundreds of miles of wild native brook trout streams in Pennsylvania.
JED HAMBERGER PHOTO

Class C waters must have at least 8.9 pounds of combined wild trout biomass per acre, but less than 17.8 pounds per acre.

Another classification that recognizes wild brook trout waters is called the Wild Brook Trout Enhancement Program. Sections of stream that receive this designation are managed for catch-and-release on brook trout; other species are regulated under standard bag and length restrictions. There are no tackle restrictions, and you must purchase a trout/salmon permit to fish these waters.

There are nine sections of stream with formal Wild Brook Trout designations, representing a total of roughly 62 miles of stream. The longest, approximately 28 miles, is on Upper Kettle Creek. These waters are located in Carbon, Forest, Monroe, Perry, Potter, Tioga, Warren, and Westmoreland Counties. All the tributaries located within the designated sections of stream are afforded the same protection as the mainstem. This increases the total miles of protected water exponentially.

Pennsylvania's stream-dwelling wild brook trout live in two types of waters: small mountain freestone headwater streams and limestone creeks. These two environments vary radically, and, in general, life is much easier in limestone creeks than it is in freestone streams.

Limestone creeks have a better forage base, are less susceptible to floods and droughts, and have temperatures that remain consistent throughout the year, never getting as cold or as warm as their freestone cousins. These fertile streams provide access to a much wider variety of food, and more of it, than the relatively infertile freestone streams. Hatches are much more robust and varied on limestone creeks than those found on freestone streams. Fish living in limestone creeks also have access to sow bugs, or cress bugs, a high-protein food source. Both types of waters have terrestrials and minnows, mostly sculpin, dace, and juvenile trout.

There are exceptions, but as a rule Pennsylvania trout streams open to fishing April 4 or April 18 depending on the county. They close after September 7. Numerous exceptions include waters that remain open until the end of the year or are open year-round.

Pennsylvania has a large inventory of wild brook trout streams. While the freestone streams are similar to those found elsewhere, the limestone creeks are unique to the area and rarely found outside the state. Both are worthy of your attention.

total wild trout biomass, there must be a combined biomass of at least 35.6 pounds per acre. Class A waters are not stocked. There are just over 20 Wilderness Trout Streams with a Class A designation. The largest concentration is in Potter County with six.

Class B waters must have at least 17.8 pounds of brook trout per acre, but no more than 26.7 pounds per acre. In waters where brook and brown trout overlap, the lower end of the range remains the same, but the upper end is increased to 35.6 pounds per acre.

Rangeley, Maine

angeley, Maine, is much more than simply the Rapid, Magalloway, Kennebago, and Cupsuptic Rivers, Upper Dam, and Kennebago Lake—all of which are covered earlier in the book. It would be fair to call it the "Brook Trout Capital of the United States." Nowhere in the country is there a better concentration of native brook trout rivers and lakes, many of which are self-sustaining. Nowhere in the country do you have a better opportunity to catch wild native brook trout measured in pounds not inches, especially in a river. When it comes to native brook trout, there is no place better than Rangeley, Maine.

Metallak, "The Lone Indian of the Magalloway," hunted, trapped, fished, and guided in the area in and around Rangeley. Parmachenee Lake, a State Heritage Fish water, was named after his daughter, as was the classic Parmachenee Belle wet fly, designed to imitate the fin of a brook trout.

Carrie Stevens invented her fabled Gray Ghost streamer and many other patterns at historic Upper Dam. Herb Welch, a noted taxidermist from nearby Mooselookmeguntic Lake, Maine's largest State Heritage Fish water, invented the popular Black Ghost streamer. Cornelia "Fly Rod" Crosby, the first Registered Maine Guide, plied her trade in and around Rangeley. President Eisenhower fished the Magalloway River in 1955—a streamside plaque commemorates his visit. President Herbert Hoover fished in Rangeley as well.

A large wild native brook trout caught from the Rapid River near Rangeley, Maine. The Rapid is the finest native brook trout river in the nation. KRIS THOMPSON PHOTO

The Rangeley Outdoor Sporting Heritage Museum in Oquossoc, Maine, is the home of White Nose Pete, a collection of original Carrie Stevens flies, and other historical items. BOB MALLARD PHOTO

White Nose Pete, the mythical brook trout of Upper Dam, is housed in the Rangeley Outdoor Sporting Heritage Museum, as is a taxidermy mount of an 11-pound brook trout caught at Upper Dam in 1897, which is 2 pounds heavier than Maine's official state record.

The classic wooden Rangeley Boat, a favorite of fishing and hunting guides since the turn of the last century, was as elegant as it was practical. Lower Dam on the Rapid River was long synonymous with fly fishing in Maine, and one of the most recognizable landmarks in the state. Louise Dickinson Rich wrote her book *We Took to the Woods* while staying at Forest Lodge just below the dam; the structure is still intact.

Rangeley was also famous for its now extinct population of blueback trout, a distant relative of the brook trout now referred to as Arctic charr. These fish served as the primary food source for the strain of giant "humpback" brook trout found in Rangeley, Mooselookmeguntic, and Upper and Lower Richardson Lakes.

While not covered in this book due to its admittedly seasonal nature, the Rangeley River, which connects Rangeley Lake with Cupsuptic and Mooselookmeguntic Lakes, offers spring and fall fishing for large lake-run brook trout.

Rangeley is also home to the finest concentration of large native brook trout lakes in the country including Aziscohos, Cupsuptic, Mooselookmeguntic,

A poster featuring White Nose Pete, the mythical giant brook trout that haunted Upper Dam Pool for a generation or more. DIANA MALLARD PHOTO

Fall fishing for brook trout in the Rangeley region of Maine. It doesn't get any better. DIANA MALLARD PHOTO

Parmachenee, Rangeley, Upper and Lower Richardson Lakes, as well as Kennebago Lake, which is covered earlier in the book.

Other quality brook trout fisheries in the Rangeley area include the Little Magalloway and South Branch Dead Rivers, South Bog Stream, Bemis Brook, Pond in the River, and Little Jim, Little Kennebago, Round, Sabbath Day, Tea and Little Tea, and Quimby Ponds. Countless small brooks and streams throughout the region contain healthy populations of wild brook trout as well.

There are several museums and historic sites in or near Rangeley. Of particular interest to the fly fisher, or any outdoor enthusiast, is the Rangeley Outdoor Sporting Heritage Museum in Oquossoc. The museum is home to a restored Rangeley Boat, vintage fly-fishing tackle, a collection of original Carrie Stevens flies, and a few Herb Welch trout mounts.

The Rangeley region has a number of traditional sporting camps, as well as hotels, motels, rental cabins, and campgrounds. There is a grocery store, numerous restaurants and pubs, gas stations, two fly shops, gift shops, a post office, and a hospital. Many fishing guides work out of the area as well.

Rangeley is a tourist-friendly town with a robust tourism infrastructure. The downtown section is roughly two miles long, with many of the businesses located along Main Street. Most importantly, it is a great town to fly-fish for native brook trout—nothing even comes close.

Sea-Run Brook Trout

Sea-run brook trout are a form of diadromous fish, migrating between freshwater, brackish water, and saltwater. They differ from sea-run, or anadromous, Atlantic salmon, which live in saltwater and only enter freshwater to spawn: Sea-run brook trout live and spawn in freshwater but move into brackish and saltwater to feed and seek thermal refuge. They are commonly referred to as salters, and occasionally sea trout.

When Europeans first arrived on the East Coast, salters were extant in hundreds of coastal streams from the Canadian Maritime Provinces to Long Island Sound. All coastal New England states, along with New York and New Jersey, boasted populations of sea-run brook trout, and, based on early reports, lots of them.

Massachusetts had a famous sea-run brook trout fishery in the early 1800s. Rivers such as the Agawam, Mashpee, Monument—now buried beneath the Cape Cod Canal—Santuit, and Quashnet, along with Red Brook, were well known for their salter fishing. The Connetquot and Carmans Rivers on Long Island, New York, were famous sea-run brook trout fisheries.

Daniel Webster is purported to have caught a sea-run brook trout of over 14 pounds from the Carmans River in 1827, formerly known as the East Connecticut River. The fish is one of the most, if not the most, written about brook trout in history. Born in New Hampshire, Webster was an ardent angler. He caught the historic trophy on a 15-foot rod and a brace of wet flies, a carving of which still exists today.

While early sea-run brook trout averaged a pound or so, fish up to and even over 10 pounds were occasionally caught. This resulted in the creation of fishing clubs on

A sea-run brook trout from the Chandler River in Downeast Maine. On one outing with Ted Williams and Emily Bastian, we caught close to 75 fish from the river. EMILY BASTIAN PHOTO

A sea-run brook trout from a small stream in Downeast Maine. We caught endangered Atlantic salmon parr from the stream as well. EMILY BASTIAN PHOTO

some of the more popular salter rivers and streams to cater to the rich and famous and movers-and-shakers of the era.

By the mid-1880s Massachusetts had become an industrial giant. This led to demands for power, and the state's rivers and streams were the easiest place to get it. Dams built to harness the rivers and streams for power generation greatly fragmented and reduced sea-run brook trout habitat by the late 1800s. The industrial boom pushed south and north, destroying even more salter habitat.

Streams that had escaped the dam-building rampage soon succumbed to agriculture. Cranberry farming took its toll, and still does today, replacing native vegetation with a managed crop, turning streams into irrigation ditches, and stripping them of valuable sun-blocking canopy. Blueberry farming had a similar, but less extreme, effect in some areas. The use of fertilizers, herbicides, and pesticides negatively affected water quality as well.

Many sea-run brook trout streams fell victim to pollution, siltation, canopy removal, and other forms of habitat degradation that are by-products of development. Fish husbandry in the form of nonnative invasive fish introductions and stocking took its toll as well. Other waters were subjected to high levels of angler exploitation by an ecologically illiterate population that viewed brook trout as nothing more than table fare.

Attempts to restore or even maintain sea-run brook trout populations through stocking were largely unsuccessful.

By the mid-1900s it was clear that fish-husbandry was not the answer. Apparently, the domestication of the hatchery fish left them incapable of surviving in a world that required they move between freshwater and saltwater to find forage and thermal refuge.

Sea-run brook trout utilize freshwater, brackish water, and saltwater. They leave the relative safety of their natal streams to feed in the dangerous transition zone between freshwater and saltwater, and even bays and sometimes open ocean. Regardless of the type of habitat they utilize, salters rarely venture more than a few miles from their natal stream.

When sea-run brook trout migrate into saltwater varies geographically and, to some degree, based on weather. As brook trout on Mount Desert Island in Maine are dropping down to the ocean in search of thermal refuge, fish on Cape Cod are moving back into streams for the same reason. Some salters spend winter months in saltwater, returning to freshwater in the spring or summer in search of thermal refuge. Others winter-over in freshwater. But all sea-run brook trout spawn in freshwater.

Ocean temperatures off Mount Desert Island in Maine remain conducive to brook trout throughout most of the year, allowing sea-run brook trout to remain in saltwater for up to two years before returning to their natal stream to spawn. Conversely, those found on Cape Cod must retreat to their natal streams by late spring to find thermal refuge.

A National Park Service sea-run fish kiosk at the mouth of Stanley Brook in Acadia National Park, Maine. Interestingly, the stream was not on a list of sea-run brook trout streams I got from the state. BOB MALLARD PHOTO

While in saltwater sea-run brook trout adopt a silver-like coloration, and their markings fade as well. Within a couple of weeks, or even days, of returning to freshwater, they look like any other brook trout. Salters attain sizes, especially weights, larger than their purely fluvial cousins. Sea-run brook trout feed on minnows, eels, marine worms, and small crustaceans and spend up to three or more months a year doing so.

While salters spawn in the same streams that resident brook trout do, they sometimes don't move as far upstream as the home-based fish do. In addition, like the coasters found in the Great Lakes region, fish born in the same stream, and even from the same parents at the same time, may or may not become sea-run. Why this happens is not completely clear.

While significantly reduced, sea-run brook trout can still be found in Maine, Massachusetts, and New York. There are populations in Maine from the Canadian border to the New Hampshire border. There are several populations on Cape Cod, and reports of fish north and south of Boston, as well as Martha's Vineyard. Long Island has a couple of populations. Connecticut, New Hampshire, New Jersey, and Rhode Island may have some remnant populations also.

Although sea-run brook trout can be found up and down the Maine coast, the best concentration of salter waters is found in Downeast Maine. Almost every river and stream has brook trout, and most places where they have access to the ocean have salters. This includes all the historic Atlantic salmon rivers as well as many lesser-known waters. Mount Desert Island has several sea-run brook trout populations as well.

Most of the sea-run brook trout in Massachusetts are found on upper Cape Cod. This includes Red Brook and the Quashnet River. Sadly, the Santuit River, also known as the Cotuit River, appears to have lost its salters as of 2015. While the exact cause is not known, it has been referred to as "death by a thousand cuts."

While sea-run brook trout may be losing ground in New York, Rhode Island, and Massachusetts, they seem to be doing quite well in Maine. But even Maine doesn't fully understand what it has as evidenced by the fact that several salter waters I am aware of were not included in a list of such that I obtained from state fish and game. If the list is correct, or even close, with more than 40 waters Maine has roughly 90 percent of the remaining native sea-run brook trout populations in the nation.

Salters live in the last place you would expect to find wild brook trout, the heavily developed and densely

Sea-run brook trout informational sign posted on a coastal stream in Downeast Maine. BOB MALLARD PHOTO

populated coastal Northeast. And we don't know nearly enough about them. Rhode Island Fish & Wildlife was quoted as saying, "We do not have any reliable information on sea-run brook trout in Rhode Island." According to the Connecticut Bureau of Natural Resources: "[I]f they [salters] still exist in Connecticut, they are exceedingly rare."

From an angling standpoint, sea-run brook trout are a great gamefish. They fight better than typical stream-resident brook trout their size, and I swear I had one jump. Salters are more likely to hit a streamer than many brook trout, and far less likely to hit a dry fly, at least until they have been in freshwater for a bit. In brackish and saltwater, they feed almost exclusively on minnows and eels, making small streamer patterns by far your best bet.

Sea-run brook trout are here today and gone tomorrow. They move due to water temperature, roll in and out with the tide, and move up and down streams at will. Salters are more accessible in the transition zone at high tide than low tide and are better fished on a rising tide than a dropping tide. They are most easily targeted in the stream or near the head of tide, but can be caught in marshes and bays at certain times. Very few sea-run brook trout are actually caught in the "sea."

Sea-run brook trout have become trendy and popular with young anglers looking to fulfill a bucket list item. This increased visibility has resulted in a higher level of interest in them from both within the conservation community as well as state fish and game agencies. We are still learning about sea-run brook trout, and we still have a lot to learn. If you haven't already had the chance to do so, give sea-run brook trout fishing a try, and admire this fish that has survived against all odds.

STATUS, THREATS, AND CONSERVATION

There is a lot to be excited about in the world of brook trout, and hope for the future in the form of growing ecological enlightenment, a burgeoning pro-native movement, and ongoing conservation and restoration efforts. Unfortunately, there have also been some significant losses, some of which have been covered earlier in the book, and some which have not.

Conservation is in trouble before it even gets started. Unlike preservation, which is maintaining something in its original or existing state, the goal of conservation is to protect something from harm or destruction, which is ambiguous at best. There is a big difference between harm and destruction, and the goals of conservation usually focus on the latter—preventing something from going away.

While preservation puts the resource first, conservation allows for use, and even consumption, of the resource. Unlike preservation, which is absolute, conservation is a balancing act between so-called multiple use or wise use and preservation. And often we lose our balance and harm, but not necessarily destroy, what we are trying to protect.

Conservation allows for some level of resource usage and depletion as long as it is sustainable. The problem is the definition of sustainable. Much forestry is referred to as sustainable, yet how can removing something that takes centuries to replace be sustainable? Are today's forests representative of what we once had? Are they even close? The same can be said about our wild native brook trout; although they are still here, in many places they have been greatly diminished or seriously compromised under the guise of sustainable harvest and conservation.

In practice, conservation is not any one thing, it is a series of actions and reactions we take and make to try to ensure the long-term viability of something, which in this case is wild native brook trout. The rules change as the game changes, and the game changes as the rules change. Today's crisis is often tomorrow's distant memory, and today's social norm is often tomorrow's taboo. And sometimes we end up back where we started.

Conservation requires hard work, vision, cooperation, compromise, concessions, money, and a bit of luck. It has to address the big picture to be effective, and when it doesn't, it isn't effective. Much of what is being done today regarding native brook trout conservation is not big picture. We are often painting the back deck while the front of the house is on fire, and addressing the easy stuff rather than the necessary stuff. And we often lower the bar to keep the peace—at the expense of the resource.

While not in imminent danger of going away, in some ways brook trout are one of the more beleaguered trout in the country. Clearly Atlantic salmon, Apache and Gila trout, Arctic charr, Arctic grayling, and certain subspecies of cutthroat are at a much higher risk of extirpation than brook trout in the United States. But brook trout are not without their own challenges, and in some cases populations could and most likely will be lost.

While some salmonids have seen their populations stabilize to at least some degree, brook trout are still losing ground—at least at the aggregate level. Maine continues to lose lake-, pond-, and river-dwelling populations of brook trout to invasive fish introductions, and the Santuit River in Massachusetts, once a notable salter stream, recently lost its brook trout for reasons that are not completely clear.

Today brook trout are facing what could be referred to as the "perfect storm." Geography, invasive fish, climate change, pollution, development, road building, logging, mining, agriculture, water use, stocking, and angler exploitation are all taking their toll on wild brook trout populations across their native range. Each is a problem in and of itself, and some drive others.

The threats faced by the nation's wild native brook trout are numerous, varied, and ever-changing. The situation changes depending on where you are, and what is a major threat in one place may not be so elsewhere. While habitat degradation is a significant problem in southern New England and climate change the bogeyman south of that, neither is the biggest threat in northern New England, where it's invasive fish and stocking.

What is a major threat to brook trout today could become a minor issue tomorrow and vice versa. For example, acid rain was a huge issue in New England and Upstate New York in the 1970s and 1980s. High-elevation pond-dwelling populations of brook trout were lost, and many headwater stream populations were severely compromised. Today you rarely hear about acid rain due to a region-wide improvement. Conversely, climate change was not even on the radar screen in the 1970s and 1980s, yet it is a major concern today.

The threats to the nation's wild native brook trout come from many sources including industry, government, private landowners, and Mother Nature, as well as from within the angling community. While the tendency is to blame the other guy, we sportsmen have done as much damage as anyone else, at least indirectly, and in some cases we are still doing so.

Like everything else, the threats to native brook trout are subject to interpretation and debate. For every position there is a counter-position, and you must peel back the onion to truly understand what is going on. Many studies

Round Pond, Somerset County, Maine. There was once gold at the end of that rainbow, but now there's highly invasive golden shiners. BOB MALLARD PHOTO

regarding the impacts, or nonimpacts, of activities on native fish are funded by industry, including aquaculture, hydropower, resource extraction, agriculture, and recreational angling. These groups all have an agenda, and that is to protect their turf. Studies that contradict each other are common and used by both sides of the argument to discredit the other side and confuse the masses.

In general, I think we have become too trusting of what we see as science and reluctant to use common sense and observations afield. Much of this science comes from state fisheries managers who use stocking as the primary tool for dealing with our declining wild native trout stocks. Is stocking over wild fish good science? Introducing nonnative fish? Allowing nonnative fish to be used as bait?

The loss of wild native brook trout populations is not just a number on a report, a color on a map, a story in a magazine, or internet chatter between anglers, biologists, and advocates—it's real, and for me, damn real, as I have lost several of my favorite brook trout waters over the years. Others I fish have been noticeably degraded.

In some cases angler exploitation compromised waters I fished. In others it was stocking, including one pond lost to hybrid splake. In still other instances it was a nonnative fish introduction. And as was the case with Ash

Swamp, my first brook trout home water, it was habitat degradation.

My personal knowledge, experience, and loss are by no means definitive or in any way all-inclusive. In fact, it's just the tip of the iceberg. Most anglers have their own horror stories, and those who don't, eventually will.

While we have stopped the bleeding in some areas, and even regained lost ground in others, we are still losing wild native brook trout populations and will continue to do so until we have a paradigm shift in how we view, treat, and manage these invaluable resources.

My hope is that we will see the error in our ways before we lose too much more, as two steps forward and one step back is almost as harmful as it is helpful. Hopefully, this will happen before you lose *your* favorite brook trout water.

Paradise Lost

For me, nothing drives home the loss of wild native brook trout like Round Pond in Chase Stream Township in Somerset County, Maine. While I have fished many great wild native brook trout stillwaters, Round Pond stands out, or stood out, above all others. I had never seen anything like it before, and I haven't seen anything like it since.

The brook trout in Round Pond averaged over a foot in length, fish between 14 and 16 inches were not at all uncommon, and fish larger than that were regularly caught. And the numbers were equally impressive. The pond also had the finest hatches I have ever seen. To say Round Pond was the quintessential wild native brook trout pond would be fair.

One year we encountered surveyor's string—known as "hip chain"—ribbons of colored plastic tape, and hatchet-marked and spray-painted trees a couple of hundred feet from the water. It was obvious this was not going to be a cut, but a road, and dangerously close to the pond. The new road resulted in a noticeable increase in fishing pressure. Lured by stories of large brook trout, anglers swarmed on the pond like flies to a discarded sandwich. With them came illegal, and dangerously effective, live minnows for use as bait.

While the loss of large fish to poaching was a concern, it was the least of the problem. Soon the pond became overrun with nonnative and highly invasive golden shiners. The alien minnows competed with the native trout for food and space, preyed on juvenile brook trout, and seriously compromised the food supply, especially insects.

Sickened by what had transpired at Round Pond, after 30 years of storing a canoe at the pond, I removed it and surrendered my prime shoreside spot. If there is a better wild native brook trout pond than Round, I haven't seen it. To have something so precious and treat it so poorly is selfish and wrong-headed. To stand by and do nothing about it is criminal. Can Round Pond be fixed? I believe so, if we act before we lose the pond-specific strain of trout. Do we have the will to do it? I'm not so sure, as we seem to have lost our appreciation for wild native things.

By the Numbers

By some estimates wild native brook trout populations in the United States have been reduced by as much as 90 percent. I think the Trout Unlimited estimate of 45 percent is probably more accurate. The situation in Canada, while not perfect, is, however, much better.

According to Eastern Brook Trout Joint Venture, intact populations—those where wild brook trout occupy 90–100 percent of their historic habitat—of stream-dwelling brook trout can be found in only 5 percent of subwatersheds in the United States. Self-sustaining populations have disappeared or been greatly reduced in nearly half of subwatersheds. Much of what is left are fragmented populations located in the headwaters of streams.

Healthy wild brook trout subwatersheds are rare in many eastern states. Per Eastern Brook Trout Joint Venture, they represent only 14 percent of Maine's subwatersheds, 14 percent of Vermont's, 9 percent of Virginia's, 8 percent of New Hampshire's, and 5 percent of New York's. Brook trout have been extirpated from 58 percent of Georgia's subwatersheds, 57 percent of Maryland's, 44 percent of South Carolina's, 40 percent of North Carolina's, and 38 percent of New Jersey's.

Very few large lakes in the United States still have self-sustaining populations of native brook trout. Most that do are in Maine, and these are at risk due to development, angler exploitation, stocking, and nonnative fish introductions. The situation in Canada is much better due to fewer of the risk factors noted above.

Self-sustaining native brook trout ponds are rare outside Maine. Neighboring New Hampshire has just three formally designated Wild Trout Management ponds, and per Vermont Fish & Wildlife: "Most of Vermont's brook trout pond fisheries are supported entirely by stocking. . . . A few ponds are not stocked at all." New York, second to only Maine in regard to wild native pond-dwelling brook trout, states that "the vast majority of our brook trout ponds are stocked. Ponds totally sustained by natural reproduction probably total less than 50." And I think this number is high.

Most large native brook trout rivers in the United States no longer support self-sustaining populations. Even in Maine, home to most of the remaining large wild native brook trout rivers in the United States, many waters no longer have self-sustaining populations. Outside Maine, most states have fewer than five notable self-sustaining large brook trout rivers, if they have any left at all. While in better shape than the United States, river populations in Canada are being lost to hydropower as well.

While there are numerous wild brook trout populations in the Adirondacks, including some lakes and ponds, the situation in and around the fabled Catskills is troubling. Most of the historic rivers and streams, including the Beaverkill, Esopus, Neversink, and Willowemoc, are stocked with nonnative brown and rainbow trout. And while the branches of the Delaware are mostly wild fisheries, they too are primarily brown and rainbow trout waters.

Except for Big Spring Creek, most of the famous Pennsylvania limestone creeks are now brown trout fisheries or, in the case of Falling Springs Branch, a rainbow trout fishery. Penns Creek, Slate Run, Spruce Creek, Spring Creek, both Fishing Creeks, and Yellow Breeches are brown trout fisheries for the most part as well. And many rivers and streams are being stocked. From Virginia to Georgia, many small streams have self-sustaining nonnative brown trout or rainbow trout populations, and in some cases both.

Many historic native brook trout waters are being stocked. In New Hampshire's White Mountain region, most rivers and streams within striking distance of a road receive at least some level of hatchery fish. The same thing is happening in Vermont, central and western Massachusetts, Connecticut, and Rhode Island. In many cases these waters could support at least some level of wild brook trout under different regulations and expectations.

Maine stocked nearly half its remaining never-stocked brook trout lakes and ponds in just over a decade. Per Ted Williams in an early 1990s article in *TROUT* magazine, there were close to 500 never-stocked brook trout lakes and ponds in Maine at the time. Just over a decade later, that number had shrunk to roughly 275, according to research done in support of Maine's State Heritage Fish law. At one time there were probably well over a thousand.

In many states the only uncompromised wild native brook trout populations left are found in high-elevation headwater streams away from the road and above natural barriers that have blocked the passage of stocked and nonnative fish. With most native brook trout lakes and large rivers in the United States in trouble, the last stronghold for wild native brook trout could become these small headwater streams. If we lose our lake and river brook trout, large wild native brook trout could become a thing of the past in the United States, and in many areas they already are.

There are, however, still waters where brook trout are not only wild but have never been stocked over. These fish represent some of the last genetically pure native trout in the country, and where they live some of the least compromised waters in the nation. Maine alone has over 275 never-stocked brook trout lakes and ponds, as well as countless miles of never-stocked streams. The only species with a larger inventory of never-stocked waters is likely lake trout, and most of that is found in Canada.

And large wild native brook trout can still be found without going to Canada. Maine, New York, and to a lesser degree New Hampshire still boast brook trout that would be considered trophies under any definition of such. Other states still put up the occasional large brook trout as well, and with any luck, we will find a way to bring big brook trout back to even more waters.

Range Expansion

Unlike many forms of wildlife that are moving into areas not previously occupied by them due to changing weather, there is no natural range expansion occurring regarding brook trout that I am aware of. The reason is because most weather-influenced range expansions involve wildlife taking advantage of warming trends, something that negatively impacts brook trout.

While brook trout have been introduced across America, they haven't been moved around to the extent that rainbows and browns have. Although brook trout have been introduced to Europe, South America, and New Zealand, their invasion of foreign soil, or more appropriately water, has not been nearly that of Europe's brown trout, which can now be found throughout the contiguous United States and parts of Canada, South America, and New Zealand.

Nonnative brook trout introductions have probably been limited to at least some degree by the fact they already had a large footprint, plus they were long considered inferior to rainbows and browns, arguably the two most popular trout in America today. The only major species of trout that has been moved around less than brook trout is cutthroat trout, which are relatively uncommon outside their native range.

Brook trout are not popular with tailwater fisheries managers, and most man-made reservoirs are managed for species that get bigger than brook trout because that's what the primary users of large lakes, mostly trollers and ice anglers, want. While brook trout may be experiencing a bit of a surge in popularity in pro-native fish circles, I doubt it

will result in any noticeable increase in their use by state fisheries managers.

Brook trout have also become a pest in many of the places they have been introduced. With a few notable exceptions, they have often overpopulated in the fertile conditions found outside their native range and become stunted, while forcing out native fish and more "desirable" species by competing with them for food and space.

Finally, the habitat requirements of brook trout are more specific than those of rainbow and brown trout, making them less attractive to fisheries managers than other species with more general requirements.

Because of the issues noted above, I do not believe there will be any noticeable increase over the current nonnative brook trout range. In fact, I suspect some states will walk away from brook trout, and even go as far as to eradicate them where already established. Others could be replaced with brook trout hybrids, which grow larger and are easier to manage.

Husbandry

While brook trout have been deliberately hybridized with lake trout and brown trout, they have not been manipulated to the degree that some species have. You rarely see triploid brook trout, nad-zapped sterile fish, or pigment-deprived brook trout like so-called palomino or golden rainbows. No one I am aware of has developed a spring-spawning strain of brook trout like they have with fall-spawning rainbows. This may again be because brook trout are not as popular with today's anglers as other species of trout.

Triploids and pigment-deprived trout have unfortunately become popular with certain anglers and many fisheries managers. The cover of the West Virginia fishing regulations book, an important native brook trout state, features a pod of palominos, often referred to as the "unofficial state fish," in a hatchery tank. Pennsylvania, another native brook trout state, has promoted palominos on the Fish & Boat Commission Facebook page. This could lead to the manipulation of brook trout as well.

State fisheries managers and some factions of the angling community have become enamored with hybrids. Fisheries managers love them because they grow fast and are often, but not always, sterile, making their populations easy to manage. Anglers like them because they grow large and are usually easy to catch due to their piscivorous tendencies.

The use of splake, a brook trout/lake trout cross, has increased noticeably in the last 20 years. Look up "splake" on the internet and you will see references to Colorado, Idaho, Maine, Michigan, Minnesota, New Hampshire, New York, South Dakota, Utah, Wisconsin, and Wyoming. Maine, the last stronghold for wild native brook trout, currently stocks over 50 waters with roughly 90,000 splake a year.

Tiger trout, a hatchery cross between a brook trout and a brown trout, are also becoming more popular. Colorado, Connecticut, Illinois, Indiana, Massachusetts, Michigan,

Over 40 wild brook trout gathered around a shallow spring during low water. It would be very easy for anglers to seriously compromise the population under these conditions. DIANA MALLARD PHOTO

Minnesota, Montana, Nevada, South Dakota, Utah, West Virginia, and Wyoming, some of which are native brook trout states, all have tiger trout stocking programs.

While some states have reeled hybrids in—excuse the pun—and some have even suspended their programs, splake and tiger trout appear to be here to stay. There are also states experimenting with splake/lake trout back-crosses. I do not, however, expect to see any significant expansion of these hybrid programs as they are already pretty well saturated.

Geography

Native brook trout are often found at relatively low elevations. Many are found at just hundreds of feet above sea level, and some at far less. This is especially true for sea-run fish, as well as lake, pond, and river-dwelling fish. While some populations are found up to a few thousand feet above sea level, very few live much higher than that. Trout found elsewhere in the country live at elevations that are two to three times higher than what would be considered high in native brook trout range.

Except for acid rain, which thankfully has been greatly reduced in the last 25 years or so, elevation is usually a friend of wild trout because it helps keep the water cool. Not only does water at high elevations typically not get as warm as that in low-lying areas, but the warm-water season tends to be much shorter. While trout can survive

warm water to some degree, the longer they are subjected to it the more stressed they become.

In moving water, high elevation usually means high gradient, and this means high oxygen content. Unless they are spring fed, low-gradient streams can become oxygen-deficient during the warm summer months. High-gradient flows are also less hospitable to nonnative fish such as bass, perch, sunfish, and shiners. And they are less likely to be affected by siltation, at least in the long term, which can negatively affect spawning and insect life.

With some notable exceptions such as Pennsylvania limestone country and parts of Cape Cod and Downeast Maine, native brook trout range is not known for an abundance of springs. Most streams are classified as freestone and get much of their water from precipitation. Many rivers get their water from lakes. Temperatures and flows in these types of waters fluctuate much more than they do where the water comes from springs. Freestone rivers and streams are also subject to extreme flooding on one end and extreme droughts on the other, both of which can negatively affect wild trout.

Nonnative Fish

Make no mistake about it, nonnative fish are the biggest short-term threat to wild native brook trout across much of their range. Once established they are costly to remove at best, and impossible to remove at worst. Small reclamation projects cost tens of thousands of dollars, and projects costing over a million dollars are not unheard of. And many reclamation efforts fail, or the water is re-infected later.

There is some confusion as to the meaning of the term *invasive*. While many see it as being synonymous with nonnative, that is not necessarily the case. When applied to plants and animals, invasive means "not native to an ecosystem and causes harm," with "causes harm" being the key point. While all invasive fish are nonnative, not all nonnative fish are invasive.

While nonnative smelts, white suckers, and golden shiners are highly invasive to brook trout, many chubs and dace are not. Big Reed Pond in Maine, a recently reclaimed native brook trout and rare Arctic charr water, was found to be infested with six species of nonnative minnows. Only one, smelt, was considered invasive.

Invasive fish affect a water in multiple ways. They can prey on native minnows, including juvenile trout, and compete with native fish for food and space. They can affect the food supply as well. Specifically, schooling minnows such as golden shiners can devastate aquatic insect populations by feeding heavily on emerging nymphs and thus reducing recruitment. Smelts can tax zooplankton and cause a bottom-up disruption of the food web. Invasive fish can also disrupt spawning, and even hybridize with native species in some cases.

Maine is experiencing what is arguably the worst invasive fish epidemic in the country, and as goes Maine so goes wild native brook trout. Unlike other states where the damage was done decades ago, Maine is losing waters to invasive fish now, and at an alarming rate.

The St. John River in Maine, once the longest and most remote wild native brook trout stream in the nation, is now home to nonnative and highly invasive muskellunge and all but devoid of brook trout. A decade or so ago it would have been included in this book.

Nonnative and highly invasive smallmouth bass can now be found throughout Maine's fabled Rapid River. The Rapid is not only the finest trophy wild native brook trout river in the state and nation, it's also one of the finest wild native trout fisheries in the country irrespective of species.

Maine Department of Inland Fish and Wildlife has worked with dam owners to try to find flows that are unfriendly to bass. They also approved a one-time bass harvest event that included temporarily lifting the strict fly-fishing-only regulation, so anglers could use spinning rods and lures to try to catch and kill as many bass as possible. While the flow changes have helped to some degree, the bass in the Rapid River are here to stay. Like the lake trout in Yellowstone Lake, we can never get rid of them; the best we can hope for is to control them.

Will the brook trout in the Rapid River be able to coexist with bass? The short answer is yes, to at least some degree. And the situation will likely improve somewhat as it has elsewhere once things level off. But to be clear, the Rapid River will never be what it once was. That this could happen to the water most synonymous with brook trout fishing in Maine is tragic.

While a worthy gamefish and native to many waters in historic brook trout range, smallmouth bass and brook trout don't mix well. KING MONTGOMERY PHOTO

A large wild native brook trout from the Rapid River. This is what is now at risk due to the introduction of highly invasive nonnative smallmouth bass. KRIS THOMPSON PHOTO

Nonnative bass can also be found throughout the upper Kennebec River system, including historic Moosehead Lake. Both the river and lake are covered in this book. With bass in Moosehead Lake, it's just a matter of time before they move into the Roach River, also featured in this book.

While it happened 35 years ago, I remember the first bass I caught in the Kennebec Gorge as if it were yesterday. Stunned by what I was holding, I felt physically ill. I remember wondering to myself how people could be so careless and uncaring.

Invasive bass, pike, and muskellunge have all taken their toll on native brook trout. White and yellow perch have as well. Walleye are becoming increasingly popular with some anglers in the East and are likely to find their way into native brook trout water via state-sponsored stocking and bucket biology.

While anglers get much of the blame, not all invasive gamefish are the result of bucket biology. Much of the current invasive epidemic has been government-sponsored. Prior to states taking control of their natural resources, the federal government threw nonnative fish around like confetti. Records from the late 1800s show numerous introductions of bass and various species of salmon into Maine waters. Thankfully, much of this did not take hold.

When states took over fish and game management, they often simply continued what the feds had started—and that meant moving fish around. The state-sponsored introduction of nonnative brown trout, rainbow trout, lake trout, and landlocked salmon has compromised brook trout populations throughout their native range. In total the government has introduced far more nonnative fish than anglers have, and continues to do so.

You can now find self-sustaining populations of rainbow and brown trout throughout the Appalachian corridor from Maine to Georgia. Browns can be found throughout the Midwest. Brown trout are highly piscivorous—they are to brook trout what wolves are to coyotes. Nonnative steelhead, coho and king salmon, and brown trout now enter many Great Lake tributaries to spawn.

Anglers are, however, behind many nonnative fish introductions. Deliberate acts of bucket biology have accounted for many, but certainly not all, recent non-salmonid invasive gamefish introductions within native brook trout range. In other cases sunfish, perch, and most likely even bass have entered our waters as a result of species misidentification associated with the use of self-trapped live fish as bait. Juveniles of these species can be tough to tell apart from baitfish.

The legal and illegal use of live minnows as bait is behind many baitfish introductions. In other cases baitfish have been deliberately introduced in an ill-advised attempt to grow bigger gamefish. The use of live minnows as bait is a problem because it can, and does, result in the

A battle-weary Kennebec Gorge brook trout; note the damaged tail and healed scar on its flank. Life is hard enough in the Kennebec Gorge without having to compete with nonnative smallmouth bass. CHRIS RUSSELL PHOTO

A wild rainbow caught from a small native brook trout stream in New Hampshire. Years of state-sponsored stocking have resulted in several self-sustaining populations of nonnative rainbows that compete with native brook trout for food and space. NATE HILL PHOTO

Trouble by the Bucketful

Northern Pike

Black Crapple

Smallmouth Bass

Please help stop the illegal stocking of fish.

Illegal introductions can destroy native fish populations and alter the ecology of Maine's waters, _FOREVER!_

Introducing any fish species or _possessing_ or _transporting_ any live fish (except baitfish) without a permit is <u>illegal</u>. These are Class E Crimes punishable by a fine of up to $10,000 and may result in the suspension of all Department licenses and permits.

To report any suspected illegal stocking activity Please call:

Operation Game Thief

1-800-ALERT-US

There is a $2,000 reward for information leading to a conviction.

Thank you!

To learn more about Maine's fisheries, log on at:
www.mefishwildlife.com

spread of nonnative and often invasive minnows. As they say, "to use bait is to lose bait"; lose enough and you can establish a population. Some, me included, believe that unless it is trapped from the water where it is being used, live bait should not be allowed anywhere near wild native brook trout.

In Maine much of the fabled Allagash Wilderness Waterway, the finest concentration of large wild native brook trout lakes in the country, is still open to the use of live bait. This includes 17 species of minnow, more than 10 of which are not native to the watershed. Nonnative sunfish, illegal to use as bait, were recently confirmed in one lake. I suspect they got there via their illegal, but most likely accidental, use as bait.

Of the 17 species of fish that are legal to use as bait in Maine, three are highly invasive to brook trout: smelts, white suckers, and golden shiners. One, the eastern silvery minnow, is nonnative to Maine and therefore everywhere it is legal to use them. Others, while native to the state, are nonnative to many of the waters where they can be legally used, and smelts are nonnative to most.

In New Hampshire there are 16 legal baitfish, including smelts, golden shiners, and white suckers, that are highly invasive to brook trout, as well as emerald shiners, which have been linked to outbreaks of viral hemorrhagic septicemia (VHS) in the Great Lakes. Many are nonnative to many of the waters they can be used on, and some are nonnative to the state. Profile Lake, a popular stocked brook trout pond in the White Mountains, is now overrun with yellow perch, even though it is closed to the use of bait.

In New York there are 20 species that are legal to use as bait anywhere open to such. This includes golden shiners, emerald shiners, and white suckers. Smelts, alewives, mummichog, herring, and menhaden are legal to use in select waters.

While some bait used by anglers is procured from commercial dealers, much is trapped by anglers who in many cases don't know, or care, what they are using. In fact, at a legislative hearing in Maine, the director of Fisheries at the time defended the use of emerald shiners, saying that game wardens could not tell the difference between them and smelts. If wildlife professionals can't tell the difference, how can we expect anglers to?

There are two ways to deal with invasive fish: proactively and reactively. In theory, addressing the former can lessen the need for the latter. However, in practice we will have to do both, as we cannot completely prevent invasive fish introductions.

Proactive management is far less risky and costly than reactive management. Unfortunately, we have fallen well short of what is needed to prevent or even lessen nonnative fish introductions, forcing us to operate in a reactionary manner, or a perpetual state of firefighting.

Stronger laws, more restrictions, better enforcement, faster responses, and more information and education regarding invasive fish are needed if there is to be any hope of stopping this dangerous and damaging trend. Unfortunately, these reforms have been slow to come and are often opposed or ignored by anglers and resisted by state fish and game agencies.

Once invasive fish have entered a water, they can spread throughout the system. The longer you wait to address it, the worse things get. States should be required to establish "rapid response" policies that mandate they act immediately upon confirmation of an invasive fish introduction that could imperil a native fish population—the sooner the better.

When it comes to invasive fish introductions, there are two options: control or eradication. When eradication is not feasible for environmental, economic, legal, or social reasons, you can at least control an invasive fish population if you have the will and resources to do so. Man has proven to be pretty effective at reducing native populations; why not apply the same pressure to nonnative species?

For example, while invasive lake trout can never be completely removed from Yellowstone Lake, keeping their numbers down has allowed the native cutthroat to rebound. The project is ongoing and can never be stopped or the lake trout numbers will bump up again. The same thing could be done for the invasive nonnative bass now imperiling Maine's Rapid River, a native brook trout water of national significance.

Hatchery space should be reserved for housing native fish from waters infected with nonnative fish, so they can be artificially reproduced and reintroduced after chemical reclamation or control measures where applicable. To date this has not happened.

Chemical reclamation is one of the best tools we have for eradicating invasive fish populations, and in some cases it is the only option. Where possible it is a one-time event and often cheaper than ongoing control projects. It is, however, still expensive, time-consuming, and risky and often comes with at least some level of public opposition, including costly lawsuits to try to prevent it.

We need to do a better job of educating the public as to what chemical reclamation is and isn't. We need to explain what gets killed and what doesn't, and how what gets killed is returned to the ecosystem. We need to explain the short-term and long-term impacts of piscicides and address any health and public safety concerns in a clear, thorough, concise, and sensitive manner.

The fish advocacy world needs to stop using names like "chemophobe" to refer to people who oppose chemical reclamation. We need to start addressing the legitimate concerns of the public regarding chemical restoration if we are to have any chance of expanding its use. Last I checked, you don't win people over to your side by calling them names.

And it would help if state fish and game agencies would stop using chemical reclamation as a way to create sport fisheries, especially stocked ones. When we use it as a way to restore nonnative and stocked fisheries, we lose credibility and it becomes harder to defend its use when it is really needed—to restore native fish, frogs, insects, and so forth.

Unfortunately, both control and eradication treat the symptom, not the cause. They are reactive, not proactive, and in far too many cases we end up back where we started due to a subsequent introduction that happens for the same reason as the initial infestation.

While true bucket biology and the illegal use of live fish as bait are tough to address because they are deliberate criminal acts, there are things we can do. We need to establish, and be willing to impose, stiff fines that reflect the cost of undoing the damage regardless of whether it was a deliberate act of bucket biology or the result of the illegal use of live fish as bait, as the impact is the same and in both cases a deliberate violation of the law. Lengthy license suspensions should be imposed as well, as nothing gets the attention of sportsmen like losing the privilege to partake in the sport they love.

We can, and should, address the legal use of live bait, as it is a huge problem in native brook trout range and a primary cause of nonnative fish introductions. No state should allow the use of nonnative fish as bait, yet many do. And highly invasive species such as smelts, white suckers, and golden shiners should not be allowed on or even near wild native brook trout water—the risk is simply too high.

When it comes to invasive fish, *management by reclamation* is a losing hand because you can never get out in front of it. As soon as you clean up one mess, another mess pops up. Give it enough time and the last mess you cleaned up becomes the next mess you have to fix, as reinfection rates are troublesomely high.

Like the fly in the soup, nonnative fish have degraded the aesthetics and quality of many of the nation's native brook trout waters, diminishing their appeal to brook trout anglers and negatively affecting other forms of wildlife. Unless addressed—and many, in fact most, are not addressed—these waters will never be the same.

Climate Change

Climate change is the 10,000-pound gorilla. It could be a real game changer, and left unchecked could be the biggest long-term threat to native brook trout. Because brook trout are often found in habitat that would be considered marginal for other species of salmonids, a change in the wrong direction could have a serious negative impact or, worse, prove fatal in some cases.

Climate change is defined as a measurable change in weather patterns over an extended period. It can be measured in decades, centuries, thousands, or even millions of years. Climate change can be seen in weather patterns as well as at the event level. The faster the change, the harder it is for living things to adjust to it, or evolve. Evolution is a race against time—fail to run fast enough and you go extinct.

Climate change can take many forms. In some cases it can result in extreme weather such as prolonged periods of drought, excessive rain, or low or high snowfall. While one area is burning another could be drowning, and while snowpack is high in one area it can be low in another. Climate change can also affect the timing of events, which in turn can change their impact. It can cause gradual changes in the mean temperature, and longer or shorter seasons as well.

While you can debate what causes climate change, a subject for another time and place, and even whether it can be stopped, it would be tough to argue that our climate is not changing. It seems as though so-called 50-year floods now come around every five years or so. These floods turn rivers and streams into raging torrents threatening roads and structures. States and municipalities send heavy equipment into the streams to try to stem the rising tide. Streams are straightened, banks destroyed, canopy lost, and streambeds scoured, and many are left with a coating of silt that can take years to flush away.

Previously occurring primarily in the early spring, my home river, the Kennebec in Maine, now sees flows exceeding 10,000 cfs in midsummer. A giant log deposited on an old bridge abutment during the flood of 1986 was recently dislodged from its perch like Excalibur and deposited somewhere downstream. Hurricane Irene in August 2011 damaged New England rivers and streams to an extent I had not seen in my 60 years of living in New England.

A late October flood in New Hampshire in 2017 appears to have had a significant effect on the next season's brook trout. Recently laid eggs that were barely settled into the gravel at the time were likely washed away. I suspect many current-year fish were lost as well, as the receding water trapped them in pockets and dry channels.

Southern Appalachia has seen unprecedented flooding that pushed rivers and streams to historically high levels. And the unseasonably dry summer weather has resulted in some of the worst fires I can remember, causing erosion and siltation.

For decades the word "drought" was about as foreign to me as "tsunami." Primarily a western problem, it was just not something we worried about in the Northeast. But in the last decade or so I have seen wells go dry, and last year I saw streams go intermittent for the first time in my lifetime.

Ice-out often comes a couple of weeks earlier than it did when I was young, and some larger lakes like Sebago in Maine don't always completely freeze over anymore. This has resulted in the cancellation of long-standing ice fishing tournaments, and in one recent case a first-ever emergency early fishing season opener.

For roughly a decade in the early 2000s, I told my fly shop customers to target June 5–15 if they wanted to take advantage of the spring mayfly hatches on the river. By the time I closed my shop five years later, we were telling people to show up between Memorial Day and June 5. Maine's popular early summer Green Drake hatch, actually a *Hexagenia*, seems to start and end earlier than it used to as well.

Fall fishing has also changed noticeably in my lifetime. For years I took the month of September off to pursue spawning brook trout and landlocked salmon near Chesuncook Lake in northern Maine. As my old fishing logs attest, I was typically into migrating fish within a day of arriving. As the years went on, the spawning fish started showing up later, until early to mid-September was no longer reliable.

A late October flood in New Hampshire's White Mountains damaged numerous backcountry roads. The US Forest Service issued emergency permits to allow municipalities to "fix" them so they could gain access to public water supplies. Unfortunately, they bulldozed the streambed to do so. BOB MALLARD PHOTO

While talking to a friend who, incidentally, doesn't believe in climate change, we discussed the early hatches and late fall brook trout and landlocked salmon spawning runs we are experiencing in northern Maine lately. His response was, "May is the new June and October the new September," a shocking admission from a climate denier.

The current impact climate change is having on brook trout varies depending on where you are. Low-lying areas in warmer parts of its native range have been hit the hardest. While Maine has somewhat dodged the bullet for now, Rhode Island has apparently recorded measurable changes in mean water temperature in some cases.

By most measures temperatures are getting warmer, and staying warm longer, over much of brook trout native range. Any noticeable rise in temperature is dangerous, and if the trend is permanent, or even lingers too long, climate change could be, and many think it is, the biggest long-term threat to the nation's wild native brook trout.

Habitat Degradation

Habitat degradation is kind of a catch-all and comes in many forms, including river and stream straightening, warming water, canopy removal, bank destabilization, and the loss of instream structure, all of which takes a toll on wild brook trout populations. Activities such as development, logging, and mining all contribute to the problem.

But habitat degradation is a symptom, not a problem in and of itself. Habitat degradation is also more of an issue in some areas than it is in others, and while often tagged as the "number one threat" to wild native brook trout, this is not always the case.

To effectively address habitat degradation, you must delve into its root causes; otherwise you are just putting out fires. You also need to look at the big picture to make sure that habitat, not some other factor or combination of factors, is the true cause of the decline in the fishery you are witnessing. Like most things it is rarely that simple, and it is often far more complicated than it looks.

Logging, mining, and other resource extraction practices need to be changed to better protect brook trout habitat. The same holds true for farming and water use. Development and road building near critical habitat need to be done in ways that minimize their impact on wild native fish.

Addressing degraded habitat can reap huge benefits and help offset other things that negatively affect wild brook trout. It can increase holding capacity, improve spawning habitat, and allow passage. This in turn increases population size and improves distribution. Habitat work can also cool the water, prevent siltation, and stabilize banks, as well as lessen avian predation and even improve forage.

Some habitat work is enhancive and some corrective. Replacing poorly designed bridges and culverts, adding

A severely damaged section of stream resulting from recent flooding. While you can debate the cause, you cannot debate the impact. BOB MALLARD PHOTO

Guide Nate Hill and the author inspecting some questionable "chop-and-drop" on a small stream in the White Mountain National Forest. Cutting live trees from the streambed is never a great idea. DIANA MALLARD PHOTO

This low-wall dam is located on a small wild brook trout river in New Hampshire. While downstream fish passage is possible, upstream passage is not. Many such dams still exist across much of native brook trout range.
BOB MALLARD PHOTO

woody debris and structure, creating meanders, repairing damaged banks, and planting shade trees can all yield positive, and even significant, results.

Federal agencies such as the US Forest Service, National Park Service, and Bureau of Land Management dedicate a significant amount of money and resources to fish habitat improvement. Unfortunately, most state fish and game agencies do not. Much of the money spent at the state level must come from the private sector and nonprofits. Thankfully, habitat work has very few enemies, and what few it does have very few friends. This makes it a safe place for large national conservation organizations and small grassroots groups to work, as the opposition is minimal and the noise level low.

Addressing habitat is a complicated proposition. It requires permits, input from hydrologists and other experts, and the ability to get equipment and manpower to the source. It is almost as hard to prepare for as it is to get it done. It is also expensive, with even small projects costing in the thousands of dollars. Many projects cost tens or hundreds of thousands of dollars, and some can even push the million-dollar mark.

Habitat work costs as much to do it wrong, or in the wrong place, as it does to do it right and in the right place. Some of what I have seen clearly benefited trout, some had no noticeable impact, some may have harmed fish, and some failed altogether due to its inability to withstand what Mother Nature threw at it.

If we are going to spend time and money on habitat work, we need to make sure it's going to accomplish what we want it to—increase wild native fish populations. And we should ask state fish and game agencies for some concessions regarding protecting the fish we are doing it for from exploitation. We owe it to those footing the bill to spend their money in a way that will achieve the highest benefit possible.

Fragmentation

Stream fragmentation is a form of habitat degradation, and is also a symptom, not a problem in and of itself. Some of it occurs naturally, at least indirectly, and some is manmade. And like other forms of habitat degradation, it needs to be addressed at the root cause.

Obstructions in rivers and streams can prevent brook trout from reaching critical thermal refuge and important spawning areas. In other cases it can prevent fish from getting back to where they came from. This can reduce gene flow, which can negatively affect genetic diversity. While some forms of blockage are bidirectional, others prevent upstream movement only.

An ineffective, at least for passing brook trout, fish ladder in Downeast Maine. There are brook trout above the structure and brook trout below; connecting the two populations would help gene flow and recruitment.
BOB MALLARD PHOTO

While we are removing far more dams than we are building today, many fish-blocking dams still exist across native brook trout range. Because the East was settled long before other parts of the country, many of the dams in the region are old, and most were not built with fish passage in mind. As they come up for relicensing, many dams are modified to pass fish, or removed altogether for cost reasons.

Due to aging infrastructure in the East, dams that are not a problem today could become a problem in the future as they deteriorate and fall into disrepair. And those that were relicensed in the last couple of decades but not modified for fish passage may not come up for relicensing for another several decades.

While fish ladders provide some relief, they are never as good as unimpeded passage. Hike around our rivers and streams enough and you will eventually bump into a nonfunctioning fish ladder. Some have grown in with vegetation or been damaged by the elements, and others are poorly designed and not effective in passing all species of fish.

Poorly designed culverts can also block fish passage, at least upstream. So-called perched or hanging culverts are suspended above the water, making it impossible for brook trout, a species not known for its athletic prowess, to pass through. Others are too long and sans structure that allows fish to rest as they work their way through. And like any choke point, culverts can be tough to negotiate during high water.

Like culverts, but less commonly a problem and not as obvious to the untrained eye when they are, poorly designed bridges can hamper fish passage or even prevent it in extreme cases. This is especially true regarding small bridges that are narrower than the streambed. Others have rock pads that cause erosion and can become perched.

Culvert design has come a long way in the last 20 years. So-called box, arch, and bridge culverts are much more fish-friendly than the old-style pipe culverts. The same is true for bridge design, with newer bridges built longer than older ones to allow for a more natural flow.

Mother Nature can cause stream blockage as well. Blowdowns and mud and rock slides can create small waterfalls that can block upstream fish passage, and strainers can impede passage in either direction during low water. But these are usually temporary and typically get blown out by a subsequent high-water event.

And beavers, nature's civil engineers, are seeing population increases across much of native brook trout range due to declines in trapping driven by low fur prices and demand. While their impact on brook trout is a mixed bag, and often temporary, beavers can block fish passage at times. But beavers and brook trout have been coexisting peacefully for thousands of years, and it all works out in the end.

Connectivity is important to the short- and long-term survival of wild native brook trout. It helps mitigate other problems by keeping the gene pool healthy and making sure brook trout have access to critical thermal refuge and

This badly perched culvert in New Hampshire blocks upstream fish passage between a small river and small stream, both of which are home to brook trout. At certain times of year, the water temperature in the stream is noticeably cooler than the river and could provide thermal refuge if accessible. BOB MALLARD PHOTO

This century-old backcountry railroad bridge likely blocks upstream fish passage in both low and high water due to the small waterfall and long, narrow, tilted chute above. BOB MALLARD PHOTO

important spawning habitat. People are starting to understand how important this is and are finally doing something about it.

Pollution

Pollution can wreak havoc on fish populations and has accounted for the loss of numerous wild native brook trout populations. Thankfully, things have improved noticeably over the last few decades. In fact, many rivers and streams are cleaner today than they were when I was young. The days when many of our rivers and streams were too polluted to step in appear to be behind us. Many rivers and streams that were once devoid of fish are now home to healthy fish populations.

This is not to say that pollution is no longer a threat to brook trout, just that it is better than it once was, and much of what we do experience is more localized than it once was.

There are two primary types of pollution: point source and nonpoint source. Most of the former is man-made and ongoing, while the latter is usually event-driven and triggered by rain and snowmelt. Accidents can cause pollution as well, albeit usually temporarily, and can fall into either category depending on how, where, and when they happen.

Point source pollution is best described as "coming from a single identifiable source." This includes outflows from businesses, factories, farms, mines, power plants, sewage treatment facilities, stormwater systems, and, interestingly, aquaculture facilities and fish hatcheries, which release uneaten food, urine, excrement, and tissue into the water. For example, while walking a stream in Acadia National Park looking for sea-run brook trout, I came upon a half dozen or so dead brook trout fry just below a rust-colored trickle coming from some sort of municipal sewer pipe. While I could not determine what it was, it was pretty clear it was the cause.

Nonpoint source pollution, however, comes from multiple sources and is often a cocktail of poisons. This includes contaminated precipitation, ground seepage, storm runoff, and windblown debris. But most nonpoint source pollution originates from point source pollution that is difficult to track down as it weaves its way to the water by indirect routes.

Herbicides and pesticides are still used on farms, many of which border rivers and streams. Some municipalities and private landowners use herbicides as an alternative to more resource-intensive brush trimming. There is a wide swath of dead vegetation running along the border of a large private land I fish in Maine that could only be the result of herbicide spraying. And if you pay attention you will notice what look like fall leaves along dirt roads in Maine's "working forest" in the summer, many of which show signs of spraying.

Some municipalities and private landowners spray insecticides as well. While staying at a fishing lodge in Montana last year, I was driven inside by a small truck spraying the yard for mosquitoes, which by eastern

standards would be a nonissue. When I was in my late 20s, large landowners in Maine carpet-bombed the woods with insecticides to get rid of spruce budworm. Interestingly, Rachel Carson wrote an entire chapter on this in her book *Silent Spring*, noting that spruce budworm spraying was responsible for the death of entire year-classes of brook trout and Atlantic salmon in Canada.

Last year while fishing for sea-run brook trout in Downeast Maine, I encountered four or so recently deceased frogs with no sign of trauma in a very short section of river. Interestingly, and maybe not coincidentally, the section of river was bordered by a blueberry farm. While I cannot prove it, I couldn't help but wonder if contaminated runoff did my amphibian friends in.

Fertilizers are used on lawns, farms, football and baseball fields, and golf courses. Water quality, especially in lakes and ponds, can be negatively affected by fertilizer runoff because it increases nutrients, particularly nitrogen and phosphorus, which promote algae and weed growth. This is referred to as eutrophication and can negatively affect brook trout and things they feed on by blocking light and reducing oxygen levels.

Most of native brook trout range experiences at least some level of winter, and in the case of northern New England, a whole lot of winter. Roads are treated with salt to help reduce accidents and make them passable. Much of this finds its way into lakes, ponds, rivers, and streams via storm drains where it can cause salinization. While brook trout can usually adapt to increased levels of salt, some of what they feed on cannot. And while not deliberately applied like salt is, our roads get a constant dose of leaked oil, gas, and other automotive fluids that are flushed into our lakes, ponds, rivers, and streams by runoff.

As populations increase, traffic increases. As traffic increases, accidents increase. Some accidents result in petroleum and other chemical spills that can enter our waterways. When they involve large trucks transporting chemicals, the effects can be devastating on brook trout and what they feed on. The same is true for trains, which have accounted for some of our worst chemical spills. Ruptured oil pipelines have resulted in fish kills as well.

Waters can suffer acidification as the result of pollution carried in precipitation. While not the problem it once was, so-called acid rain caused by emissions of sulfur dioxide and nitrogen oxide from power plants can change water chemistry and result in the loss of brook trout. This has been most prevalent in the Adirondacks of New York and high-elevation ponds in northern New England. Contrary to what the name implies, these contaminants can also be carried in snow, sleet, and fog as well as rain.

Sadly, while we have made a lot of progress regarding pollution in the last few decades, we seem to be backsliding at both the state, especially rural states, and federal level under what is best described as a "commerce at any cost mentality." When environmental restrictions are relaxed or removed, as is now happening, industries take advantage of the opportunity to push the envelope in an attempt to increase profits.

Development

The recent Great Recession brought development to a screeching halt across much of the economically hard-hit native brook trout range. But as the region claws its way out of the economic abyss, the construction industry is rising up in its wake like Godzilla after being knocked down by King Kong.

While Maine dodged a bullet when Plum Creek abandoned their wilderness development plans, there are movements to lessen restrictions on development in the unoccupied townships, home to most of Maine's wild native brook trout. And besides Baxter State Park, the new Katahdin Woods and Waters National Monument, a few small state-owned parcels, and land owned by organizations like The Nature Conservancy, much of Maine's prime brook trout habitat is still in private hands.

The White Mountains of New Hampshire, the Green Mountains of Vermont, and western Massachusetts are in the crosshairs as well. Skiing and outdoor recreation, and their proximity to New England's big cities and suburbs, make them prime targets for developers. Fortunately, much of the best brook trout habitat in New Hampshire and Vermont is somewhat, but not completely, off-limits due to the two large national forests.

Southern Appalachia in and around Great Smoky Mountains National Park and the surrounding national forests is a hot commodity right now. Blessed with much more favorable weather than New England, a growing population and economy, and a lower cost of living, areas such as greater Gatlinburg and Johnson City in Tennessee and Bryson City and Brevard in North Carolina have become popular with second-home buyers. Thankfully, while the edges will be eroded and some prime brook trout habitat lost, there is a lot of protected public land.

In general, much of native brook trout range is lacking in public, read "protected," land when compared to other areas of the country. At 814 square miles, Great Smoky Mountains National Park is the largest national park in the East, but only the 19th biggest in the country. The same holds true for most of the eastern national forests; they pale in comparison to their western cousins when it comes to size.

Creating more public lands through acquisition and donation will be key in preserving wild native brook trout. And stricter laws regarding what can and cannot be done within riparian zones will be needed as well. There are not many places left in the Northeast to build, thus putting what's left in the crosshairs of those looking to develop land for businesses, homes, second homes, and tourism infrastructure.

Logging

Timber harvest can have both short- and long-term negative effects on wild brook trout. While best-in-class practices can reduce the impact, they cannot entirely eliminate it. And as an industry that has experienced severe financial stress over the last couple of decades, best practices are not always economically feasible or justifiable.

Much of what is done under the guise of commercial logging can be, and often is, detrimental to wild brook trout. In some cases we are cutting too close to the water, which can cause erosion, siltation, and bank destabilization. In other cases we are removing canopy from headwater streams that provides shade at critical times of year, which can cause the water to warm and promote algae growth.

Skidders and other heavy equipment used in commercial logging cause soil compaction, which reduces absorption and increases runoff. Roads are built to get the equipment into the woods and the logs out of the woods. Insecticides and herbicides are used to protect the "crop," and diesel fuel is leaked and spilled as part of daily operations. Like most forms of natural resource extraction, logging comes with a price, and wild native brook trout are often the ones that pay it.

State and local shoreline zoning laws are rarely strict enough to truly protect our waters. While full of fancy language and glowing promises of protection, most shoreline zoning laws are weak in practice and fall well short of what is needed. Enforcement is an issue as well, and I have seen some flagrant violations go unaddressed. And these policies regulate development more than they do logging and other forms of resource extraction.

Originally written in 1971, Maine's shoreline zoning laws have not changed much in the last 45 years. While the shoreline zone is 250 feet of the normal high-water mark for ponds greater than 10 acres and most large rivers, the buffer drops to just 75 feet for streams. And most shoreline zoning laws don't mean you can't cut trees, just that you cannot cut all of them.

These quotes are from *Maine Shoreline Zoning: A Handbook for Shoreline Owners*: "No more than 40 percent of the total volume of trees over 4 inches in diameter in the buffer area may be harvested in any 10-year period. . . . Within 100 feet of great ponds [waters over 10 acres] and rivers flowing into great ponds, and within 75 feet of all other water bodies and streams: no opening in the forest canopy may exceed 250 square feet. . . . Selective cutting is allowed, provided a well-distributed stand of trees remains." And commercial harvest is held to an even lower standard.

The draft management plan for Maine's newly acquired Cold Stream Forest public land, home to seven State Heritage Fish waters and the best wild brook trout stream in the area, calls for a mere 100-foot no-cut buffer along the ponds and streams, implying that everything else is up for grabs.

Mining

While historically viewed as a problem affecting central Appalachia only, mining can, and is, affecting other areas as well. While coal is king across most of native brook trout range, sand, gravel, and granite are also being mined. Recently, recreational gold mining has become popular in the region, and while small-scale compared to coal mining, it can cause significant damage to streams—enough so that legislation has been submitted to reel it in.

When most people think of mining, they think of what is known as underground mining, where dust-covered men in helmets with lights attached to the top drop like worms deep into the earth to remove and haul out whatever it is they are mining for. Tunnels, or mineshafts, are dug to reach the prize. What is pulled from the tunnels is deposited elsewhere. Hazardous gases and dust are released, which can find their way into water via precipitation.

There are somewhere around 15 active coal mines across native brook trout range. They are centered in the Allegheny and Appalachian Mountains, home to important native brook trout habitat. West Virginia has the most with roughly six, with Pennsylvania right behind at approximately five. Coal mines can be found in Kentucky and Ohio as well. West Virginia also produces the most coal at 112.2 short tons, with Kentucky coming in second at 77.3 tons and Pennsylvania next at 60.9 tons.

So-called mountaintop removal is the most destructive of all mining. This form of surface mining starts at the top of a mountain and works its way down, leaving a stub behind. As the mountain is chewed down to extract the coal, unwanted fill, referred to as overburden, is pushed off to the side and on top of tiny headwater streams. One study stated that more than 700 miles of stream in Appalachia were buried between 1985 and 2001 alone.

The deforestation and loss of topsoil resulting from mountaintop removal mining has caused severe floods and erosion that have badly damaged rivers and streams. Once the mining operation has been abandoned, the now flat land is used for agriculture or some other form of economic development, which can result in other threats to brook trout.

Other forms of surface mining, such as strip mining and open-pit mining, aren't a whole lot better than mountaintop removal. While strip mining goes wide, open-pit mining goes deep. Both leave a barren landscape not fit for man or beast, especially fish, as well as settling, or tailing, ponds laced with toxic mining waste. These man-made ponds can leach into the aquifer, and have breached their dams and spilled tons of sludge into nearby rivers and streams.

Not only is the extent of damage done by mining a problem, but much of it is permanent. Have you ever seen a fully restored sandpit? Granite quarry? Strip mine? Open-pit mine? Mountaintop removal site? The answer is pretty much no, with most remaining seriously degraded in perpetuity. And while there are laws that require companies mitigate the damage they do, many culprits are given waivers or allowed to do less than the law requires, which is usually less than what is needed.

In general, rivers and streams near mines often suffer from pollution. Many have lower levels of biodiversity than those found where mining is not happening. Fish in some of these streams have experienced reproductive failure, physical deformities, and even death. The impacts have been traced to downstream lakes and ponds as well.

Fracking

Hydraulic fracturing, better known as fracking, is the new kid on the block when it comes to resource extraction. While it's been around since the 1940s, it has really ramped up over the last decade or so.

Fracking is a process where rock is fractured by injecting pressurized liquid into the ground. This releases gas and petroleum, which is drawn to the surface for collection. The liquid used in fracking, known as fracking fluid, is mostly water with some sand and thickening agents in it. But it can also contain things like 2-butoxyethanol, acetic acid, borate salts, citric acid, ethylene glycol, glutaraldehyde, hydrochloric acid, isopropanol, isopropyl alcohol, methanol, polyacrylamide, sodium chloride, and sodium and potassium carbonate, all of which can negatively affect living things.

Fracking also sometimes involves injecting radioactive tracers into the ground to determine the location of fractures and what they look like. They are bonded to sand or synthetic beads and injected like fracking fluid to help identify the exact location of fractures. Known as radiotracers, they contain detectable levels of radiation.

The bottom line is that, like most forms of resource extraction, fracking has the potential to contaminate groundwater and surface water, and in some cases has done exactly that. It is also water-intensive and reported to use as much as 8 million gallons of water per well over its lifetime. Some also believe that fracking can trigger earthquakes, which can cause mud slides that can negatively affect rivers, streams, lakes, and ponds.

Interestingly, and I believe tellingly, Maryland, New York, and Vermont, important native brook trout states, have banned fracking due to public safety and environmental concerns. Massachusetts has imposed a 10-year moratorium. Unfortunately, Michigan, Pennsylvania, Virginia, and West Virginia have not followed suit.

Road Building

Road building goes hand in hand with development, logging, and mining. Bridges and culverts are built to get vehicles, equipment, and supplies into places we did not have access to before. Some of these structures are poorly designed and block upstream fish passage, which I discussed at length under "Fragmentation" earlier in this chapter.

Roads can also reduce soil absorption and change runoff patterns. This can result in siltation and the conveyance of contaminants into rivers, streams, lakes, and ponds. You can read more about this under "Pollution" in this chapter.

Not covered earlier is the fact that more roads mean more access, and when it comes to fish, more access means more pressure. At best, increased pressure results in increased incidental mortality. And if the now easily accessible water is liberally managed, it can mean a higher level of angler exploitation in the form of increased harvest.

Increased access also makes it easier for anglers to transport live fish into areas where they could not easily do so before. In Maine we have seen a noticeable increase in nonnative fish introductions, both gamefish and baitfish, as road access has increased. According to former Fisheries director Michael Brown: "Development that allows vehicle access facilitates the possibility of invasive introductions." He went on to say that native salmonid waters were "at risk, in part due to increased public access."

Agriculture

While native brook trout range does not have the sprawling cattle ranches and industrial mega-farms found in many other parts of the country, it is not without agriculture.

New England is well known for its picturesque family-owned dairy farms. They can be found elsewhere in native brook trout range as well, including New York, Pennsylvania, and Virginia. While relatively harmless looking, these small farms can, and do, negatively affect native brook trout, albeit at what is often, but not always, a somewhat localized level.

Cows can damage streambeds and banks, which widens streams and makes them shallower and, in turn, warmer. The loss of banks also removes critical habitat for brook trout. Cows eat streamside vegetation, which can cause erosion. They urinate and defecate in the water, which increases nutrients and promotes algae and vegetation growth. And of course, cows need to eat, with land-intensive hay and corn making up much of their diet.

In Downeast Maine, home to a high percentage of the nation's wild native sea-run brook trout as well as critically endangered Atlantic salmon, blueberry farming is a major contributor to the local economy. The largest producer of blueberries in the world, Washington County has over 50,000 acres of blueberry barrens. While naturally occurring, many have been converted to managed lands that barely resemble natural barrens.

Maine is also the 10th-largest grower of potatoes in the country. With approximately 60,000 acres of land dedicated to the production of potatoes, Maine has nearly four times more than North Carolina and New York, which have over 10,000 acres of land being used to grow potatoes.

Apples are also grown throughout native brook trout range including New York, Pennsylvania, Virginia, and North Carolina, all of which are in the top 10 producers in the country.

Wisconsin and Massachusetts are the two leading producers of cranberries in the United States. Wisconsin is home to rare coasters, and Massachusetts is home to the majority of salters found outside Maine. One of the problems with cranberries is that they are grown in man-made cranberry bogs, many of which are on coastal streams. Few crops affect waterways as badly as cranberries, and they have been the cause of more than one lost native brook trout population.

While less than what is needed in other more-arid areas, agriculture in native brook trout range requires water. This water is often siphoned from rivers and streams, and sometimes the aquifer. While much of it is absorbed into the ground, some is flushed into rivers and streams carrying herbicides, pesticides, and animal waste along with it.

Farming also requires land, and that land needs to be cleared to be productive. Readying land for agriculture means removing trees and other vegetation, which can cause erosion, runoff, and a loss of canopy. Erosion causes siltation, runoff transports pollutants, and the loss of canopy results in the warming of streams, all of which can harm wild native brook trout.

Water Use

For most of my life water use was not a big problem in native brook trout range, or at least I didn't think so. Unlike in the West, agriculture is a relatively small industry in the East, and large-scale farming and ranching is pretty much nonexistent, favoring smaller family-owned farms. As a result, unlike other areas of the country, agriculture has had a somewhat limited impact on our rivers and streams in regard to water use. Plus, the East receives much more rain than most parts of the country, which helps keep lakes and ponds high while replenishing groundwater and river and stream flows.

One form of water use that affects brook trout is municipal water supplies. Decades-old small dams and tiny impoundments can be found throughout New Hampshire's White Mountains. These remote facilities are rarely visible from the road and therefore unseen by the masses. They not only impound water but also block fish passage and isolate populations. And by default they consume water, though how much is unclear and hard to ascertain.

The first noticeable change I witnessed regarding water use was snow-making in support of downhill skiing. Water was being siphoned off small freestone rivers at a time when they were low and subject to anchor ice, extreme temperatures, and other factors that stress wild brook trout. Operating at a time when most anglers are home tying flies, the intake pipes are rarely seen in action. I call this our "dirty secret," as it is hard to detect and flies under the radar of most anglers and advocates. And state natural resource agencies and conservation organizations don't seem to be that concerned either. As ski areas expand and weather patterns change, the problem will only worsen.

For the first 40 years of my life, we got our water from a tap and our beer from a bottle. Now we get our water from a bottle and our beer from a tap. We also seem to drink more water today than we did when I was young. When I was young and thirsty I reached for milk or soda. What water I did drink usually came from a garden hose, and that was only because it was convenient. I suspect bottled water now outpaces soft drinks in some urban areas, and by a wide margin.

The first record I could find of commercially distributed bottled water in America was from Boston in 1767. While early consumer products were sold as medicinal "mineral water," today's bottled water is used mostly for hydration and often in place of soft drinks. Extracted cheap

The gate and small sign is all most people see of what is a fish-blocking dam, a small man-made impoundment, and equipment used to siphon water from this wild native brook trout stream. BOB MALLARD PHOTO

and sold steep, bottled water is now a highly profitable mega industry.

Jump-started by Perrier in the mid-1970s, it is said that bottled water is now the second most popular beverage in the United States after soft drinks. While there are technical differences between artesian, distilled, ground, municipal, purified, sparkling, spring, and well water, it all comes from pretty much the same place and is important to the environment, especially fish.

Bottled water consumption more than quadrupled between 1990 and 2005. The United States is now the second-largest consumer in the world after China, accounting for between 30 and 50 billion bottles, or over 12 billion gallons of water per year depending on whose numbers you want to believe. Fortunately, a few of the top brands sell what is known as purified water, which comes from a municipal water supply, usually surface water.

In addition to the direct consumption, it takes water to make water. One study said it requires roughly 1.3 liters of water to produce a 1-liter of bottle of water, the 0.3 liter being lost to processing. Personal products take the least at approximately 1.25 liters, while bulk home and office products take the most at over 1.5 liters. Interestingly, this is less than the water used to produce soft drinks, which is in the 2-liter range, and far less than beer, which uses 4 liters.

While the net result of the increased use of bottled water may actually be positive, the issue is where the water is coming from. While much of bottled water comes from ground sources, most of the water used to make soft drinks and beer comes from municipal surface water sources. Unfortunately, most of the best groundwater resources are found in rural areas like Maine, which is now losing millions of gallons of water a year to the new bottled water craze.

Companies like Poland Springs, owned by corporate giant Nestle, are moving into rural America to take advantage of a dangerous lack of regulations and a willingness on the part of local governments and residents to sacrifice natural resources for the promise of jobs. This has resulted in lawsuits by conservation watchdogs concerned about the long-term effects of groundwater exploitation.

Canada cracked down on the bottled water industry in 2016, including boycotting Nestle for using its huge financial resources to take control of a local water supply. Because this happened during a period of drought, it knocked folks out of their stupor. Unfortunately, most of the United States is still in that stupor.

Brook trout require colder water than many other salmonids. As the water warms in the summer, which it usually does across most of native brook trout range, many stream-resident fish become reliant on springs and seepages for thermal refuge. Changes in groundwater usage could

Bottled water is now the second most consumed bottled beverage in America. In some areas it's the first. Are we taking water out of brook trout mouths? DIANA MALLARD PHOTO

negatively affect these critical coldwater sources and, as a result, wild brook trout.

While experts disagree as to the short- and long-term impacts of high levels of groundwater exploitation, it is fair to assume it will have at least some level of localized negative impact on the resource. Whether this affects wild brook trout is yet to be determined, and apparently all we can do is wait and see.

Stocking

Stocking continues to be a problem across much of native brook trout range. It is being done over wild native brook trout throughout the region, and in some cases as a rule, not an exception. Short of an economic Armageddon, which is not out of the picture, I do not see state fisheries managers backing off stocking anytime soon.

Stocking is an expensive proposition, accounting for a large percentage of the typical state fish and game budget. Stocked fish cost from $2.50 to upwards of $10 per fish. Money spent on stocking is money that cannot be used for land acquisition, habitat restoration, reclamation, infrastructure, law enforcement, and information and education. Stocking is an economic black hole.

Hatcheries are a major expenditure for most state fish and game departments, and with declining revenue, mostly due to falling license sales, increasing costs, and little outside money available to support them, I do not believe that stocking-centric trout management is sustainable over the long-term.

Many states have stocking links on their websites, including Maine's "Current Fish Stocking Report." The page states, "The fish stocking report now features daily updates from hatchery staff. Instead of hearing when and where the hatcheries have stocked well after the season has ended, anglers now will be able to easily locate waters freshly stocked with catchable trout." New Hampshire's website states, "Updates on the location of the previous week's stocking activities are posted on this page during stocking season." Amazingly, according to the website this is protected under the law: "New Hampshire State Law allows the Fish and Game Executive Director to provide past stocking information on a weekly basis."

As for Vermont, another important native brook trout state, their website states, "Regular stocking updates will begin the first week of May and will continue until all stocking is complete. All stockings dates will be entered within 48 hours after completion." I have also encountered links stating, "See Where We Stocked Yesterday" on state fish and game websites.

Most states disseminate annual stocking reports through the local media as well. Sporting publications and the sports section of newspapers run stocking reports in the spring. My former state representative, considered pro-environment by the local media, used to mail out a trout stocking report to his constituents.

Maine is divided into North and South Regions from a regulatory standpoint. The former is home to most of the state's wild brook trout; the latter is mostly maintained through stocking. The daily limit on brook trout in the South Region is 2 fish. In the North Region it is 5 fish. This implies that the state places a higher value on stocked brook trout than it does wild ones.

There are two primary types of stocking: intraspecies, sometimes referred to as intraspecific, and interspecies or interspecific. Intraspecies is exactly that, brook trout over brook trout. Interspecies stocking means stocking something other than brook trout over brook trout, which can include brown trout, rainbow trout, lake trout, or landlocked salmon. Hybrid splake and tiger trout fall somewhere in between and have the combined negative effects of both.

Intraspecies stocking, often referred to as supplemental stocking, is a problem across much of brook trout range. Supplemental means "in addition to," which means in addition to wild fish. While fisheries managers say they use this to "enhance" the fishery, in many cases it actually degrades the fishery for many of the reasons noted above. It is also often a precursor to permanent stocking and put-and-take fishing.

In Maine, interspecies stocking usually involves landlocked salmon. In New Hampshire and parts of Appalachia, it's usually rainbow trout and sometimes brown trout. In Vermont, New York, and Pennsylvania, while rainbows are stocked, the primary culprit is brown trout. When it comes to brook trout, brown trout are the most invasive species of trout due to their highly piscivorous diet, fall spawning, and the possibility of hybridization. Landlocked salmon are as big an indirect threat as they are a direct threat, as they almost always bring highly invasive smelt with them.

Another form of stocking is called surplus or unscheduled stocking, which can be intraspecies or interspecies. This is a by-product of excess hatchery output. Hatcheries raise more fish than biologists request to protect themselves from unanticipated losses. In years where they end up with more fish than needed, they notify biologists, who lay claim to these extra fish like Wall Street brokers and stock them wherever they like, all the while claiming to be "managing" their stocked waters.

The least visible and least understood form of stocking is indirect stocking. This can be intraspecies or interspecies. Basically this means stocked fish gaining access to non-target waters due to connectivity. What happens upstream, and sometimes downstream, can affect waters elsewhere in the system. There have been many documented examples of stocked fish showing up where they were not supposed to. This includes such important wild native brook trout waters as the Rapid and Magalloway Rivers in Maine, and species such as landlocked salmon, splake, browns, and rainbows.

It is well documented, nearly universally accepted, and almost unchallenged that stocking over wild fish creates competition for food and space. It can also disrupt spawning, negatively affect the genetics of wild fish, and even result in hybridization. Stocked fish can also prey on juvenile wild fish. Stocking can introduce diseases such as whirling disease and furunculosis, as well as parasites. It can also result in the introduction of nonnative fish.

The negative impacts of stocking are generally agreed upon by the scientific community, yet it is the scientific community—specifically state fish and game biologists—that is doing it. And while better than most states (and in fact very good in the case of the National Park Service), the federal government is a perpetrator of ill-advised stocking as well.

While preparing for a legislative hearing to try to stop stocking over wild fish in Maine, we culled numerous quotes from the Department of Inland Fisheries and Wildlife website and internal documents regarding the negative impact of stocking over wild fish. Interestingly, the reason we were there is that the department was doing exactly that.

In the time between Ted Williams's article, "Twilight of the Yankee Trout," in TROUT magazine in the 1990s and the State Heritage Fish law hearings in the early 2000s, Maine lost nearly half its never-stocked brook trout lakes and ponds to first-time stockings. An analysis of the last 25 waters stocked for the first time showed that all went from general law fishing—5 fish, 6 inches, unrestricted bait—to stocked with no interim step to try to mitigate the problem, a declining fishery, with regulation changes.

In New Hampshire's White Mountains, including White Mountain National Forest, most rivers and streams that can be reached from the road and all but two lakes and ponds are stocked. In most cases it is being done over wild native brook trout. The situation is so bad that a recent delay in spring stocking caused by high water sent local anglers into a panic because they couldn't find any fish.

Practically every river, stream, lake, and pond in Pittsburg, New Hampshire, is stocked. Nestled against the Canadian border in the northern extreme of the state, it is otherwise one of the most wild, remote, and undeveloped places in New Hampshire, and the closest thing to Maine you can find without going there.

Even in cases where their own data shows an abundance of wild fish, New Hampshire Fish & Game has been reluctant to suspend stocking. And in at least one case where they did, they started up again a few years later for reasons that are not clear, but clearly unnecessary.

Maine is stocking Upper and Lower Richardson Lakes with brook trout and landlocked salmon. This is the source of the fabled Rapid River, the finest wild native trophy brook trout fishery in the country. Both species leak into the Rapid, and from there they have access to the Magalloway River, the second-finest wild native brook trout river in the nation, and the Dead Diamond River in New Hampshire, possibly the third-finest wild native brook trout river in America.

The same thing is happening on historic Rangeley Lake and Little Kennebago Lake in Maine, giving stocked fish access to Mooselookmeguntic and Cupsuptic Lakes and the fabled Kennebago River. Nonnative landlocked salmon are also being stocked over wild native trophy brook trout on Pierce Pond of Dud Dean fame, as well as fabled Moosehead Lake.

The Swift River in Massachusetts, arguably your best shot at a wild native trophy brook trout in the state, is heavily stocked with nonnative rainbow trout even though the brook trout population is relatively robust, self-sustaining, and easily visible to anyone paying attention.

Rhode Island is actively stocking the Wood River, considered by many, including Eastern Brook Trout Joint Venture, to be the finest, and one of just a few, wild brook trout rivers in the state. Attempts to get the stocking suspended by a small local group were opposed by the large trout-centric nonprofit.

I have encountered stocked fish on top of wild fish in many other states, including Connecticut, Maryland, New Jersey, New York, North Carolina, Pennsylvania, Tennessee, Vermont, Virginia, and West Virginia. In fact, the list of stocked waters that do, or could, support populations of wild native brook trout that are being stocked is lengthy.

Often stocking levels exceed, and in some cases by a wide margin, the natural holding capacity of the water. This creates crowding and can force wild fish out of what is often prime habitat and even critical refuge. It also pressures food supplies, albeit in a localized and temporarily manner, due to overcrowding.

Stocked fish are often larger than what occurs naturally in the respective water. The 8- to 10-inch brook trout stocked in many small streams in New England are often the largest fish in the system and by default the apex aquatic predator. Trout are cannibalistic, and these large fish can prey on juvenile wild brook trout, especially in what are often relatively infertile freestone streams with limited forage.

Even some wild trout advocacy groups have jumped on the stocking train, posting pictures on the internet of members proudly posing in front of stocking trucks while writing about the day's events. Local grassroots groups are not only actively involved in stocking, including stocking on top of wild native fish, many are funding it. Others are paying to reclaim put-and-take trout ponds while compromised wild trout waters sit unaddressed.

Having initiated a float-stocking program on my home water a decade and a half ago, a decision I now regret, I am guilty as charged. It took me several years to understand that while it was economically better than dumping all the fish at boat launches as was being done, it had no real environmental benefit and may in fact have been detrimental. As a result I walked away and never looked back, but the program lives on.

While the severity varies from state to state and even area to area within a state, the situation is more or less the same from Maine to southern Appalachia and in the Great Lakes region as well. Stocking has become an accepted management practice, and stocking over wild fish barely

A fin-clipped stocked brook trout caught from the Rapid River in Maine. Stocked brook trout don't belong anywhere near the Rapid River. KRIS THOMPSON PHOTO

causes a raised eyebrow. In many places stocked fish are now unfortunately the norm, and wild fish a rarity.

Stocking has become a crutch for many state fisheries managers trying to balance the desires of anglers who want to harvest fish with the need to maintain acceptable levels of fishing to keep the noise level to a dull roar. Unfortunately, the reluctance and refusal to address harvest to maintain fishing quality often results in them going to "Plan B," which is stocking.

In many cases waters that are currently being stocked could be self-sustaining native brook trout fisheries if managed accordingly. Far too often state fish and game biologists and the governor-appointed bureaucrats who call the shots succumb to public and political pressure and use stocking rather than tackle, length, bag, and season restrictions to mitigate declining wild fish stocks. Anglers show up at public hearings and, rather than agree to concessions, suggest that they stock more, enabling what is a bad practice.

State fish and game agencies need to stop stocking over wild native brook trout. There are better, cheaper, and safer

A large stocked nonnative rainbow trout from a small New Hampshire native brook trout river. How many juvenile brook trout could this fish eat? DIANA MALLARD PHOTO

A stocked brook trout caught from a stream in New Hampshire with a robust wild brook trout population—note the shredded tail. Stocking over wild fish is bad science. DIANA MALLARD PHOTO

ways to maintain what they refer to as a "viable fishery." Stocking is a Band-Aid and a quick fix, not a long-term solution. Economic realities are going to force our hand eventually, so why not get out ahead of it now?

Stocking should be the last resort, not the first line of defense. To go from bait, a high creel limit, and a low length limit to stocking in one step is not "management." We should always address tackle, creel, length, season, and temporary closures before we resort to stocking.

In Maine it took a legislative action to stop fish and game from stocking over never-stocked self-sustaining brook trout in lakes and ponds. The law was expanded to protect waters not stocked in 25 years as well. Other states should take Maine's lead and consider using the legislative hammer to force stocking reform if negotiations don't work.

Fisheries Management

Brook trout are in some ways the Rodney Dangerfield of trout—they get no respect. Within their native range they are often the least protected gamefish in their respective states. Even at the water level they often receive less protection than other, often nonnative species. In states that differentiate between trout species, which many do not, brook trout rarely if ever come out on top.

It is important to note that the specific numbers presented in this chapter reflect the laws and regulations in place at the time the book was written. The numbers are subject to change. However, the underlying message holds true: Many, though not all, states treat their nonnative trout better than their native trout. And they sometimes treat their stocked trout better than their wild brook trout. It would seem reasonable that wild would trump stocked, native would trump nonnative, and wild native would trump all, yet that is unfortunately and frustratingly not always the case.

In coastal waters in Maine, native sea-run brook trout, or salters, are subject to a 5-fish daily limit. The limit is reduced to 2 fish for nonnative brown and rainbow trout, which are usually stocked, as well as for what are usually nonnative and stocked landlocked salmon.

In inland waters in Maine, the daily limit on brook trout in lakes, ponds, rivers, and streams in the North Region, home to most of the state's wild brook trout, is 5 fish. In the South Region it is reduced to just 2 fish in lakes and ponds, which are almost exclusively maintained through stocking. Statewide the limit for lake trout and landlocked salmon, the latter of which are usually nonnative, and nonnative brown and rainbow trout is just 2 fish. Nonnative bass are granted a 2-fish limit in the South Region as well.

In New Hampshire the daily limit on "trout," which includes brook trout, in rivers and streams is 5 fish. The limit is 2 fish for native lake trout and lake whitefish and nonnative landlocked salmon and walleye. It is 2 fish for what are often nonnative smallmouth and largemouth bass for 8 of 12 months of the year. The limit drops to 1 fish for highly invasive nonnative pike. The situation on lakes and ponds is roughly the same.

In Vermont the daily limit on native brook trout in rivers and streams, many of which are wild, is an astounding 12 fish, the highest in the East. The limit drops to just 6 fish for nonnative rainbow trout and brown trout, most of which are stocked. Trout in lakes and ponds, including brook trout, most of which are stocked, are managed under a 6-fish daily limit. According to Vermont Fish & Wildlife: "Most of Vermont's brook trout lake and pond fisheries are supported entirely by stocking. . . . A few ponds are not stocked at all."

Trout in Massachusetts are managed under a 3-fish limit in lakes and ponds and an 8-fish limit in rivers and streams. The daily limit for lake trout is 2 fish or 3 fish depending on where you are; landlocked salmon 3 fish; pickerel, bass, and walleye 5 fish; and nonnative pike and muskellunge 1 fish.

Rhode Island has a daily limit of 5 fish for trout, bass, and pickerel. The limit is just 2 fish for landlocked salmon and pike.

At 5 fish, Connecticut's brook trout get the same protection as carp, slightly more than bass, pickerel, and catfish, but less than pike and walleye.

New Jersey, an anomaly in native brook trout range, is providing more protection to wild native brook trout than most states and treating them as good or better than they are any other species. (See the section on New Jersey wild trout for specific examples.)

In New York, "trout" includes brook trout, which have the same 5-fish daily limit as bass, pickerel, and pike. Lake trout and landlocked salmon are afforded more protection at 3 fish, and muskellunge much more at just 1 fish.

Pennsylvania has a combined "trout" daily limit of 5 fish. They extend a 4-fish limit to bass and pickerel, a 6-fish limit to walleye, a 2-fish limit to pike, and a 1-fish limit to muskellunge.

Maryland is another anomaly in native brook trout range, extending more protection to trout, including brook trout, at just 2 fish per day, than it does any species other than pike and muskellunge at 2 fish and 1 fish, respectively.

Virginia allows the harvest of 6 fish a day for trout including brook trout. Bass, pickerel, and walleye have a 5-fish limit, inland stripers a 4-fish limit, and pike and muskellunge a 2-fish limit. It also gets the award for the most complicated website.

West Virginia has a 6-fish limit on "trout" and smallmouth and largemouth bass, a 4-fish limit on striped bass, a 2-fish limit on pike and muskellunge, an 8-fish limit on walleye, and, oddly, a 10-fish limit on frogs, displayed right there along with the other "fish."

Tennessee has a 7-fish daily aggregate limit on "trout," all of which can be brook trout, a 5-fish limit on bass and walleye, a 2-fish limit on inland stripers, and a 1-fish limit on muskellunge.

In North Carolina "wild" trout are wisely afforded a 4-fish daily limit and "stocked" trout a 7-fish limit, both of which apply to brook trout. This is better than bass at 5 fish and walleye at 8 fish, but not as good as it is for muskellunge at just 1 fish.

South Carolina extends a 5-fish daily limit to its "trout," including brook trout. This is the same as they do for smallmouth and largemouth bass, lower than it is for walleye at 8 fish, and way lower than it is for pickerel at 30 fish.

Georgia has an 8-fish daily limit on trout and walleye. This is high, but better than the 10-fish limit on bass and 15-fish limit on pickerel.

In Michigan trout, bass, and walleye have a 5-fish daily limit and pike a 2-fish limit. On Brook Trout Restoration waters, a name that implies things are not in good shape, it drops to 1 fish, but a recent change bumps it up to 10 fish on the aptly named but ill-advised 10 Brook Trout Possession Limit Waters, affecting nearly 400 streams.

Minnesota has a 5-fish daily limit on "trout" that includes brook trout, a 2-fish limit on lake trout, a 6-fish limit on bass and walleye, a 2-fish limit on pike, and a 1-fish limit on muskellunge.

Last but not least is Wisconsin, with a 3-fish or 5-fish limit on "trout" depending on where you are, a 5-fish limit on bass and walleye, a 2- or 5-fish limit on pike, and a 2-fish limit on lake trout.

As you can see, in most cases the daily limit on native brook trout is higher than, or as high as, it is for any other species. Is this because brook trout are less susceptible to angler exploitation? More desirable as table fare? Or is it something much deeper, something that makes us value our wild native fish less than we do our nonnative and stocked fish? I personally believe that it is due to the fact we can attach a cost to stocked fish, but not a value to wild native fish.

The situation with regard to length limits is pretty much the same as it is with bag limits, with brook trout having a lower length limit than most other species in most states. For example, while brook trout have a 6-inch minimum length limit in coastal waters in Maine, the limit on nonnative brown and rainbow trout is 14 inches, both of which are usually stocked. On lakes and ponds, it is 6 inches for brook trout, and 12 and 14 inches, respectively, for nonnative and usually stocked rainbow and brown trout.

In many cases the low, or nonexistent, minimum length limits associated with brook trout does not guarantee that any fish will live long enough to reproduce. And minimum length limits often result in the top being taken off the population and the loss of the largest fish, fish that have proven to be superior to others in the system.

Many states within native brook trout range, including Vermont where they are the official State Cold Water Fish, do not have formal "wild trout" programs. Those states that do have programs often have arbitrary inclusion criteria, random application, and/or weak protections.

Maine's State Heritage Fish law applies to brook trout and Arctic charr. Unfortunately, it only covers lakes and ponds, and rivers and streams are ineligible. Only waters that have never been stocked or have not been stocked in 25 years or more qualify, the latter of which is not based in science, as five-year-old brook trout are rare in Maine. And all it prohibits is stocking and the use of live fish as bait, which, while two of the biggest threats to Maine's wild native fish, are not the only threats.

New Hampshire's Wild Trout Management program has best-in-class inclusion criteria and protections. It applies to lakes, ponds, rivers, and streams, and is based on published and measurable biomass metrics. Unfortunately, it has only been applied to 16 waters statewide—three ponds and 13 streams—which doesn't even pass the straight-face test when you consider that the White Mountains alone has more wild trout waters than that. And they haven't added a water since 2006 even though numerous waters meet the criteria.

Note that these programs are subject to change and are as likely to go backward as they are forward these days. The bottom line is that it was accurate at the time I wrote the book and is a fair representation of how we currently view and treat our native brook trout.

It is also important to note that many brook trout waters are subject to special regulations and are not managed under the general law. The degree to which this happens varies depending on the state, and in cases like Maine, the type of water, as lakes, ponds, and large rivers are far more likely to be managed under special regulations than are streams.

Angler Exploitation

The term *angler exploitation* has become a four-letter word in some circles. State fish and game agencies and consumptive anglers shun the term as do some advocacy groups that count on angler memberships and donations to survive. Basically, in the eyes of some in our ranks, everyone and everything else is to be blamed for our fish and fishing woes, not us.

Six states within native brook trout range are in the top 10 in the nation regarding population size, and 12 are within the top 20. From a population density standpoint, the numbers are similar, with seven in the top 10 and 13 in the top 20. Where there are people there is fishing pressure, and where there is fishing pressure there is incidental mortality and deliberate harvest.

I believe it would be fair to say that East Coast and Great Lakes anglers are harder on their fisheries resources than their western peers, at least those in the Rocky Mountains, as the situation in parts of the Pacific Northwest is similar. Steeped in a tradition that sees trout as table fare and eating them as a rite of passage, brook trout anglers are often more consumptive than other anglers.

I have logged a lot of time out west, and I rarely if ever saw a trout harvested. Unlike the Rocky Mountains where trout fishing is a huge economic driver, and trout are revered for their sporting qualities and considered more valuable alive than dead, trout in the East, especially brook trout, are often coveted for their culinary qualities and viewed as more valuable dead than alive.

While not as common as they once were, fish stringers and creels are by no means rare in native brook trout range. Commonly used terms such as *mess of trout*, *feed of trout*,

Tackle restrictions such as fly fishing only helps to reduce incidental mortality. Why waste fish? DIANA MALLARD PHOTO

limit of trout, *keeper*, and *pan-sized* imply harvest. And when a brook trout angler says, "I caught my limit," he or she actually means they "killed" their limit, as there is no limit when you are releasing your fish.

Conservation writer Ted Williams stated in a late 1990s article in *TROUT* magazine that releasing brook trout was "akin to leaving food on your plate in some parts of the Northeast." In this case he was talking about Maine, but I have witnessed the same attitude elsewhere in the East, from Maine to Georgia.

Arguably the most telling expression I have heard is *fished-out*, which is a common term in the rural Maine brook trout angler vernacular. Mention a pond to a local Mainer who knows it's not worth fishing and they often reply by saying it's been "fished out." They don't say the habitat was degraded, climate change did it in, or invasive species compromised it, but that we anglers ruined it.

I ran a fly shop in Maine for 15 years. Many of my customers routinely harvested wild native brook trout. Some viewed fishing without harvesting as somehow nonsensical and a waste of time.

Once when discussing at a public hearing a proposal to impose a catch-and-release restriction on a pond that had seen a noticeable drop-off, several anglers suggested that we close it instead, stating, "If we can't fish it, why should anyone be able to?" That they saw a prohibition on harvest as a prohibition on fishing speaks volumes.

High creel limits and low length limits add to the stress already placed on our wild native brook trout fisheries. Changing these to be more in line with that applied to other species of trout such as nonnative rainbows and browns would help reduce pressure on wild native brook trout. It would also be wise to embrace more slot limits to protect important larger fish.

Incidental mortality, fish that die after release or are unintentionally killed, runs between 2 and 35 percent by most estimates. Fly fishing has the lowest incidental mortality and bait the highest. And while most studies say fly fishing and spin fishing are very close, those of us who have done both know better. What happens in a lab where people are trying not to harm fish is not necessarily representative of what happens in the field with anglers sans waders, nets, or the proper tools for removing hooks.

While anecdotal, I believe the eastern trout angler is more likely to spin fish or use bait than his western counterpart. I say this because while I see a lot of spin fishing in the East, I seem to see far less when I travel to other places. And lures and bait come with a price, a price paid by our brook trout.

Very few easy-to-access wild native brook trout fisheries can withstand long-term exposure to bait fishing, especially smaller ones. Bait is simply too effective. Plus, with an incidental mortality rate in the 25–35 percent range, far too many fish are inadvertently killed and wasted. Artificial lure or fly restrictions should be imposed on easily

No-kill and low-impact tackle lessens mortality. Is that too much to ask? DIANA MALLARD PHOTO

accessible small wild brook trout waters. Single-hook, single-point, barbless lures and flies should be required on more delicate waters.

Ice fishing, arguably the most impactful of all types of fishing due to its bait-centric nature and the fact that it occurs when outside temperatures can be very harmful to fish, has experienced a noticeable increase in popularity in the East. In Maine where many wild native brook trout lakes are open to ice fishing, the state now sees more angler-hours during the ice fishing season than it does during the open-water season.

After years of growing acceptance, catch-and-release is now being called "extreme" and "unnecessary" by certain factions in the angling community as well as some of the agencies and organizations that represent us. While no wild native trout population I am aware of has ever been ruined by catch-and-release, some have been saved by it, and many others greatly improved. Is it a coincidence that many of our finest trout fisheries are catch-and-release? I don't believe so.

Others are insisting that eating trout is some sort of rite of passage and failing to do so is somehow "missing the boat." This new threat comes mostly from within our ranks and, more specifically, from consumptive anglers and certain factions in the trout conservation world and fly-fishing media looking to appeal to a broader audience.

And there is a new bogeyman in the room: those who say that catch-and-release is a form of torture or "playing with your food." While some consumptive anglers use this to try to justify their own behavior, this is mostly coming from outside the angling community. While being interviewed for an "eating wild" podcast, the host hit me with this one. In reply I asked him if he just took his limit of fish and went home? He said no. I said case closed.

While often overlooked or ignored, I believe angler exploitation is one of the primary drivers of stocking. When faced with a declining fishery, state fisheries managers often take the easy way out and back up the truck rather than confront an angling community that is often opposed to and unwilling to accept stricter tackle, bag, length, or season restrictions.

And while I can't prove it, I believe compromised native fish populations caused by angler exploitation are responsible for at least some of the illegal nonnative gamefish introductions we have suffered across native brook trout range. Faced with declining fishing, some anglers apparently have taken matters into their own hands and resorted to bucket biology to address the problem.

We are still using lethal gill nets to survey wild native brook trout in some cases. Used by state fish and game as a cheap, light, and easy-to-transport alternative to nonlethal traps and electrofishing, they are often associated with surveys of what have been identified as stressed populations or populations of unknown densities. This seems almost counter to what we are trying to do—save fish.

Environmental DNA, or eDNA, is a nonintrusive way to determine the presence, but not necessarily absence, of species of fish by analyzing water samples for discarded tissue and waste. While the bugs have not all been worked out of it, eDNA holds great promise for helping reduce the number of fish killed in the name of science.

Depressed populations of fish are more susceptible to catastrophic failure due to disease, parasites, drought, or warm water than natural populations. Recruitment, or spawning success, can be negatively affected as well. Reduce a population enough and their genetic diversity also decreases, and this can affect growth rates, fertility, adaptability, and survivability.

Conservation

Preserving, or even conserving, the nation's wild native brook trout is a challenge. Threatened on many fronts, it will require a concerted effort on the part of many individuals, organizations, and agencies to make it happen. While no one can do everything, everyone will have to do something. The key is for each party to do what they do best, while supporting the efforts of others.

IDENTIFICATION

You can't protect what you don't know is there. While we have made huge strides regarding the identification, cataloging, and mapping of the nation's wild native brook trout waters, there is still a lot of work to be done.

Maine has dozens of unsurveyed ponds that may or may not contain wild native brook trout. These waters have never been stocked, and if they do have brook trout, they are by default genetically pure fish. A quick tour of the White Mountains of New Hampshire and Green Mountains of Vermont using Google Earth will show dozens of small, remote ponds off the beaten trail. Many are not stocked and may contain wild native brook trout.

Shenandoah National Park, Great Smoky Mountains National Park, and many East Coast national forests have miles of hard-to-reach and relatively unexplored streams, many of which are home to wild native brook trout. And we are just scratching the surface regarding our coastal streams and whether they are home to populations of wild native sea-run brook trout.

Identification is best addressed by large groups with access to grassroots volunteers and the staff and infrastructure to pull it off. Many of the identification projects now going on utilize volunteer "citizen scientists" who hit the woods and water on their own time and dime to help figure out what is out there. Without their help this important work would never get done.

Maps and lists depicting wild native brook trout habitat need to be complete and accurate to be truly useful. While attending an event at a nonprofit, a member of another nonprofit pointed to a third nonprofit's map and referred to it as "junk." Seeing what looked like a wild brook trout nirvana in an area I knew firsthand to be seriously compromised, I couldn't disagree. Overstating the situation is not much better than understating it, as it gives people a false sense of security and makes them complacent. Understating the situation leaves important wild brook trout resources unprotected.

PROTECTION

Once identified, we need to protect what we find. Stopping at identification, as is often the case, is like fighting your way up the field only to drop the ball at the 5-yard line and walk away. What level of protection a population of wild native brook trout warrants varies depending on the type of resource, abundance, where it is, and how accessible it is.

In some cases protection means regulating logging, mining, agriculture, or water use. In others it means stopping stocking and the use of live bait. Other times it means tackle, creel, or season restrictions. In extreme cases it means some combination of the above. Like identification the key is to do it right and apply meaningful protection that will achieve the goal—sustaining wild brook trout.

INFORMATION AND EDUCATION

We need to do more to inform and educate the masses as to the threats faced by our wild native brook trout. Signage at the source is often weak or nonexistent. The Maine

chapter of Native Fish Coalition undertook a 575-water, 1,000-plus sign initiative to let anglers know they are at a State Heritage Fish water, what the threats to these fish are, and what is expected of them. The New Hampshire chapter tried to do the same regarding their Wild Trout Management waters, but the project was shot down by state fish and game.

State fishing rule books often gloss over important conservation issues that should be given far more space than they are getting. While departments often dedicate a page to the use of live bait, a major cause of nonnative fish introductions, they often allot just a paragraph to the threats posed by it. States should dedicate an entire page to things like the use of baitfish, proper fish-handling, voluntary catch-and-release, and so on.

Advocacy

Advocating for wild native brook trout, or any fish for that matter, is not easy because it is tough to get people excited about something they cannot see, and unless you fish for them, or cruise the internet looking for pictures, you won't see brook trout.

Brook trout aren't cute or cuddly like bears, they're not fun to watch like beavers and otters, they don't jump out

A State Heritage Fish sign hangs on a tree at a remote wild native brook trout pond in central Maine. It tells you where you are, why it's special, and what's expected of you. BOB MALLARD PHOTO

of the water like whales, soar high above like eagles, or step out into the open like deer or elk. They swim away when they see you and otherwise make themselves scarce.

Fish are not on the radar screen of many conservationists, and most water protection advocates are focused on exactly that—water—and not necessarily what lives in it. In most cases, once people can safely swim in it, a water is deemed "restored," even though it may have lost its native fish, been infected with nonnative fish, or be subject to ongoing stocking.

Fish advocacy is dangerously weak in many areas, and in others poorly focused. Some of our advocacy groups have shifted away from conservation in favor of outreach and are more focused on fishing than fish. Many fish advocates are actually fishing advocates. Often the focus is on wild trout, regardless of origin, not native trout. And some defend, participate in, and even fund stocking.

We need to go beyond identification and work to gain protection for what we find, as just knowing brook trout are there does not ensure their survival—and in some cases can actually do harm by drawing attention to them. The emphasis of one project I was involved in was changed from *identify and protect* to just *identify* when it became apparent that doing the latter would require ruffling some feathers at state fish and game, greatly lessening its effectiveness.

One conservation nonprofit website says, "The information collected by volunteer anglers—verified by biologists—will help inform future fisheries management decisions. This data will be used to set policy and implement effective conservation strategies to protect, restore, and enhance native Eastern Brook Trout populations." Unfortunately, after six years of studies the only management decisions made were those required by law, and even this was done arbitrarily and inconsistently.

We need to protect fish as well as their habitat. Addressing habitat degradation without addressing angler exploitation, or vice versa, is like putting gas in your lawnmower but not oil; while it will work for a while, it won't work forever. Ditto for stocking, as fixing habitat but ignoring stocking is not going to save our wild native fish. Just as our once exploitation- and stocking-centric approaches were flawed, so is the new habitat-centric approach, and for the same reason: It addresses only part of the problem.

Recognizing that habitat is critical to wild native brook trout survival, and doing something about it, represents one of our greatest successes. Refusing to accept, or admit, that angler exploitation is one of the greatest threats to wild native brook trout is one of our biggest failures. Again, stressed populations are not good, and would there be stocking over wild native brook trout if we were not exploiting the population?

When we deny that angler exploitation is a problem, we are validating the flawed ideology of state fish and game agencies and some in the angling community that any brook trout that dies of natural causes is somehow wasted. When we deny that angler exploitation is a problem, we are also ignoring the aggregate impact of the masses, focusing instead on the desires of the individual.

Like those who came before us and rescued the nation's wild trout populations from the brink, we need to accept that while we will ruffle some feathers by asking our peers to lessen their impact on the resource, it is necessary to ensure the long-term viability of wild native brook trout. The same goes for state fish and game agencies; we need them to stop doing things that harm wild native brook trout populations.

Make no mistake about it, the best friend brook trout have today is anglers, but unfortunately, not all anglers are friends. No one appreciates fish like we do, and we need to get more involved so we can influence management, policy, and law. We need to direct the efforts of our advocacy groups toward programs that focus on wild native fish, low-impact angling, and total solutions. While the preference is always to find voluntary solutions, we cannot be afraid to use the court of public opinion, legislation, or even litigation when nothing else is working. If we are to pass on to our grandchildren what was passed on to us, we must be willing to get our hands dirty. Do you think the protections we have today came easily? No, they were hard fought.

Sportsmen and fisheries managers need to stop viewing wild native brook trout as table fare and start recognizing them as the unique, beautiful, and irreplaceable resource they are. Like golf where you don't have to eat the ball to enjoy the sport, eating wild native trout, while OK in some cases, is not a necessary rite of passage. Bird watchers don't eat songbirds; we don't have to eat wild native brook trout. Our legacy should be one of improving the situation regarding wild native brook trout, not further degrading it.

EPILOGUE

I never set out to be a brook trout advocate—it just happened. While I had been a strict catch-and-release, low-impact fly fisher for years, I was never very active regarding trout conservation. Sure, I did a bit of preaching, but that was about it.

But then something happened: I started to change how I viewed native trout and the places they lived. Unlike other states that had little left worth protecting, my home state of Maine still did: wild native trout living in natural environments. I didn't want Maine to become like the rest of New England—heavily reliant on stocking and nonnative fish—and I wanted to try to do something about it.

After formal affiliations with several local trout advocacy groups and some successes such as helping to pass Maine's State Heritage Fish law, I joined several others in the formation of Native Fish Coalition. As a New England–based native fish non-prof, brook trout were by default a primary focus.

While I still endorse the notion, "take care of the fish, and the fishing will take care of itself," I don't believe that protecting fishing will protect fish. In fact, in many ways fishing has become part of the problem, as anglers are moving around nonnative fish, pushing wild trout populations to the point where they need to be stocked, and creating the demand for nonnative fish and hybrids.

While it was never in my plans, I see wild native fish advocacy as a natural progression for someone who loves trout and trout fishing as much as I do, because what is good for fish is good for anglers, and if you protect fish you by default protect fishing. And as I see it, fly fishing for wild native trout represents fishing in its purest form.

While there is no nationally known book called "Brown Trout," "Rainbow Trout," or even "Cutthroat Trout," there is a nationally known book called *Brook Trout*, a seminal piece written by Nick Karas in 1997 and still in print today. There is a reason for this—brook trout are special, and very much so.

Wild native brook trout are important ecologically and socially. They belong where they are found. They are beautiful. They survive against all odds, and in habitat that is

The author standing under the first informational sign posted on a State Heritage Fish water in Maine. It all starts with information and education. JEFF MOORE PHOTO

often marginal for salmonids. They are America's first gamefish, and "America's Trout." Brook trout are where it all began as far as recreational angling in America goes.

Brook trout likely are, however, the most exploited wild native gamefish in America. They are pursued as much for their culinary qualities as their sporting qualities. This needs to change.

Brook trout are also usually the least protected gamefish where they are found. Minimal tackle restrictions, high bag limits, and low length limits are the norm, and conservative regulations the exception. This needs to change, too.

Whether wild native brook trout persist into the next century is very much up to us—anglers. The challenge has been issued, and we must heed the call or pay the price. We were given a gift, and we need to pass it on to the next generation as it was passed on to us.

Can brook trout anglers, and all anglers for that matter, get past the "bigger is better" mantra and learn to accept small fish in natural densities where applicable? Can we get away from the belief that "any trout is a good trout" and wean ourselves off nonnative trout and other alien fish?

Will we figure out that hatcheries are not a cure-all to our fishing woes, at least fishing as it is meant to be? Will we get tired of shredded fins and rounded tails, and develop an appreciation for wild fish with intact fins and tails? Will we be willing to make concessions regarding tackle and harvest?

Things like fly fishing, catch-and-release, or other forms of low-impact fishing are not elitist or selfish; rather they are selfless and smart business, as they help preserve that which we all love—wild native brook trout. When someone releases a wild native brook trout, he or she is giving someone else the chance to catch it later, the ultimate form of multiple use.

Will we stand up for public lands, as they may be our last best hope? Will we oppose those who exploit our natural resources? Can we be convinced that "access at any cost" actually comes with a very high cost? Or that *multiple use* is just a catchy phrase for resource abuse?

Will federal agencies such as the National Park Service and US Forest Service step up and start protecting wild native brook trout living on federal land when state fish and game agencies refuse to do so? Will we support them if they try?

Will we accept that the mantra "united we stand, divided we fall" is a falsehood when it comes to conserving the resource, and that breaking ranks with those who exploited our wild native fish is what saved them from the brink decades ago?

No group of sportsmen has become more accepting of and dependent on stocking than trout anglers. What can be done to break our reliance on stocked fish? Will it be ecological enlightenment or economic hardship at the state fish and game level that forces our hand?

Likewise, no group of sportsmen has become more accepting of nonnative species and man-made hybrids than trout anglers. Can anything be done to change this?

Will the new pro-native fish movement led by small nonprofits be enough to change anglers' perspectives? Will these groups be able to live off the crumbs left behind by the corporate conservation groups? Will the big conservation groups get fishier, and will those that are fishy change their focus to a more native-centric one?

Brook trout face an uphill battle if they are to survive in an ever-changing world, in what are often not ideal environments. Nonnative species, climate change, stocking, development, and angler exploitation are taxing our wild native brook trout stocks. How much more can they take? What is the tipping point?

The game has yet to be played out, and what happens to our wild native brook trout is yet to be determined. But there is change in the wind, and anglers are starting to understand that while all trout offer good recreation, wild native trout are different and special—especially brook trout.

There is hope for the nation's native brook trout, and it comes in the form of groups like Downeast Salmon Federation, Eastern Brook Trout Joint Venture, Native Fish Coalition, Protect Rhode Island Brook Trout, Sea-Run Brook Trout Coalition, and Trout Power. Please support them as they support our wild native brook trout.

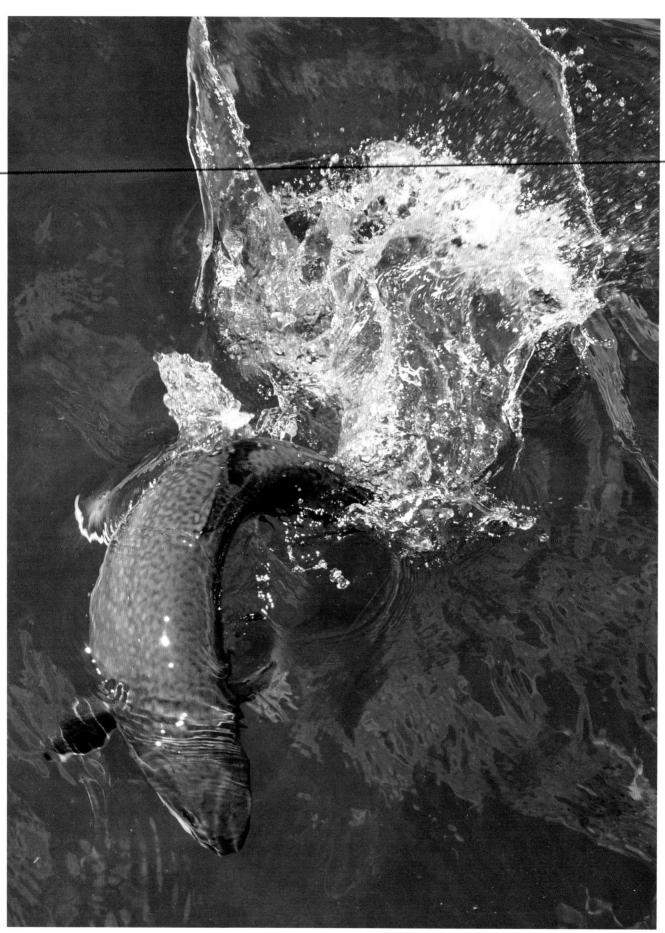

A large wild native brook trout released to fight another day. Reuse is the real multiple use. DIANA MALLARD PHOTO

RESOURCES

CONSERVATION ORGANIZATIONS

Downeast Salmon Federation: mainesalmonrivers.org
Eastern Brook Trout Joint Venture: easternbrooktrout.org
Maine Wilderness Watershed Trust: mwwt.org
Native Fish Coalition: nativefishcoalition.org
    ME: nativefishcoalition.org/maine
    NH: nativefishcoalition.org/new-hampshire
    VT: nativefishcoalition.org/vermont
Protect Rhode Island Brook Trout: protectribrooktrout
    .org
Sea-Run Brook Trout Coalition: searunbrookie.org
Trout Power: troutpower.blogspot.com
Trout Unlimited: tu.org
    Connecticut: cttrout.org
    Georgia: georgiatu.org
    Iowa: facebook.com/IowaTU
    Maine: tumaine.org
    Maryland: maryland.tu.org
    Massachusetts and Rhode Island: ma-ri-tu-council.org
    Michigan: michigantu.org
    Minnesota: mntu.org
    New Hampshire: tu.org/blog/welcome-to-the-new
        -hampshire-council-site
    New Jersey: njtu.org
    New York: nytu.org
    North Carolina: nctu.org
    Pennsylvania: patrout.org
    Tennessee: tctu.org
    Vermont: vttucouncil.org
    Virginia: virginiatu.org
    West Virginia: wvtu.org
    Wisconsin: wisconsintu.org

STATE FISH AND GAME AGENCIES

Connecticut Department of Energy and Environmental
    Protection: ct.gov/deep
Georgia Department of Natural Resources/Wildlife
    Resources Division: georgiawildlife.org/fishing
Iowa Department of Natural Resources: iowadnr.gov/
    Fishing
Kentucky Department of Fish & Wildlife Resources:
    fw.ky.gov/Pages/default.aspx
Maine Department of Inland Fisheries and Wildlife:
    state.me.us/ifw
Maine Department of Marine Resources: maine.gov/dmr
Maryland Department of Natural Resources:
    dnr.maryland.gov/Pages/default.aspx
Massachusetts Department of Fish and Game:
    mass.gov/eea/agencies/dfg
Michigan Department of Natural Resources:
    michigan.gov/dnr
Minnesota Department of Natural Resources:
    dnr.state.mn.us/fishwildlife/index.html
New Hampshire Fish & Game Department:
    wildlife.state.nh.us
New Jersey Division of Fish & Wildlife: state.nj.us/dep/
    fgw
New York Department of Environmental Conservation:
    dec.ny.gov
North Carolina Wildlife Resources Commission:
    ncwildlife.org
Ohio DNR Division of Wildlife: wildlife.ohiodnr.gov
Pennsylvania Fish & Boat Commission: fishandboat
    .com/Pages/default.aspx
Rhode Island Division of Fish & Wildlife: dem.ri.gov/
    programs/fish-wildlife
South Carolina Department of Natural Resources:
    dnr.sc.gov/fishing.html
Tennessee Wildlife Resources Agency: tn.gov/twra.html
Vermont Fish & Wildlife: vtfishandwildlife.com
Virginia Department of Game and Inland Fisheries:
    dgif.virginia.gov/fishing
West Virginia Division of Natural Resources: wvdnr.gov
Wisconsin Division of Natural Resources: dnr.wi.gov

PUBLIC LANDS

Acadia National Park: nps.gov/acad/index.htm
Adirondack Park: visitadirondacks.com/about/
    adirondack-park
Appalachian Trail: appalachiantrail.org
Baxter State Park: baxterstateparkauthority.com/
    index.htm
Great Smoky Mountains National Park: nps.gov/grsm/
    index.htm
Green Mountain National Forest: fs.usda.gov/
    greenmountain
Katahdin Woods and Waters National Monument:
    nps.gov/kaww/index.htm
Monongahela National Forest: fs.usda.gov/mnf
Pisgah National Forest: fs.usda.gov/nfsnc
Shenandoah National Park: nps.gov/shen/index.htm
White Mountain National Forest: fs.usda.gov/main/
    whitemountain/home

MISCELLANEOUS

North Maine Woods: northmainewoods.org
Maine Sporting Camps Association: mainesportingcamps
    .com
Maine Wilderness Watershed Trust: mwwt.org/pierce
    -pond-wildlife
Rangeley Lakes Heritage Trust: rlht.org
Rangeley Outdoor Sporting Heritage Museum:
    rangeleyhistoricalsociety.org

INDEX

ABOUT THE AUTHOR

Author with a large pond-dwelling brook trout from a remote water in central Maine. CECIL GRAY PHOTO

Bob Mallard has called New England home for 60 years. He has lived in Massachusetts, New Hampshire, and Maine, residing in each state for over a decade and living in Maine for the last 20 years. This, along with a 20-year career in software, information technology, and business consulting that allowed him to travel extensively, has exposed Bob to the finest fly-fishing for brook trout the continent has to offer.

Bob is about as singularly focused as anyone can be. His passion is fly-fishing for trout. Bob is on the water more than 100 days a year and has been for as long as he can remember. While he occasionally fishes for stripers, salmonids—especially wild native ones—are his real passion. Bob travels all over the country in search of trout and salmon and has caught them in 25 states and three Canadian provinces.

Bob is a Registered Maine Guide. He owned and operated Kennebec River Outfitters, a full-service fly shop, in Madison, Maine, from 2001 to 2014. One of five fly shops on the fabled Kennebec River, Bob's shop was the last one standing after a notable crash of the popular brown trout fishery on the middle river.

Bob has served on the pro staffs of several tackle manufacturers including R. L. Winston and Scientific Anglers. He works closely with many other tackle manufacturers due to his writing and work with *Fly Fish America* magazine and *Southern Trout* online magazine.

Bob has been featured in newspapers (including the *Wall Street Journal*) and regional and national sporting and fly-fishing publications. He, or more accurately, a trout he caught, was on the cover of *Fly Fishing & Tying Journal* magazine.

Bob has appeared on numerous local television and radio shows including *Chronical* (Boston), *Bill Green's Maine*, *Wildfire*, and *The Maine Outdoors*. He was the "shadow caster" on a Maine Department of Tourism television ad that ran in the Northeast and Mid-Atlantic markets.

Bob's photographs have appeared in several books as well as in *Eastern Fly Fishing*, *Fly Fish America*, *Fly Fisherman*, *Fly Fishing New England*, *Fly Rod & Reel*, *Fly Tyer*, *OrvisNews*, *Outdoor Life*, *Southern Trout*, *Tenkara Angler*, and *The Maine Sportsman* magazines and ezines.

Bob has written extensively about fly fishing, fly tying, fisheries management, conservation, and outdoor products. His work has appeared in *Angling Trade*, *Eastern Fly Fishing*, *Fly Fish America*, *Fly Fisherman*, *Fly Fishing New England*, *Fly Fishing & Tying Journal*, *Fly Tyer*, *Northwoods Sporting Journal*, *OrvisNews*, *Outdoor Life*, *SoMuchWater*, *Southern Trout*, *Southern Trout Ozark Edition*, *Tenkara Angler*, and *The Maine Sportsman*.

Bob had a regular column, *The Technical Fly Fisher*, in the *Northwoods Sporting Journal*—a Maine-based sporting publication—for several years. He currently has a column called "Gearhead" in *Southern Trout* online magazine. Bob maintained a Maine fly fishing blog for roughly a decade. He is currently the publisher, Northeast regional editor, and a regular contributor to *Fly Fish America*.

Bob contributed two chapters, "Rapid River" in Maine and "Deerfield River" in Massachusetts, to the book *50 Best Tailwaters to Fly Fish* (Gunn/Gunn). He wrote the "Acadia National Park" chapter for *25 Best National Parks to Fly Fish* (Gunn/Gunn). Bob contributed a chapter on Red River Camps to *Maine Sporting Camps* (Smith) as well. He also contributed a chapter on the Rapid River to *The Hunt for Giant Trout* (Mayer).

Bob's first book, a collaborative effort called *50 Best Places Fly Fishing the Northeast*, was released in 2014. His second book, *25 Best Towns Fly Fishing for Trout*, came out in 2015. He is currently working on a yet-to-be-titled collaborative book about fly fishing in Maine.

Bob is a staff fly designer at Catch Fly Fishing in Billings, Montana, with over 30 cataloged patterns. His flies have been featured in the books *Guide Flies: How to Tie and Fish the Killer Flies from America's Greatest Guides* and Fly Shops (Klausmeyer), Caddisflies: A Guide to Eastern Species for Anglers and Other Naturalists (Ames), America's Favorite Flies (Bryan/Carter), as well as Fly Tyer and American Angler magazines.

Bob was a founding member and the first president of Somerset County Chapter of Trout Unlimited in Maine, a founding member of Dud Dean Angling Society, and a member of Sportsman's Alliance of Maine's Fishing Initiative Committee. He is also a founding member, national vice chair, and Maine board member for Native Fish Coalition.

Bob has been a tireless and some would say relentless advocate for New England's wild native salmonids. Maine outdoor writer Ken Allen once referred to him as "the most feared coldwater conservationist in the state." Former director of Information & Education at the Maine Department of Inland Fisheries and Wildlife, Bill Pierce, called Bob a "pitbull on a porkchop." Conservation icon Ted Williams wrote that Bob was "Maine's busiest and most passionate brook-trout defender" and "[Maine's] most energetic and outspoken native-fish activist." Upon being introduced to Bob, esteemed fly-fishing writer and author Dave Hughes said, "Oh, you're the Maine brook trout guy."

Bob has testified in front of the Maine legislature on behalf of wild native brook trout, rare Arctic charr, fishing regulations, stocking, and the use of live bait on wild salmonid waters. He was instrumental in helping to establish, and amend, Maine's State Heritage Fish Law that prohibits the use of live bait and stocking on more than 575 self-sustaining native brook trout and Arctic charr lakes and ponds. Most recently he was part of a group that tried to strengthen the language for adding waters to program and extend the protections to the tributaries of so-designated waters.

Few people have fished as much brook trout water as Bob Mallard. Anchored in Maine, he is within striking distance of roughly 90 percent of the nation's remaining wild native pond-dwelling brook trout, sea-run brook trout, and large river-dwelling brook trout, as well as a lot of stream-resident brook trout. His regular forays into New Hampshire, Vermont, and Massachusetts have put him in contact with a lot of brook trout as well. And Bob makes a point of sampling the local brook trout fishing wherever and whenever he can.

Few people are as familiar with brook trout as Bob Mallard, and few are as capable of writing their story as him. He fishes for them, advocates for them, guides for them, and writes about them. Bob's knowledge of, and passion for, Salvelinus fontinalis shows in his ongoing advocacy efforts, and is evident by what he has presented in this book.

Ted Williams is an avid fly fisherman and nationally known fly-fishing, conservation, and nature author, writer, and blogger. He is the former conservation writer for Fly Rod & Reel magazine, and a columnist for The Nature Conservancy. In 2015, Ted was the recipient of the Outdoor Writers Association of America's "Excellence in Craft Award" for his "Incite" column in Audubon magazine, which ran from 1988 to 2014. He is the author of three books: Something's Fishy, The Insightful Sportsman, and Wild Moments. Ted is also a founding member and national chair for Native Fish Coalition.